The Civic Organization and
the Digital Citizen

Oxford Studies in Digital Politics

Series Editor: Andrew Chadwick, Royal Holloway, University of London

Expect Us: Online Communities and Political Mobilization
Jessica L. Beyer

The Hybrid Media System: Politics and Power
Andrew Chadwick

Tweeting to Power: The Social Media Revolution in American Politics
Jason Gainous and Kevin M. Wagner

The Digital Origins of Dictatorship and Democracy: Information Technology and Political Islam
Philip N. Howard

Democracy's Fourth Wave? Digital Media and the Arab Spring
Philip N. Howard and Muzammil M. Hussain

The MoveOn Effect: The Unexpected Transformation of American Political Advocacy
David Karpf

Taking Our Country Back: The Crafting of Networked Politics from Howard Dean to Barack Obama
Daniel Kreiss

Bits and Atoms: Information and Communication Technology in Areas of Limited Statehood
Steven Livingston and Gregor Walter-Drop

Digital Cities: The Internet and the Geography of Opportunity
Karen Mossberger, Caroline J. Tolbert and William W. Franko

Revolution Stalled: The Political Limits of the Internet in the Post-Soviet Sphere
Sarah Oates

Disruptive Power: The Crisis of the State in the Digital Age
Taylor Owen

Affective Publics: Sentiment, Technology, and Politics
Zizi Papacharissi

Presidential Campaigning in the Internet Age
Jennifer Stromer-Galley

News on the Internet: Information and Citizenship in the 21st Century
David Tewksbury and Jason Rittenberg

The Civic Organization and the Digital Citizen

COMMUNICATING ENGAGEMENT IN A NETWORKED AGE

CHRIS WELLS

OXFORD
UNIVERSITY PRESS

OXFORD
UNIVERSITY PRESS

Oxford University Press is a department of the University of
Oxford. It furthers the University's objective of excellence in research,
scholarship, and education by publishing worldwide.

Oxford   New York
Auckland   Cape Town   Dar es Salaam   Hong Kong   Karachi
Kuala Lumpur   Madrid   Melbourne   Mexico City   Nairobi
New Delhi   Shanghai   Taipei   Toronto

With offices in
Argentina   Austria   Brazil   Chile   Czech Republic   France   Greece
Guatemala   Hungary   Italy   Japan   Poland   Portugal   Singapore
South Korea   Switzerland   Thailand   Turkey   Ukraine   Vietnam

Oxford is a registered trademark of Oxford University Press
in the UK and certain other countries.

Published in the United States of America by
Oxford University Press
198 Madison Avenue, New York, NY 10016

Cataloging-in-Publication Data is on file at the Library of Congress.
ISBN 978-0-19-020361-0 (hbk.); 978-0-19-020362-7 (pbk.)

9 8 7 6 5 4 3 2 1
Printed in the United States of America
on acid-free paper

To Jennifer

Contents

Acknowledgments

Over the several years this book has been in progress, I've had the good fortune to encounter a great number of advisers, friends, advice-givers, draft-readers, coders, and more. I would like to do my best to acknowledge and thank the many people—and places—who played roles in the book's creation.

It started at the University of Washington in Seattle. When I was working in the city and considering graduate school, I began reading books on media and politics in the beautiful Seattle Public Library on 4th Avenue. One of the books I found was *Mediated Politics: Communication in the Future of Democracy*—exactly the topic I was interested in. After photocopying about two-thirds of the book, at some point I happened on the editors' bio pages and saw that one was at the University of Washington, only a few miles away. I hadn't realized that there was such a field as political communication, much less that the UW might have a strong program in it. I consider it a stroke of luck that I found my way to that book, and then to Lance Bennett, the UW's Department of Communication, and the work I got to do over the next five years.

That included research in the Center for Communication and Civic Engagement (CCCE). Especially important for this project were several years I spent designing and coordinating the Becoming Citizens program there, which placed undergraduate interns in local community youth organizations. I am so grateful to the students, organizers, and funders (mainly the Nancy Bell Evans Center, and UW's Carlson Center and Pipeline Project), who opened my perspective on how young people and organizations interact.

The CCCE's Civic Learning Online project was a first initiative into research on this topic, and in that connection I must thank the John D. and Catherine T. MacArthur Foundation for providing funding, as well as my collaborators Allison Rank and Deen Freelon, and undergraduate assistants Melissa Aar, Jorunn Mjos, and Lauren Snyder.

Later, working on my dissertation, I was fortunate to have support from the Department of Communication's Graduate Student Research Fund, which allowed me to hire five excellent assistants: Tim Carlson, Cory Eng, Kiyomi Higuchi, Lily Ly, and Caitlin Marassi. Their careful work made Chapter 5 possible. Soon after, a University of Washington Graduate School Dissertation Fellowship gave me a quarter to focus on the first pass of what would become this book. All along, Diana Smith helped it all to happen with her support and guidance, especially when working with research assistants.

I can't overemphasize the supportive experience I found at the UW's Department of Communication—support that has made its mark on this book. I would like to thank all my instructors and peers, though there is only space to name a few of them here: Patricia Moy's voice continues to have a prominent place in my mind when I am thinking about careful concept explication, operationalization, and research design. More than once—on this project and others—John Gastil gave me smart suggestions and advice that would turn out to be invaluable. A seminar I took with Chip Turner on political theory has stuck with me as I continue to wrestle with the gap between theory and empirical work. Walter Parker assured me that my dissertation would be "terrible . . . because all dissertations are terrible." This was strangely liberating in exactly the way he intended. I hope he finds this book something more like . . . . mediocre.

David Domke, Kirsten Foot, and Phil Howard also offered advice, insights, and suggestions on this project and the research enterprise. Deen Freelon, Muzammil Hussain, Penny Sheets, and Justin Reedy had the closest exposure to this work, and were generous and direct sounding boards. Jamie Moshin was the ideal writing buddy. Rich Cook was the ideal tennis buddy. Gretchen Snoey, Jen and Scott Gerdts, Todd Jarrell, Branden Pfefferkorn, Analisa Calderon, and Anita Hernandez were and remain lovely, supportive friends.

At the University of Wisconsin-Madison, I have found another department with which I could not be happier. And again, conversations with members of our faculty and others have been hugely beneficial in developing my understanding of what I am saying and how. Here, Lew Friedland has had the greatest hand: his positive influence will be seen at several points in this manuscript. I am grateful for the depth my conversations with him have added to my understanding. Among many others, Jim Baughman, Young Mie Kim, Louise Mares, Dhavan Shah, Stephen Vaughn, and Mike Xenos especially have all offered generous suggestions and support. My students, especially in my seminar Mass Media and Political Participation, have responded to my ideas and provoked new ones. From the world beyond Madison, others who have given a word of encouragement or advice include Bruce Bimber, Homero Gil de Zuniga, Matt Hindman, Russ Newman, and Michael X. Delli Carpini.

Andrew Chadwick, Angela Chnapko, and Princess Ikatekit have been wonderful editors. Maya Bringe has provided assistance with the production of the manuscript. Mark Mastromarino wrote an excellent index. Three anonymous reviewers gave their time to craft many valuable suggestions to a draft of this manuscript; thank you.

The mobility afforded by digital media and laptops allowed me to encounter a number of different spaces as I was working, which I would like to recognize as social institutions—public, nonprofit, and commercial—where reflection and writing took place. In Seattle, the University of Washington libraries, the Center for Communication and Civic Engagement, Victrola Coffee and Caffe Vita were primary locations. The public library and food co-op in Belfast, Maine, also offered their space during two crucial summers. KEXP-Seattle often provided the soundtracks.

Several people I am flattered to call peers, including Mike Wagner, Shawnika Hull, Molly Steenson, Lucas Graves, Katy Culver, Karyn Riddle, Sue Robinson, Dave Karpf, Daniel Kreiss, Karolina Koc Michalska, Kjerstin Thorson, Emily Vraga, Stephanie Edgerly, and Leticia Bode, have offered tremendous moral support as well as substantive suggestions. Creating our new community in Wisconsin with Mike Thalasinos, Marwa Bassiouni, Ben and Amanda Dreyer, Bill and Denise Buenzli, Jill and Andy Bean, has been a pleasure and welcome retreat from busy junior faculty work.

Every acknowledgment section says it, but in this case it is no exaggeration to say that this book would not have been possible without my family. First Theo, then Fred, arrived during some stage of this work's creation and are daily, joyful inspirations. My parents, Joan and Peter, and Jenni's parents, Ann and Dave, have made it possible to write a book while being a new dad. By being there, and especially by being there for Theo and Fred, their indefatigability and strength of spirit allowed me to run out early in the morning, fly back and forth between Wisconsin and Seattle, travel to conferences, stay late at work . . . and on and on. Nick, Nat, Kitty, Myra, Katie, Derek, Meghan, Kevin, Fred, Connie and Grandfather John also did their share of baby-holding, encouraging, and beer-opening. Most of all, I thank my wife Jenni, to whom this book is dedicated, who witnessed, enabled, and tolerated a book's long development—all while delivering scores of babies as a physician and two of her own as a mom. We are always doing way too much, but it couldn't be any other way. I love you.

The Civic Organization and
the Digital Citizen

1

Young Citizens and the Changing Face of Civic Information

The year 2011 was a turning point in the empowerment of young people around the globe. Confronted by repression and brutality in the Middle East, austerity in Europe, political gridlock in the United States, and worldwide economic stagnation, and empowered by an array of digital media tools for communicating and organizing, by the end of the year young activists had made themselves a political force to be reckoned with.

In Egypt, mass protests beginning January 25 resulted in the overthrow of President Hosni Mubarak three weeks later. Eight months after that, in the elections they had demanded, the young activists mobilized in the formation of a new political party that won a small plurality of seats in the Egyptian government. Today it governs in a loose coalition with the Muslim Brotherhood's Freedom and Justice Party, and the Egyptian president is very aware of the youth bloc. The activists are using their newfound leverage to advocate policies to address high unemployment among young people and develop a small but vibrant high tech sector in Egypt's economy.

On May 15, several thousand young "Indignados" camped in Madrid's Puerta del Sol to protest the dearth of economic opportunities for young people and increasing calls for austerity measures in Spain. Throughout the summer they negotiated ties with the center-left Social Workers' Party, eventually convincing them to adopt core elements of the Indignados' platform. In the November elections, the energy and organizing of young Indignados was widely credited with ensuring the Social Workers' Party's resounding victory. Since then, they have played a leading role in renegotiating the terms of Spain's responsibility to the Eurozone.

In the United States, Occupy Wall Street began on September 17 as a small occupation of a downtown Manhattan park. Bolstered by supportive occupations across the country, the protesters built a powerful base of citizens supportive of the movement's aims. By the spring of 2012, local Occupy chapters were holding regular meetings and electing officers, and a national board of directors, backed by an impressively distributed digital opinion architecture, were in close contact with President Obama. That fall, the Occupy caucus of the Democratic Party could take credit for the election of twelve new Representatives and two Senators and was personally thanked by the president on the night of his re-election.

In a universe not terribly different from our own, the scenarios above describe recent political history. For us, they are just about half true. Young Egyptian activists *did* take the streets and overthrow Mubarak in one of the most remarkable periods of modern Egyptian history, but they have since struggled to remain relevant in that country's politics: in the elections following Mubarak's downfall, the Muslim Brotherhood won the presidency and nearly half the seats in the People's Assembly. The hard-line Salafists held another 24%, and the liberal New Wafd only 7.6%.[1] After less than a year of the administration of the Brotherhood's Mohamed Morsi, the Egyptian military ousted him, leaving democracy in Egypt very much in question.[2] Spanish youth *did* occupy the Puerta del Sol and other locations around Spain at various times since May 2011; however, they called for a boycott of the major parties in the November 2011 national elections, which were handily won by the conservative People's Party that subsequently followed many of the austerity policies so opposed by the Indignados.[3] Occupy Wall Street *did* occupy Manhattan's Zuccotti Park and other locations across the United States, but as winter approached the majority were forcibly deconstructed or abandoned, and the movement has yet to produce a widely endorsed policy platform. Though protests and actions on various scales continued through the summer of 2012, they soon tapered off, its legacy as a force in American politics has been left very much in question—a striking contrast to its conservative cousin the Tea Party.[4]

In each of these examples, the half that is true is that young citizens have proven their political interest, eagerness, and courage to claim a stake in the process of governing their countries. They have adeptly mobilized and protested, using both innovative digital tools and courageous on-the-ground demonstration—an inspiring rebuttal to years of accusations that youth are apathetic and disinterested. What has remained unfulfilled is what came next: when the locus of contention moved from streets to elections, party politics, platforms, negotiations, and so forth—in short, the dirty business of everyday democracy—the innovative protest movements have been remarkably inert.

How is it that we have arrived at this peculiar juncture? Our institutions of democracy try in vain to attract the participation (and, of course, credulity) of youth, while young activists themselves prefer displays of outrage and frustration with paltry institutional leverage. Indeed, recent movements have not infrequently *explicitly* rejected opportunities to interface with institutional processes. Prime examples include the Indignados' call for boycotts of Spain's viable parties in the 2011 elections, and Occupy Wall Street's dedication to a powerfully antihierarchical ethos.[5] Why such a dramatic disconnect between emergent civic practices and established democratic process? Is there any way to reconcile them in a way that enhances youth civic participation?

These questions are the impetus for *The Civic Organization and the Digital Citizen*. Its contribution to answering them comes from looking at the space that could potentially connect young activists with the political structures they ambivalently address—a space sometimes referred to as the "organizational layer in American politics."[6] This layer has long been of interest to scholars of civic life, and in the American context in particular, associations inhabiting the layer have been recognized as essential to connecting citizens to meaningful political action.[7]

More specifically, the book concerns itself with the state of the *communicative relationships* between young citizens and civic organizations, as both contend with the digital era. This means looking to both the formal civic organizations that were once dominant in structuring engagement in the Western democracies and the emergent forms of collective action that often appear in our RSS, Facebook, and Twitter feeds, and analyzing the communication dynamics established as they communicate engagement to their publics. The aim is to understand how the decline in the kinds of organized group activity celebrated since Tocqueville can be reconciled with the vibrant if not successful movements of Tahrir Square, the Puerta del Sol, and Zuccotti Park.[8]

These are areas rich for exploration. Although writers have lamented perceived civic decay for at least centuries,[9] in recent decades scholars have become especially concerned about the health of civic life in the United States and other developed Western nations. At the forefront of this conversation have often been concerns over the decline of formal civic organizations, and the falling engagement of younger citizens. Though there is some disagreement over details, on the whole the evidence is strong that Americans participate less in civic membership associations than they did in the mid-twentieth century. Robert Putnam's famous studies link this decline to a variety of unfortunate civic and personal outcomes, including falling social capital, social trust, and inclinations to be civically engaged. A similar story has been told from the organizational side of the story, with Theda Skocpol and others documenting the graying and decline of many of the groups that once offered formal connections to the political process for millions of Americans.[10] Strikingly, it is among younger citizens' participation patterns that the declines are most obvious, with the lowest rates of engagement in formal political activities such as voting, participation in civic organizations, and habits of following news.[11]

Changes in the communication processes and dynamics of civic life have been no less compelling, as today we also see great interest in the significance of new media technologies to civic engagement.[12] The focus here has also often been on youth, as young people have been recognized—accurately if often hyperbolically—to be at the forefront of many of the most exciting and innovative uses of digital media for engagement.[13] Work in this area has shown how the contours of individual experience, organizational form, and civic practice are transforming in the early twenty-first century. And accounts of social media–enabled organizing, including the examples above, have highlighted how the logics of digital media, with their capacity to reduce communication costs, enable remote activism, and allow the expression of complex individual identities, are reshaping the possibilities of collective action.[14]

Yet there is a significant gap in this literature: in our excitement over new possibilities, the study of digital media and civic engagement has too often neglected the major civil society organizations that have been a critical component of participatory political society for the past 150 years. As scholars concerned over their decline have emphasized, these institutions have provided essential points of common reference for citizens, social opportunities, and streams of communication that have helped Americans make sense of the political world, locate themselves in it, and find opportunities to act.[15] This point highlights the need to understand the future of civil society's institutional structures in the digital era. But with a few significant exceptions, the network-focused research agenda has neglected staid and established organizations in favor of dramatic new movements and networked activism that seem to break all the rules: the "organizing without organizations."[16] These are unquestionably fascinating, important, and forward-looking. And yet the mixed histories of recent networked activism suggests that we should be cautious about proclaiming a whole new era of political organization: politics is a complicated, messy, and prolonged process, and there remain essential roles for formal groups and institutions to play in citizen engagement. What is far from clear is how such institutions can or will adapt to communicating with twenty-first-century young citizens in a drastically changed information and political landscape.[17]

The Argument of the Book

The field of political communication is in need of conceptual tools for connecting the startling implications of digital media with democracies' institutional players. *The Civic Organization and the Digital Citizen* dedicates itself to the development of those tools by examining the challenges faced by organizations using digital media to communicate with young citizens about civic action. The argument presented here holds that an essential and theoretically underdeveloped component of youth disaffection from politics is communicative in nature, as established organizations engage in a pattern of civic communication practices that are increasingly unattractive to many young citizens. As we shall see, a new set of preferences for receiving and interacting with civic information, traceable to late modern civic identity shifts and habitual digital media experience, is currently emerging, most clearly among younger citizens. This set of preferences prizes participatory opportunities, diverse and shareable content, and self-expression in the context of civic communications; not coincidentally, these communication attributes are often on display in contemporary networked social movements as well as in youth digital practices more generally.

They are much less the norm in the communications of many established organizations, whose institutional, hierarchical, professionalized, and specialized (in short, "bureaucratic") structures originated,[18] and remain rooted in, the communication logics of the mass media era. Despite the participatory, shareable, and self-expressive inclinations of younger publics, the lessons learned by legacy civic groups—and, crucially, their leaders, board members, and funders—in a previous media-engagement period privileged vigilantly guarding mass media–bound messages, cultivating partnerships with other civic groups and government agencies, developing relationships among members based on trust, duty, and excludable goods, and the need to capture and leverage member input through elite-directed strategic actions.

This account of a communicative divide may help to explain younger citizens' disaffection from traditional modes of participation, and raises the critical question of how—or whether—civic organizations are adapting to communication styles diametrically opposed to those practiced in late twentieth-century media politics. This book offers two studies of digital communication by civic organizations, in the online contexts of organization websites and Facebook presences, to shed new light on these questions.

On the whole, the results reveal what I refer to as a *disconnect*: a set of circumstances in which young citizens and many of the democratic institutions that appeal to them speak different languages of civic life and communication. From most conventional organizations of civil society most of the time, we find low levels of the communication attributes likely to appeal to young citizens. Through both websites and Facebook, organizations primarily reproduce a twentieth-century, mass media approach to engaging citizens much more than they embrace the participatory and networked norms of digital media. Yet important qualifications to this overall pattern deepen our understanding of the dynamics of this area and suggesting possibilities for improved practice—and research. For one thing, there are notable differences between different sorts of organizations: for example, we will uncover more digital-friendly patterns in the communications of organizations that exist only online, likely reflecting those organizations' unique orientations to digital culture—even making them appear intriguingly like networked social movements.[19] Further, we uncover evidence that among organizations of the most staid and traditional variety there is evidence of a shift in how members are conceptualized: we find a trend toward mobilizing supporters as autonomous actors in personally defined social networks, and not solely as formal members of a discrete organization. Finally, differences in civic organizations' communication practices on websites and in Facebook leave some reasons to believe that the social media space in which organizations operate matters—and that many of the digital platforms on which organizations try to reach youth may come with signals that spur some reconceptualization on the part of organizers.

The book's findings call for a refreshed agenda of research and practice on the nature of citizen participation in organizations in the digital era. Young citizens no longer inhabit the world that made participation in classic membership organizations attractive a century ago, and the practices of late-twentieth century "checkbook" membership appear to never have been satisfying as civic action.[20] What must be rethought is how the legacies of historically rich, vital, and proficient organizations can be made relevant and meaningful to the sensibilities of contemporary young people. The kinds of emerging forms of civic action like those that opened this chapter seem to illustrate modes of communication attractive to a set of motivated and courageous young people, though those movements have foundered when it came to participating productively in the day-to-day processes of governance.[21] What we are looking for is in a seemingly underoccupied space between these poles: a space in which movements develop and maintain institutional presences while inspiring the continuing excitement and involvement of their networked publics; or, conversely, where organizations both engage young digital citizens accustomed to individualized expression and information seeking *and* engage with institutions of government that remain decidedly institutionalized. The communicative perspective on which this book's theory and empirical results are built offers a unique way of reconciling some of these challenges.

This chapter serves as an introduction to the book's key concepts, perspective, and structure. We first consider the book's conceptualization of the concepts of civic information, civic information paradigms, and civic information styles. Next, we turn to a brief history of civic information dynamics to illustrate the contribution of those ideas. As it brings our depiction of civic information into the present this launches a discussion of contemporary changes in communication and collective action, and the theories and perspectives scholars have brought to bear on them. The chapter concludes with an overview of the chapters to come.

Key Concepts

The overarching framework of *The Civic Organization and the Digital Citizen* is a communicative perspective on the relationships between young citizens and the entities—organizations, associations, movements—that facilitate engagement in political activity. The communication-centered view is especially useful as the political communication environment fragments and citizens receive potentially civic information from a wider array of sources and over more channels than ever before. In the digital communications infrastructure, civic communicators of all sorts reach potential constituents directly, through personally and socially curated online information networks, often without the mediation of designated news-making institutions. Civic organizations thus become information actors alongside news sources and other outlets in their relationships with their supporters. This brings the importance of how civic organizations communicate with their constituencies into sharp relief.

The book's communicative perspective is developed via three related concepts. The first is *civic information*. Civic information is conceptualized as *the continuous flow of facts, opinions, and ideas that help citizens understand matters of potentially public concern and identify opportunities for action.* By "continuous flow," we are referring to the information that is exchanged through society—communicated from one entity to another—on an ongoing basis, and thus distinguish it from society's (and citizens') relatively static store of accumulated knowledge. By "facts, opinions and other ideas" we are allowing for a quite unrestrictive understanding of information, remaining agnostic as to the sorts of information that will be most significant to any individual's opinion or action. By "matters of potentially public concern" we are focusing on information that pertains to a collective of people beyond the individual citizen and his or her immediate associates. And by "opportunities for action" we make explicit the potential connection between communications and engagement.

This is a broad definition to be sure, but its breadth well suits the project. By using the generic "civic information" I mean to explicitly draw attention to the fact that our habitual conceptualization of citizens' experiences of political communication as coming primarily from "the news" reflects a narrowness that we must overcome. The news, as we shall see, is a particular incarnation of civic information practice that happened to be dominant in the high modern era—an era that featured a particular set of circumstances, including relative political consensus and a limited number of major media organizations committed to offering public affairs content.[22] The logics and norms supporting that information structure have largely broken down, and consequently, equating the information people need to function as citizens with "news" confuses our thinking about our own time, as contemporary debates over "what is news?" reveal.[23] *News* is something that is produced by credentialed producers and consumed by good citizens motivated to responsibly consume news for some later civic action. But we are increasingly seeing that this is not how contemporary citizens are most inclined to interact with *civic information* and the political world.

Adopting the more general "civic information" arms us with a higher-level concept that can be applied across sociopolitical-communicative contexts. As the heyday and decline of the news illustrate, civic information does not operate immutably through the ages; on the contrary, what is considered estimable civic information, who is supposed to produce it, and how citizens are supposed to use it has changed considerably over the years.[24] Whereas the paradigm of news defines civic information as produced by journalists, the more generic conception allows that civic organizations may also be significant producers—just as their posts may appear alongside those of news organizations in a Facebook or Twitter feed. The concept of civic information thus allows us to leave the question of "what has happened to the news?" and instead ask, "what is civic information like in our own time?" This is essential to our challenge of describing how citizens in different eras relate to information about politics and civic life.

Building on this logic, I refer to sets of sociopolitical-communicative circumstances as *civic information paradigms*. A civic information paradigm is a time period in which there is some rough similarity, even consensus, in relevant actors' conceptions of civic information's meaning, purpose, and uses. For instance, in the high modern era there was at least general agreement on the part of citizens, journalists, and civic groups about what news was—allowing one set of actors to engaged in practices of production, another in practices of consumption, and so forth. In such a context, different elements of society find useful conversation in civic information; as a result, because citizens' experiences of politics are inherently mediated by civic information, productive civic involvement is a possible result. A key argument of the book is that our civic world is currently caught in the midst of a transition between paradigms, and that the unsettled nature of this transition can help us understand contemporary patterns in civic involvement.

Becoming more fine-grained, the set of civic information preferences and habits of a particular individual, or group of individuals such as a generation, I refer to as a *civic information style*. As developed in Chapter 2, civic information styles are orientations to political communications deriving from individuals' experiences of self-identity, civic life, technology, and communication. In times of relative stasis in a society's civic information paradigm, we might expect to find many citizens sharing similar civic information styles: in such times there is rough agreement about what constitutes civic information, its legitimate producers, consumers, form, and uses. In times of paradigm transition, we find different actors within society displaying different civic information styles, potentially resulting in civic information disconnects. We are experiencing such a period now, which is what makes civic information styles such a useful framework for analyzing young citizens' interactions with civic groups' communications.

Finally, a brief note on who, exactly, young citizens are. Young people have been a perennial interest of observers of civic engagement, for two main reasons. The first is the sense that young people are the future in any society, and that they will necessarily carry forward the legacy of existing civic institutions and cultures. There has thus always been substantial anxiety about whether young people are sufficiently prepared to carry this legacy forward.[25] The second is that within the theme of social change that has accompanied social scientific—and especially sociological—research for the last century, young citizens are understood to be the group furthest out on the curve of change. From this perspective, it is often assumed that they exhibit characteristics most representative of what a given society is becoming.

My interest in this book is in studying young citizens' engagement in civic life for these reasons—more so than in young people per se, and even less in a group defined by a narrow age range. To give a quite broad range that fits this book's purpose, what can be said is that the literature on youth civic life, and the intended audience of the organizations described in Chapters 4 and 5, span a range of ages from early teens, when youth are conceptualized as developing their early conceptions of political life, to late twenties, typically the upper range in survey research contrasting young people with older generations.

But my greater interest is in comparisons between generations that have experienced different forms of civic opportunity, a concern we can pair with the question of what young people's experiences and preferences can tell us about the trajectory of civic life. As a result, the book will move between discussions of exactly what young people are doing at a given moment and more general comments on changes in civic life. Similarly, it will employ somewhat varying definitions of young person, as it traverses literature and research that define age groups slightly differently.

A Brief History of Civic Information

To elaborate the meaning of these concepts, let us briefly consider the history of civic information. The historical development of the relationship between information and civic life has received treatment from several perspectives: Bruce Bimber identifies four "information revolutions" that have helped to shape the dynamics of American politics since the founding; Michael Schudson sees several distinct eras of American civic life, each contributing its own notion of who the "good citizen" is and what he or she does, and interactions with communication constitute a not inconsequential subset of a good citizen's activities; Bruce Williams and Michael Delli Carpini put their focus on the notion of "media regimes," periods of relative stability in which norms and expectations of media and citizens are in synch; and Paul Starr places communications innovations in the context of historical periods' civic and political life.[26] Each of these authors, and others, inform the current discussion. Especially, they help us to recognize that civic information in different periods has been shaped by the particular political, social, and technological contexts in which it operates.

In drawing on them, I wish to highlight the tight relationship between how civic information is conceived and how citizenship is understood. In our current time of rapid change in communicative forms and technologies, it may seem as though communicative processes dominate our lives, and our civic lives, more than they ever have before. And there may well be some truth to this sense; yet we will see that how information about politics is conceptualized, and how a society manifests its understanding of civic information in institutions, processes, and norms, has been essential to the practices and possibilities of citizenship for the great part of democracy's history—at least since the Enlightenment democratic forms dating from the eighteenth century.

That last qualification is important, because the idea of civic information as we think of it today would have been inconceivable to citizens of the city-states of classical Greece to which we usually trace early democracy.[27] In fifth-century B.C. Athens, the typical citizen should have been fully informed all of the time, because by participating and regularly attending gatherings and participating in the events of the polis he (and it was "he") directly experienced the bulk of the city's goings-on.[28] This is the meaning of the *vita activa*—a life dedicated to participating in the public square: the essence of citizenship was the ability to entirely devote one's time and energy to public life because life's other necessities were attended to by noncitizens such as women and slaves.[29] For noncitizens civic information would have been equally meaningless, since they were so formally excluded from civic practice. Aristotle's belief "that the true ideal of good citizenship might only come to pass in a relatively small community" reflects his skepticism of substitutes for the regular interactions that made it possible for citizens to be "familiar with the character of other citizens, and engaged in the training and practice for a good and virtuous public life."[30] Under such conditions, citizens needed to be educated in the knowledge they would use as citizens, and surely exchanged information about the political world they were concerned about, but the fact of never being detached from it—and thus never needing to *attend to* consuming it—would have made civic information unrecognizable as a concept.

That possibility of full information awareness of all citizens has been disrupted by at least several factors: the franchise of citizenship expanding beyond an elite able to devote large quantities of time to participating in politics and absorbing political information; the polity expanding beyond the size of a classical city-state in which all citizens can meet in a physical space; the diversification of the kinds of people, and types of interests, enfranchised with citizenship; the differentiation of political and other spheres of public life; and—as a consequence of these—communication media becoming the primary means by which citizens learn about political events.[31]

CIVIC INFORMATION IN THE AMERICAN REVOLUTIONARY PERIOD

It is no coincidence that we see the emergence of coherent ideas about civic information with the revolution in democratic political thought and practice of the eighteenth century. In the wake of social shifts leading to increasingly large and complex polities rooted in urban centers, increasing recognition of competing interests and the prospect of tyranny by rulers, demands for representation and political rights and the development of communication media to supplement interpersonal conversation and opinion-formation, a new context for civic life and communication was taking shape. This is the context in which Jürgen Habermas famously identified a new paradigm of conversation and communication—the "public sphere"—rooted in the coffeehouses of London and salons of Paris and supplemented by the publications of participants.[32]

The American version similarly consisted of a rich interaction between a variety of characters such as tradesmen and merchants who met in public spaces like taverns and pubs to discuss current affairs and see what was happening in the area. Political communication in this society was firmly rooted in the interpersonal interactions that took place in such spaces and was thus inherently tied to a very real interpersonal public. As James Carey put it, "journalism was not an end in itself, but was justified in terms of its ability to serve and bring into existence . . . a particular form of democracy as discourse in a sphere of independent, rational, political influence."[33]

But the media necessary for the separation of civic information from lived social context were becoming available, and the American revolutionary period provided a catalyst for their use, development, and normalization in civic life. As printing presses spread rapidly in the American colonies in the 1760s and 1770s, opponents of British policies increasingly found them useful ways of sharing opinion and building public support within cities and between colonies.[34] Civic information, in the form of the writings of pamphleteers, letter-writers, and newspapers, was revealing its potential to make possible civic exchange beyond interpersonal settings.[35]

Having participated in and benefited from the exchange of political ideas through printed material, the architects of American democracy were now attuned to, and eager to promote, a communicative culture that would nourish their fledgling democracy—which, they were anxiously aware, was entirely novel in the sort of territory and diversity it hoped to incorporate.[36] But exactly what form civic information should take, and how typical citizens should be prepared to use it, was far from settled. This was a sharply stratified society in which elites exercised wide-ranging authority. The public itself was still an exclusive category, and the culture of politics still favored deference to the wise and virtuous decision-making of elites.[37] The founders were famously wary of sovereignty becoming too popular, often depicting the role of average citizens more as a check on leaders' excesses than as equals to them.[38]

In this formative period, consequently, we can detect a number of threads of thought about civic information. One is the set of ideas we now associate with a rational public sphere: that the ultimate power and responsibility of governance rests with the public, who participate in a flow of communications that yields deliberation, debate, and ultimately a public opinion.[39] In the Federalist Papers, Hamilton and Madison explicitly explore concerns about the informational capacities and needs of citizens, and the need to create systems to provide them with information so that they remain informed about political happenings. They clearly recognized that a dispersed, agrarian society would need to overcome the problem of lack of personal experience of politics. Dealing with the limits of citizens' capacity to remain informed became a critical concern of the Framers, who codified their concerns in the free speech and free press provisions of the Bill of Rights and through substantial subsidies of the postal service from the nation's first years.[40]

And yet the civic information of late eighteenth-century America was still something quite remote from our own. For one thing, a national communication infrastructure did not yet exist. For many citizens, politics was still fundamentally local and interpersonal. The detachment of information from interpersonal public life had not been completed. Civic information thus could not have had the sense of consuming information for the purposes of self-informing; it was still one element of a larger and richer conduct of public life.[41] Though elites around the country were exchanging newspapers across state lines and discussing their contents, such extralocal information was not at all a norm for most people, who were therefore largely excluded from state-level and national conversations.[42]

The Revolutionary Era offers the beginning of an understanding of civic information as consumable and separable from interpersonal experience, and its most forward-thinking writers could imagine the importance of civic information to a citizenry we might refer to as "informed." But it was not the experience of most citizens: the civic information of the late eighteenth and early nineteenth centuries was still rooted in social structure and public life, and consequently limited to local communities for all but elites. Further, the notion that citizens could—or should—be informed in the sense of developing a personal opinion about issues and policy options was far from widely held.

PARTISANSHIP AND PROFIT

By the 1830s and 1840s a number of factors were bolstering some of the more broadly democratic civic information visions of the Revolutionary period. Foremost among them was the policy decision of the adolescent US government to explicitly prioritize communication among the states with the Post Office Act of 1792. The act laid the groundwork for the development of a national postal system and heavily subsidized the carriage of newspapers, both to consumers and between newspaper publishers, soon yielding the world's premier system of intranational communication.[43]

Working and experimenting with those changes were the early parties, social service organizations, and political societies, and publishers interested in the business possibilities of producing news for a mass audience. Communication changes resulting from the possibilities offered by friendly policies, infrastructural investment, and new technologies of printing changed this, in the process transforming the relationship between citizens, civic information and political group organization.[44] Because what subsidization of newspaper certainly did do was knit together the young country: what publishers sought to do as much as anything else was reach out to and connect with other editors in other cities. John Nerone notes that in the early nineteenth century, as much as a tenth of a publisher's papers would be intended not for subscriber circulation, but for editorial exchanges with other papers. We must remember here that these are publishers and editors who have not yet embraced the profit motive: their interest is in discussing politics and gaining a voice in it.[45]

And though newspaper exchanges emerged in a printing and political culture greatly wary of any signs of partisanship or partiality, they were also, in a sense, the undoing of those norms. Because although printers frequently emphasized their impartiality, in reality they were building bases of interstate opinion and organization—in short, political parties.[46] What resulted is often referred to as the partisan press, a period in which production of the news was primarily a party affair: a way to spread their messages and build identification between citizens across the nation.[47] Jeffrey Pasley sums up the role of newspapers in the development of parties in no uncertain terms: "Party newspapers . . . contributed in fundamental ways to the very existence of the parties and to the creation of a sense of membership, identity, and common cause among political activists and voters."[48]

The same was true for organizations outside the mainstream of the party system: the 1820s to 1840s period has been widely recognized as the start of the golden age of American civic organization-building. As it did for parties, the ability to share information within nationally federated organizations, and between organizational chapters, was crucial to this transformation.[49] Indeed, in many cases it was the newspaper editor who took on primary responsibilities within the organizations emerging out of concerns their paper had addressed.[50] In this way, newspapers enabled parties and organizations to span the sheer size and scale of the nation that Madison had hoped would limit the formation of narrowly self-interested majorities while still allowing public deliberation and opinion-formation.[51]

The business of news wasn't far behind. Whereas commercial news before 1830 had been expensive to produce and distribute and thus aimed at economic elites interested primarily in mercantile content, innovations in the printing process meant that penny press publishers could greatly expand their circulations and experiment with form and content, seeking above all else to appeal to masses who could afford newspapers for a penny.[52] It would be a mistake to view the penny press as oriented to informing citizens in the way mid-twentieth-century news would aspire to do. But the penny press did deliver an experience of politics that had not before been possible for many citizens. It enabled the possibility of being informed about—and, coupled with the development of far-flung parties of political allegiance, taking political action relevant to policies being invented far away—above all, in Washington, DC.

This stage in the development of the press was thus a major step closer to the idea of civic information as we understand it today. With the development of the first mass media, civic information was detached from the social structure, enabling citizens to experience politics as mediated from far away. Further, increasing participation in political parties and large civic groups, often built with federal structures mirroring those of the government, gave citizens outlets for their civic energy. This was a new relationship between citizens and civic information: consuming civic information was becoming an important component of public life, and associated with active citizenship—though that often involved riots and social violence as well as the positive characteristics we tend to ascribe to active citizenship today.[53]

At the same time, there was much about this era of civic information that still differed greatly from later understandings. This had much to do with the rise of powerful national political parties: the citizen norms of the nineteenth century did not incline citizens toward rational and dispassionate evaluation of political facts. Instead, this was an era of party loyalty, patronage, and participation: the norm was to be an enthusiastic *participant*—in a party context—rather than an independent citizen.[54] This conception of citizenship is mirrored in the meaning of civic information: what a citizen was supposed to do with civic information in this period was much more about affirming one's views and becoming mobilized than about weighing competing facts and arguments.

THE PROGRESSIVE ERA AND THE ORIGINS OF INFORMED CITIZENSHIP

By the last years of the nineteenth century a number of trends were converging to create a time of major change in Western societies. Industrialization meant profound economic and demographic shifts, including urbanization, as millions of workers moved from farms and small communities and into cities in search of factory jobs. The jobs, work, and social environments those workers found in cities had new practices and routines—and were dictated by the logics of industrialism and capitalism, rather than small-time farming. Concepts of professionalization and rationalization were particularly important, insisting that scientific study, division of tasks, and careful allocation of resources could increase the efficiency of labor. And in the United States, a period of intense immigration was taking place, as especially southern and eastern Europeans arrived to work jobs in the growing cities. These transformed what had been a relatively homogeneous country into the ethnic melting pot for which the nation is known today—adding new complexity to the social and political environments citizens faced.[55]

Accompanying and responding to these changes was a broad and diverse movement for social and political reform that has come to be known, rather overgenerally, as Progressivism. The range of concerns ascribed to Progressives is wide, and includes labor rights, women's suffrage, temperance, good government, and much more. For our purposes, Progressives' confrontations with the citizenship and information norms of the previous century are particularly notable. Progressives looked on the party- and patronage-dominated system of the nineteenth century as antiquated and corrupt, and felt that politics could be improved by reforms aimed at giving citizens the information and power to understand and act on issues.

The application of the concept of *rationalization* is evident here, and forms a crucial component of the civic information paradigm that took shape during the time. Although rationalization was applied most famously in industry, such as in the studies and writings of Frederick Winslow Taylor, the idea was in fact socially widespread, and its influence can be seen in the Progressives' mentality toward political structures, citizen behavior, and civic information. Under a framework of rationalization, members of society had particular duties to fulfill in the work of democracy, and they must be properly equipped to fulfill those duties. One of their most important duties was the development of well-reasoned opinions, and like workers in a factory, they were responsible for taking in the raw material of civic information, and outputting those opinions. The process forms very nearly the antithesis of the passionate political events of the previous era, which was exactly the point: the Progressives were promoting a new understanding of society, a new working model of how politics works and should work. At the core of this model was a new conceptualization of what information could do for citizens and their institutions. This vision maintained that civic information could and should be produced in a rational, professional, and nonpartisan way, and consumed similarly, enabling citizens to improve on the problems of partisanship of the nineteenth century by applying their informed reason to public officials and issues. Here we see a coherent civic information paradigm take shape: the development of new information norms and practices showed what each element of the system meant and how it should operate.

First, if the emerging ideal of information was to exist, it would need a class of producers. The new field of professional journalism took it upon itself to be the stewards of this information, and in line with the professionalizing and bureaucratizing processes of the time established the first journalist guilds, schools, awards, and routines, all of which served to solidify the norm of rational, consumable information. The transition was momentous: what the Progressive mentality called for was a transformation of this practice into an information system that could provide citizens with the information they needed to make dispassionate, informed decisions.

While the new journalism was responsible for providing a steady baseline of objective, professionalized information, citizens also would benefit from associations that could structure their concerns and convert them into productive civic activity: the voluntary association. While those organizations, especially the ones organized to pursue a particular political interest, might be viewed as little more than issue-specific parties, in fact they fit quite logically with the Progressive worldview. It was not that citizens were expected to have no interests or principles, but that the political parties that had defined participation in the nineteenth century served only as focal points of blind loyalty and instruments of patronage. In place of loyalty-based parties, interest groups were seen as beneficial ways for citizens to work together to pursue rationally evaluated political goals.[56]

The decades leading up to the turn of the twentieth century were a new watershed for the development of civic organizations of myriad kinds that to a significant degree displaced the role that parties had played in structuring nineteenth-century civic involvement.[57] Organizational participation also provided a context for understanding the civic information citizens were experiencing through interactions with the press; civic groups produced their own information, interpretations of news events, and notices of meetings and activities.[58] This provided an alternative, complementary source of information for the informed citizen that complemented the consumption of journalism and explicitly connected information to civic action. Summing up these two functions of civic associations vis-à-vis citizens and civic information, Almond and Verba write:

> Through them the individual is able to relate himself effectively and meaningfully to the political system . . . because individuals tend to interpret communications according to their memberships in social groupings . . . and because they may also receive communications from their associations and are thereby provided with alternate channels of political communication.[59]

This is a model in which the model citizen selects favored voluntary organizations on the basis of principles, participated in their activities, received their communications, and understood and interpreted civic information in light of their affiliations.

Finally, of course, in addition to the roles assigned journalism and organizations, the Progressives' paradigm of civic information reserved a special place for the tasks of the informed citizen. The informed citizen has a responsibility to consume civic information, since his or her role in democracy is to use that information, particularly at election time, to evaluate leaders—and increasingly, with the Progressives' enthusiasm for direct democracy, policy itself. Further, like any other commodity, the citizen should consume information that has been produced by the highest standards of quality, as certified by journalistic professional standards. And the citizen should consume and evaluate this information as a rational actor with principles, not partisanship: as "rational sifters and winnowers of facts,"[60] aided by the citizen's principle-driven participation and membership in social organizations. At election time, the aggregation of the knowledge and opinion that had been developed over time dutifully spent consuming news should be brought to bear on the candidate choices and policy questions put before the citizen on the ballot. This conception of citizenship is deeply intertwined with its conceptualization of how citizens use information. And it places a large burden on individual citizens, whose previous participation, as we have seen, had been channeled, in the colonial era, into the approval of elite leaders, and in the party era stimulated by the spectacles of party politics, in which the good citizen was expected to be mobilizable but otherwise not particularly "informed."

One of the paradoxes of the establishment of informed citizenship is that just as the norms described above were gaining widespread acceptance, it was becoming apparent how woefully short of the informed standard almost all citizens fell. Walter Lippmann, a prescient observer of the new mass society, was one of the first and best to articulate these concerns: he famously charged that most citizens are too busy, and prefer to do any number of things before following the news to stay informed. To the extent that citizens do attempt to follow public affairs rigorously, many are cognitively poor at it and almost all have a disturbing tendency toward generalization and stereotyping based on limited information about people and things they cannot personally experience. In sum:

> The real environment is altogether too big, too complex, and too fleeting for direct acquaintance. We are not equipped to deal with so much subtlety, so much variety, so many permutations and combinations. And although we have to act in that environment, we have to reconstruct it on a simpler model before we can manage with it.[61]

Ironically, however, these concerns had little effect on a model of informed citizenship becoming the dominant standard by which American citizens understood themselves, civic information, and the institutions of politics through the twentieth century. It continued to be represented and exemplified in the institutions, practices, and standards that constituted the high modern era that encompassed the heart of the twentieth century.[62] In fact, the informed ideal remains our society's natural starting point for understanding citizens, communication, and civic information: it is one of the Progressives' longest lasting legacies. And although scholars have worked hard to imagine an updated standard for late-twentieth-century citizens, most acknowledge that it is the informed model that still structures our (popular as well as academic) understanding of what a good citizen is and does with information: witness the self-criticism of the young people in David Mindich's aptly subtitled book, *Why Americans Under 40 Don't Follow the News*. They "know" they "should" follow the news, though it doesn't resonate with them.[63]

But though the civic information ideal may remain, much else has changed, as we are about to see. We must ask the extent to which our fixedness on a set of century-old information norms now stands as a barrier to productive reimaginings of citizens' interactions with civic information.

MEDIA POLITICS—AND WHAT COMES NEXT

In recent decades, another set of communication circumstances has slowly but inexorably replaced those of the Progressive Era. Scholars have used several names to describe it, including the "third age of political communication" or the fall of the "High Modern."[64] Here we will adopt the evocative phrase "media politics" to refer to the constellation of economic and social circumstances, journalistic norms, technologies, and strategies in which politics is dominated by, and predominantly played out via, media; in which communications media become the primary grounds for the contestation of political ends.[65] The consequences of media politics have been described in a variety of ways, but the common thread running through almost all accounts is a sort of corruption of the information relationships that underpinned high modernity. Murray Edelman has described the power of the "political spectacle" in the sense that what is portrayed in communications takes on a weight and importance often greater than what is real—and that it is being performed before citizens who are spectators but rarely actors. Timothy Cook has shown how this power turns media industries into unelected institutions of governance alongside legislatures and executives. As a result, according to Joseph Cappella and Kathleen Hall Jamieson, what we often observe in public communications is a cynical exchange between politicians and media elites, as each obtains desired outcomes in sometimes antagonistic, sometimes collusive, exchanges.[66]

The consequences for citizen participation under these circumstances are dire: the media politics perspective profoundly indicts our society's communication patterns for citizens' responses of disgust, bewilderment, and retreat: this is a "democracy without citizens" and a "crisis of public communication."[67] The role of the citizen is greatly diminished, and though civics classes and social norms still remind us of the need to perform the role of the informed citizen, more often we are called upon to be strategically and selectively mobilized for fundraising appeals and at specific election intervals. For their part, the civic organizations that once fostered local participation and informed national engagement have in large part turned their backs on citizen-members. To participate in the system of media politics, interest groups of all varieties adopted increasingly strategic and expensive tactics of communication warfare, leading them to focus work on securing funds for television advertising much more than engaging citizens in regular action.[68] A prominent result of all this is plummeting citizen faith in the major systems of communication and institutions of society.

Given this grim view of the media politics era, what is most promising about our civic communication circumstances is that they continue to rapidly change. The widespread dispersion of internetworked digital technologies, and the constant development and redevelopment of social technologies built on them, means that the seams of media politics are being stretched, often beyond their breaking points. It would be a mistake to portray the digital revolution as a quantum shift from the trajectories of media politics, as some of the trends associated with media politics, including media fragmentation, channel proliferation, and new formats for transmission are closely related technically to the underpinnings of the digital communications infrastructure.[69] Nonetheless, the development of personalization of networked digital media tools, beginning arguably with pioneering amateurs in the 1980s but becoming commonplace with the invention of the World Wide Web and first graphical browsers in the 1990s, is also something distinct.[70] Whereas media politics in many ways reduced the significance of citizens in the civic information process, some recent trends may do the opposite. The possibilities of what citizens can do with information have expanded well beyond changing the channel: they now also include constructing personalized and unique networks of news sources through RSS feeds and news aggregators; sharing and receiving news within a social network or blogging community; independently producing, sharing, and commenting on content; and much more.[71] It may be most accurate to suggest that we continue to live under conditions of media politics, but in the past decade the citizen's role in this system has been fundamentally transforming.

Every element of society is struggling to contend with the implications of these changes. News organizations and media companies are being challenged, and in some cases displaced, by upstarts from the digital world that promise their users new varieties of information experience. The giants Google and Facebook, for instance, with constant innovations and techniques for interacting with and reinventing the information superstructure, have proven themselves both competitors and tantalizing partners for existing information providers. Politicians and their consultants are striving, with attempts that span the range from comical to visionary, to reinvent their relationship with constituents. Howard Dean's 2004 campaign is typically seen as the pioneer of successful digital campaigning, and Obama's its refiner.[72] Many are learning the hard way that the playing field of civic information has been forever changed: the infamous early example came from Senate majority leader Trent Lott in 2002, when he made prosegregation comments at a birthday party for Strom Thurmond. As Lawrence Lessig described it, "[Lott] calculated correctly that this story would disappear from the mainstream press within forty-eight hours. It did. But he didn't calculate its life cycle in blog space. The bloggers kept researching the story . . . Finally, the story broke back into the mainstream press . . . [and] Lott was forced to resign as senate majority leader." Senator George Allen's lesson came when he referred to an opposition researcher of Indian descent as "Macaca"—a misguided move given that the man was holding a digital camera and taping the encounter; it cost him the election. In 2008, Obama proved that such gaffes were not only for Republicans when he told a San Francisco fundraiser crowd that many rural Americans cling to "guns and religion" because they feel threatened by change. And Mitt Romney followed in 2012 with his suggestion that 47% of the public were not interested in working, but expected to live off the largesse of government.[73] In none of these cases did the established institutions of media politics break the story. Instead, unexpected media tools, such as digital video, and sources, such as bloggers, gave rise to a major stories that either would not have been pursued by conventional journalists or lacked visceral power without live documentation—upending assumptions about who produces civic information and how it reaches the public.

Indeed, such examples highlight the fact that it is at the level of individual interaction and coordination that the civic effects of the new digital tools may be most profoundly felt. From influential bloggers creating their own audience/communities (e.g., DailyKos on the left, the late Andrew Breitbart on the right) to innovation and experimentation in the nonprofit sector, to powerful new political forces (e.g., MoveOn and various Tea Party movements), to uses of social media for political purposes, we are experiencing the experimental, discordant but exciting times of genuine change in how citizens relate to the political world and try to exercise their power in it.[74] Nowhere are the changes more apparent than in the lives of young people, widely noted for heavy use of digital tools and related innovation in information practice.[75] Within the civic information framework under development here, what this suggests is that we are in the midst of a period of reshaping, as citizens and groups experiment and rethink the nature of civic information and its possibilities. *The Civic Organization and the Digital Citizen* contends that this rethinking is profound enough to constitute a new paradigm of civic information, albeit one that is in its infancy and still incompletely formed.

It is into this context that we place the movements that opened this chapter. The claim is not that they are representative of youth digital civic experience in any strict sense, but that they exhibit characteristics of the information expectations and preferences of the emerging paradigm. At the least, there are several notable patterns of recent networked social activism that we should note.

Their speed is especially striking. This is what attracted many observers to one of the original digitally facilitated protest moments: the 1999 Seattle protests against a meeting of the World Trade Organization. The ability of those activists to coalesce rapidly, apparently out of nowhere, and to have an emergent crowd intelligence led Howard Rheingold to call them "smart mobs."[76] More recent work has specified in more detail that the 1999 protests were no aberration, but an early instance of a new class of movements able to scale and reach impressive magnitude very quickly even in the absence of the formal organizing structures that have conventionally been associated with mass movements. In fact, we appear to be seeing networked movements with features once thought to be highly disadvantageous for collective action: permeable barriers, flattened hierarchies, and ideological pluralism.

Such movements benefit from the fact that digital communication technologies greatly reduce the costs of communication and coordination for movements and their supporters. As a result, the process of crossing the private-public divide that once was so costly is greatly eased, and the collective danger posed by free-riding falls. Movements consequently have less incentive to maintain rigid boundaries between members and nonmembers, and begin maintaining communicative relationships that are much more open and fluid.[77]

At the same time, also because of the falling costs of communication, the need for a command-and-control hierarchical structure that can bureaucratically store and access information falls. Whereas Weberian institutions relied on information silos that could be organized and selectively accessed by credentialed officials, the abundance of data and sorting capabilities made possible by digital technology and networked infrastructures means that information control can be greatly decentralized. Interestingly, what this has often meant for contemporary protest movements is that decision-making processes have also been decentralized, sometimes to the point that the movement has difficulty making collective decisions or coalescing around goals.[78] Along these lines, contemporary movements have tended to allow much greater diversity of ideological commitment and meaning construction than previous mass movements could tolerate. As Bennett, Breunig, and Givens describe, participants in the pan-global movements against the Iraq War tended to be members of a variety of organizations rather than identifying with only one; further, they identified themselves as concerned with a variety of topics: few were single-issue activists concerned only about a narrow topic. All of this is a considerable departure from previous eras of collective organizing, which relied considerably more heavily on defined membership, leadership, and strategy to achieve their goals.[79]

Contemporary scholarship on networked civic organizing has tended to emphasize these structural characteristics. What this discussion should add is that networked activism also tend to offer *experiences of civic information* that are distinct from those on offer from media politics. We see in these movements opportunities for participants to experiment with and express highly individualized political identities. The personally networked opportunities of the connective media facilitate this, as they allow for both an exchange of information between network nodes and the construction of flexible identities within the network; the less formal obligations of action and membership mean that participants are not punished for pursuing their own concerns (within the broader umbrella of the issue at hand).[80] In sum, such movements offer anchoring points for acting out issues of personal concern while also accommodating diverse action repertoires, ease of entry and exit, ideological flexibility, and opportunities for self-expression. These are important clues to why the movements are successful, and what they tell us about the civic information preferences of contemporary young citizens.

A RESEARCH AGENDA FOR CIVIC ORGANIZATION AND DIGITAL MEDIA

Digitally networked social movements are intriguing and revealing indicators of the information expectations and preferences of many young citizens. But we would be hard-pressed to argue that such movements will, or can, be the extent of youth participation in politics. Especially, significant questions have been raised about the capacities of such movements to exert conventional political influence.[81] As we saw at the outset of this chapter, each of the three movements under examination has gone through a process of energy, excitement, and some success (most pronounced in the Egyptian case), followed by very painful realizations of political impotence in the conventional realm: they have found themselves stymied when the locus of action moves from streets to democratic institutions. These include the challenges faced by the liberal youth movement in Egypt, which played a leading role in the downfall of Mubarak but has struggled to effectively mobilize for elections and parliamentary government, as well as the failure of both the Spanish Indignados and the American Occupy Wall Street movement to successfully interface between large and energetic street demonstrations and electoral and policy spheres. Movements against the Iraq War, neoliberal globalization, and climate change have similarly sparse records of success. In short, such movements appear to have the complement of institutionalized civil society: large, creative, youthful, and mobilized citizen bases, but little significant input into formal political process. What are missing are connections between a young citizenry demanding autonomous and expressive communication relationships and the institutions of government that call the shots of policy.

This is where the legacy organizations of civil society are sorely missed. It was their expertise, structure, and communications that for decades helped Americans to situate themselves and act in an increasingly complex civic environment. We would be mistaken to write them off as simply archaic dinosaurs of the bygone mass-mediated twentieth century; they will be needed in our civic future. What's more, if, as I will argue, the contemporary challenge to civic involvement has a largely communicative character, civil society has a chance to return to a leading role in engagement. Considerable attention has been devoted to the *structures* of engagement facilitated by contemporary networked movements, particularly in contrast to those of conventional organizations, and these are undoubtedly important. But the civic information perspective highlights the fact that the underlying structures of engagement are not the whole story: for the typical young citizen observing the civic world through a stream of networked communication, the sorts of *communicative relationships* maintained between organizations (or movements) and potential supporters may also be crucial.[82] It is these communicative relationships, and their establishment through different styles of civic information, that we interrogate throughout the book. In the process, this perspective offers unique insight into a number of questions currently being debated by thinkers at the intersections of digital media, social life, and civic engagement.

Theorizing the Digital Information Paradigm

First, the book uses the concept of civic information to reconceptualize young citizens' orientations to the civic/communication world. The framework developed in the next chapter is built on work describing a shift away from modern-era norms of citizenship. Scholars have identified important trends, but in general have reached less agreement about exactly what is replacing those norms, as evidenced by the variety of terms describing young citizens' emergent practices, including Russell Dalton's "engaged," Lance Bennett's "actualizing," Ronald Inglehart's "postmaterialist," Cliff Zukin and colleagues' "DotNet," and others.[83]

This book adds an important and underappreciated element to this discussion. Following Kjerstin Thorson's contention that most accounts overestimate the coherence and distinctiveness of citizen norms, this book argues that the most productive approach to understanding how young citizens relate to politics may not be to continue retheorizing civic style. Instead, combining accounts of late modern civic experience with the unique set of information practices increasingly habitual to young digital citizens may reveal more about the civic world young people inhabit. The framework of the next chapter is thus one of *civic information styles*, and specifically contrasts the received, legacy style of modern-era citizenship—and, crucially, the native language of dominant social institutions—with that of digital media and young citizens.

Civic Information as the Basis for the Citizen-Organization Relationship

One advantage of thinking in terms of civic information rather than the specific form of the news is that it highlights the diverse and voluminous communication environment citizens face today. A primary challenge of political communication is understanding who, exactly, is producing the political information that reaches citizens, the channels by which it flows, and what citizens do with it.

The Civic Organization and the Digital Citizen contributes to this conversation by recognizing civic organizations as participants in the developing media ecology and potentially major sources of civic information for many citizens. This is not a wholly new role for civic organizations, as Chapter 3 makes clear: particularly in the earlier twentieth century, civic organizations played major roles in providing information and interpretive resources to citizen-members. The conditions of media politics interfered with this role. But in the networked information society, this role potentially returns to the fore, as citizens once again turn to organizations and movements of interest for interpretations of an increasingly scattered news environment. Individuals' choices to affiliate with civic organizations online constitute conduits in their experiences of civic information also contribute to the further blurring of the lines between information consumption and civic participation.

What the empirical results of the studies presented in the book show, however, is reticence on the part of many legacy civic organizations to embrace the digital media ecology of which they are now a part. This finding supports the book's early chapters' description of the disjuncture between many young citizens' civic information styles and those of the institutions of politics. And it highlights the gulf between young citizens and key elements of civil society. The result of these findings is a case for bringing citizens and civil society organizations back together—to reinvent the citizen-civil society relationship through an interaction of information flows. Importantly, this is not about returning to a dutiful era membership in the sense of the modern society. Rather, it is about civic organizations recognizing their potential as nodes in a constant flow of information, and occasional action points, in citizens' diverse social-information networks.

Connecting Institutionalism and Networked Individualism

In the process of contemplating the future of the citizen-organization relationship, this book offers a pronounced counterpoint to a dominant discourse holding that the future of engagement lies in citizens opting individually for actions at specific times on the basis of opportunistic communications coming over digital networks. This view has enjoyed a number of manifestations, including smart mobs and "organizing without organizations."[84] The idea has been especially enthusiastically applied to recent protest movements in the Middle East, though sometimes over enthusiastically, most infamously in the case of the Green Revolution in Iran in 2009.[85] More recently, this excitement has been challenged by alternative perspectives that argue that digital media should not be seen as a monolithically liberating or democratic tool, and that digitally mobilized engagement may have inherent limitations.[86]

In this book, we explicitly explore the role of civic organizations in a digitally mediated space for civic communication. Rather than abandon formal civic groups, it makes the case that organizations will continue to play fundamental roles in connecting citizens with politics. In this, it develops Kreiss and colleagues' astute criticism of the digital empowerment narrative by looking back on genuine advantages of bureaucratic organization.[87]

This is not to say that the book fails to recognize profound changes in social structure and communication context—far from it. The book's contribution in this area is an exploration of how civic organizations can better adapt themselves to a society of networked individuals who increasingly live their lives through personally, rather than institutionally, managed relationships to others.[88] It is the tension between modern-era institutionalism, or bureaucracy, and digital-era networked individualism that the book attempts to address. Its approach to the problem is to focus on communication dynamics: it insists that civic organizations must adapt to seeing themselves as sources of and sites for civic information within the networks of their potential supporters. In this, they become less stand-alone, strategic institutions focused exclusively interfacing with government and policies and more nodes in the diverse and voluminous information networks their constituents are embedded in. The studies offered in Chapters 4 and 5 point up the challenge for civic organizations here: most are highly reticent to abandon a dutiful-era one-to-many, crafted and strategic relationship with supporters. But that relationship makes less and less sense to citizens whose experience of information is dominantly one of exchange and interaction.

The advantage of viewing the relationship in communicative terms is that it is actually relatively optimistic for organizations' future in digital media. Unlike dominant work in the field of social capital and social group participation, which laments the passing of a social structure that is simply not returning, the challenge identified in this book has its roots in communication style, and thus suggests some malleability.[89] The concept of communicative autonomy is developed here as a way of assessing the dynamics of a communication relationship that is beyond media and specific social structures. Although it may be difficult—Chapters 4 and 5 suggest that indeed it is—organizations' communication practices may be adaptable in ways other elements of their relationship to supporters are not.

Plan of the Book

The preceding pages have established a framework for thinking about how citizens relate to the political world, and especially the crucial political intermediaries of civic organizations, through civic information. We have seen that the nature of civic information—and with it the roles and practices of information producers, distributors, and consumers—have taken different forms in different social, political and technological contexts. And we have made the case that we are currently in the midst of such a shift in civic information paradigm, as citizens and institutions struggle with the legacies of modern-era informed citizenship and media politics and experiment with the possibilities of the new digital media environment.

The task of Chapter 2 is to describe the transition underway today. It presents a theorization of two civic information styles currently in competition. The argument made is that the informed set of norms and practices described is increasingly challenged by a new set of practices reflective of ongoing social changes and digital patterns of information exchange, which I term *actualizing*. Further, the fact that younger citizens are more likely to embrace the norms and practices of the emerging information style puts their expectations of communication into potential opposition with established political communicators, including civic organizations. Understanding the conflict between these information styles may be key to understanding recent dynamics of civic participation.

Especially, the information styles identified in Chapter 2 raise the important question of how well the communications of civic institutions complement youthful preferences: to what extent are the organizations of civil society willing or able to adapt to the changing communication environment? Chapter 3 addresses this question, beginning with a review of a hundred years of the civic organization–citizen relationship, with an emphasis on the communication dynamics that have characterized the relationship over time. What it shows is that the direct mail check-writing memberships maintained over the decades of media politics may be a particularly anemic expression of the relationship—but that it has not always been so. Citizen members of the early modern society were situated in local organizations and local chapters of nationally federated institutions that afforded them considerable opportunity to define their own membership and influence the meanings and directions of the group. In addition to the sense of membership these engendered, an active and reciprocal communicative relationship was also essential. The chapter develops the concept of *communicative autonomy* to describe the experience of an individual, in an interpersonally grounded organization or an online network, and what it means to citizens to be able to express political identities and define their interactions within the group.

And it reiterates that one of the issues underlying late-modern civic ennui may be the disconnect between the communication styles honed by institutions in late-twentieth-century media politics and younger citizens' increasingly actualizing information preferences. The question is the extent to which digital media, with its own logics of exchange and dispersion, will change this. The chapter's end considers the ability of civic organizations to change their communication patterns, and the question of which kinds of organizations will be most able to do so.

Chapters 4 and 5 deliver detailed empirical analyses of just those communication patterns. They present two studies of the communications of a range of organizations attempting, in different forms and with different goals, to engage young people in politics. Organizations in the sample include some of the oldest and most established interest groups, such as the Sierra Club and National Rifle Association; the political parties, candidates, and government agencies; community-oriented nonpartisan organizations like the Boys and Girls' Clubs and the Girl Scouts and Boy Scouts; and cutting-edge, "online only" organizations that connect with supporters primarily online.

In Chapter 4 we examine the kind of civic communication offered by organizations when they have complete control over an Internet medium that yields considerable ability to structure the experience of their users: through their websites. To each of a diverse sample of 90 websites are applied measures for dutiful and actualizing communication patterns. The study offers validation of our conceptualization of civic information styles and the organizations that exhibit them: newer, online-only organizations are the most likely to present engagement opportunities that are participatory and expressive of individual identities. Such opportunities are quite rare on the websites of other types of organizations, suggesting considerable reticence to embrace the emerging information style.

Websites, however, are far from the only digital space in which organizations may interact with supporters—and they likely are no longer even the primary place. To address this issue, Chapter 5 considers what happens when organizations, habituated as they are to a communication logic that prizes message control and instrumental, strategic action above all else, enter a communication context that exudes interactivity and information exchange. Specifically, it considers how organizations adapt their communication patterns when they are communicating to young people not on their websites, but through the social media giant Facebook. The possibility raised is that on Facebook a set of information norms closer to those of young citizens is inscribed, and civic organizations there may be more likely to adapt their communications in that direction.

Tapping into organizations' Facebook presences, and the information they disseminate to supporters' news feeds via status updates, thus offers a unique opportunity to assess how they are communicating in this medium. Building on the study of website communications in Chapter 4, Chapter 5 identifies the 60 organizations from that study that established presences using the Facebook Page functionality. It then uses similar measures, adapted to the Facebook status update, to identify differing patterns of civic communication. Here, although the evidence suggests that they remain deeply hesitant to expose themselves to the considerable risks that true interactivity and openness entail, we do detect some indications that organizations are beginning to reconceptualize the role of their members. In particular, we find that organizations offer a variety of engagement opportunities through Facebook rarely offered in websites—especially, encouragements to members to be active in shaping their own information experiences and those of the people around them.

Chapter 6 concludes the project and explores the implications of the empirical studies. In light of their findings, it reconsiders literature on late twentieth-century organizational practices and draws parallels between the organization-building era of the turn of the twentieth century and the potential of the early twenty-first. It also reflects on the consequences of political organizations' struggle to adapt to participatory and networked communication modes. And it raises and attempts to answer a central question: how do we reconcile a civic-political system fundamentally rooted in institutional bureaucracy with a society whose citizens increasingly display the characteristics and preferences of networked individualism?[90] The book's findings point toward communication dynamics as a key element of this issue. It develops the importance of communicative autonomy in creating spaces for citizens to make sense of the world—for themselves, but also in the context of civic organizations that can offer inputs into the political decision-making process. In this way, it is asking organizations to adapt to a communication world in which they are nodes in the multifaceted networks of their supporters—hardly the identity-grounding socially embedded institutions of the past; while at the same time maintaining their productive and strategic interface with government.

2

Two Paradigms of Civic Information

In his day, Walter Cronkite really was the most trusted man in America. A poll conducted by Roper in 1974 found that 60% of respondents respected the newsman "a great deal," while another 31% responded "somewhat." That left less than one respondent in ten who either did not know of Cronkite or did not respect his work.[1]

No newscaster today remotely approaches that level of popularity and authority. A 2009 *Time Magazine* poll found the top spot occupied by "fake news" host Jon Stewart, perhaps indicative of the current condition of broadcast news.[2] What has changed? Is it that we simply do not have an individual like "Uncle Walter" broadcasting today? Have the news media undermined their own credibility by overplaying titillation and sensationalism at the expense of hard news? Has the press too often compromised itself in its close relationships with powerful government actors? Has the "collapse of political consensus," political polarization, and media fragmentation ended the possibility of speaking to the whole of a nation? There is some truth in each of these assertions.[3] But underlying them is a deeper and more fundamental set of changes of which the decline of our broadcast news system is but one symptom. This chapter will make the case that a shift in civic information paradigm is underway, and attempt to add some specificity to what is happening.

But to begin illustrating the magnitude of this change, let us briefly return to Uncle Walter. Consider the nature of the information exchange that occurred when Cronkite was operating at his peak: at 6:30pm each day, Cronkite appeared on CBS to read the news. Literally: he sat at a desk not unlike any other in an American office, and read, off sheets of paper, the news stories he and his team had prepared. At moments of breaking news, he was handed fresh sheets by an assistant mostly out of the frame. He did so for a half-hour a day, with occasional hand-offs to a reporter in the field or a prepared segment. The production of authoritative civic information exhibited the hallmarks of modernity: it was constructed and delivered in a rational, unornamented, and dispassionate manner by professionals specialized in the trade. Cronkite was the consummate professional, and as such reflected the sort of modern ideal discussed in Chapter 1.[4]

And the audience fulfilled its end of the bargain: People came home from their professions, where they built houses or assembled cars or sold insurance, and watched Cronkite perform *his* profession. In the process, they fulfilled one of their most hallowed responsibilities of the informed citizen: to learn about the political issues of the day and prepare for future engagement moments—voting, of course, as well as organizational events and social interactions that could involve civic topics.

Were viewers consciously thinking about the civic duty they were performing by watching the news? Of course, most were not. A good number simply could not be bothered to turn off the television between entertainment programs.[5] Nonetheless, in the moment of respected newsman joined with his audience, the civic-communication values of the modern society were reified and affirmed. Cronkite performed his role as purveyor of essential civic information—and, occasionally and famously, critic of policies—and citizens performed their sacred duty to become informed. This was a cultural practice, a ritual in the temple of civic modernity, that went to the heart of defining what the press was, who citizens were, and how civic information was to be used in that relationship.

I point to this example as an illustration of how much our experience of civic information has changed in the last 50 years. The state of the news is just one facet of this change, but an illustrative one. Fewer and fewer citizens sit down in front of evening network news broadcasts, and their hair has turned almost completely white: one of the most striking and oft-cited characteristics of younger generations of citizens is their lack of interest in news.[6] Those who do tune in do not experience the sort of news product Cronkite produced: the style and practice of the news industry transformed dramatically between the 1970s and the early twenty-first century, as newscasters on a greater number of channels sought to appeal to and capture audiences with abundant choices for news, entertainment, or anything else. They no longer are captive at six in the evening. In addition, increasing profits pressures that are the result of reorganization of the economics of news production have led broadcasters to an increasingly desperate race for ratings.[7] Broadcast news has adopted practices from entertainment television—dramatic graphics, technological wizardry, and an aura of constant suspense. Geoffrey Baym concludes that these changes have left what was once a venerable institution of American democracy "a communicative form in decay."[8]

The argument of this chapter is that the same can be said for the larger civic information paradigm of the high modern era. But if that paradigm is decaying, what is taking its place? How does civic information operate in the early twenty-first century? We do not yet have a fully-fledged information paradigm in place[9]—a key problem underlying contemporary debates over what is news, whether citizens are consuming enough of it, and the lines between information and activism. But some of its defining characteristics are taking shape,

and in this chapter we trace them, ultimately proposing that we can understand our current moment as an inflection point between two civic information paradigms: one the legacy of a modern society and modern-era media, and
one emergent from the conditions of "late" modernity and the surprisingly
related information practices developing in digital media.

To develop this civic information typology, we will draw on theory and
evidence on the civic and communicative practices of young citizens, who are
important for two reasons. First, as the future of society, their practices are
in and of themselves critical to the functioning of democracy in the future.[10]
Second, and more theoretically consequential here, as the most recent generation they have most acutely experienced the social and technological changes
that are driving much of the paradigm shift in the meaning and use of civic
information. Indications of the emerging information paradigm should thus
be most visible among younger people. Though generational boundaries are
inherently fuzzy and imprecise, in this book we conceptualize young people as
those born between about 1980 and the mid-1990s, who at the time of writing
span an age range from the teens to about 30 years old.

More specifically, in what follows we will try to describe what, exactly,
has changed since the modern civic information paradigm was at its height.
Our focus will be on two areas fundamental to the civic information shifts
we are seeing: changes in social organization that have altered basic foundations of civic life and citizen identity for many citizens of the industrialized
West, and changes in how individuals interact with information as a result of
now-habitual experiences with digital communication technologies. As we will
see, though conceptually separate processes, a close look reveals them to be
deeply and consequentially intertwined.

The Shifting Foundations of Citizenship

I will not pretend to capture in a few pages the extent of social change that has
occurred in the decades separating the lived experiences of young citizens from
those of their parents, grandparents, great-grandparents, and other members
of the high modern society. Many books have been written to explain what is
happening to the social structures that were the early products of industrialization and bureaucratization in the western democracies.[11] In what follows we
will narrow our focus to several trends that have been most consequential to
how citizens understand themselves today, in the period that has been called
late modernity,[12] and how communication is implicated in contemporary processes of civic identity formation and maintenance.

At the core of accounts charting the coming of late modernity is a story
about change in the basic relationships individuals have with one another and

with larger structures of society. In particular, one of the modern society's basic organizing logics, the organization of social processes through formal groups, is breaking down. This bureaucratic form of social organization provided a number of resources in short supply a hundred years ago: differentiation and specialization of tasks, allowing the development and application of a new level of expertise, rationalization, and use of science, all coordinated across large institutions serving (newly) mass publics. In short, the bureaucratic social form offered the ability to efficiently perform functions that other social forms could not, enabling the growth and increased efficiency of social structures as diverse as armies, corporations and civic groups.[13] Most significant to the present discussion, this means that individual social experience was largely organized through group structures: groups helped manage citizens' community interactions, economic opportunities, mitigation of risk, and participation in civic affairs. It would be incorrect to say that we live today in a postbureaucratic society—it's obvious that a great many of our society's functions are still accomplished with the aid of bureaucracies—but in the sphere of civic experience, the trend is in an indisputably postbureaucratic direction.[14] Some of the best evidence is the decline of formal civic groups: individuals appear to be losing their inclinations for creating and participating within formally organized groups for collective action. These include labor unions, fraternal organizations, parent-teacher associations, interest groups, and, as Robert Putnam has famously pointed out, bowling leagues.[15]

But why are civic group declines taking place? The answer is complex, and involves individuals in late modern society pulling away from civic organizations in two opposing directions: on the one hand, they turn their attention to increasingly global concerns—to the supranational realm in which global power is increasingly contested. On the other, they look inward and toward hyperlocal opportunities for the development of satisfying civic identity. We might say that modern-era civic organizations occupy a sort of midlevel donut hole being abandoned by late modern citizens. We will take these two trends in turn.

THE GLOBALIZATION OF POLITICAL POWER

Manuel Castells has offered the most extensive accounts of the emergence of the "network society." What he shows is that economic and cultural globalization, the information technology revolution, and consequent changes in how employment and work are experienced, are all redefining the shape of society. The result is a "network society" characterized by unprecedented connectedness across a myriad of spheres, from world finance to transnational activism. The old logics of space and time morph in the network society into something new: a "space of flows" that takes the place of older space-based organizing structures.[16]

We might expect citizens responding to this new global connectedness to reach outward toward power structures now located in the world network. And we do see this. Trends in transnational activism, for instance, demonstrate increasing cross-national affiliation of activists who share strategies, tactics, and objectives and target global corporations and trade organizations in lieu of conventional national governments.[17] Political action in the form of lifestyle politics often finds inspiration in global conceptions of issues such as world hunger, economic justice, and environmental concerns.[18] As a result, there is a distinctive cosmopolite trend to contemporary citizenship, as citizens find transnational or global relevance for action. Occasionally this also takes the form of rooted cosmopolitanism, captured in the famous phrase "think global, act local." However, such cosmopolitanism, expressed as it often is through transnational activism, poses challenges to much of the civil society of the modern era, oriented as it is to national—or even more local-level—participation and policymaking.[19]

Part of the source of this challenge is the fact that surviving modern era institutions appear increasingly unable to deal with the problems faced by their would-be constituents. For instance, as the American economy has globalized, the fortunes of a broad swath of American society have become increasingly precarious: since the 1970s wages have stagnated, layoffs have loomed, and unprecedented numbers of people have sought second or even third jobs to make ends meet. Working multiple jobs itself takes up time that might otherwise be devoted to participation in organized group activities; even more potent, as workers have become dependent on the capricious decision-making of transnational corporations and global markets, it becomes painfully obvious how little power both individuals and conventional social groups have over decisions that frequently uproot lives.[20]

To a significant extent, individuals in this society are left on their own: this is a risk society in which the precariousness of (comfortable) life is close, and the increasing impotence of social institutions to mitigate that risk obvious.[21] In the classic modern society, risk was one of many problems managed through social groups: a stable job, a responsive union, a brotherly club all offered ways to manage the many risks incurred simply by living. In the late modern society, by contrast, that burden is increasingly borne on individual shoulders as the socializing institutions have crumbled under the weight of change.[22] The sorrowful plight of labor unions in the last decades of the twentieth century offers a case in point. Unions once were essential repositories of risk insurance: a vocal advocate for workers' employment, pay, and conditions; protections and often insurance in the case of accident or illness; and, not least, camaraderie fostered on the factory floor and on picket lines. Their decline over several decades has meant that workers are increasingly at the mercy of employers no longer burdened by the need to negotiate with unions. Workers are on their own: the risk remains, but it is increasingly the individual's task to cope.

When citizens find themselves less and less able—or, in the case of many young people today, never able to begin with—to depend on institutional structures to help them find work, develop satisfying civic identities, or solve social problems, they lose identification with and trust in those structures. A large-scale social secularization has taken place,[23] meaning that the social and political institutions that once helped to structure individuals' lives—and through which individuals themselves were once afforded a structured degree of influence—have lost both their political power over social and economic processes and their credibility and authority with their former publics. A series of failures of some the largest and most visible civic institutions, such as government and the press, does not help. Events such as Watergate, official and journalist-enabled prevarication about wars from Vietnam to Nicaragua to Iraq, the Catholic Church's devastating child predation scandals, and the wrenching financial crises beginning in 2007 also suggest to many citizens that the major institutions of society are at best inept, at worst fundamentally corrupt. [24]

The result has been a downward spiral in the legitimacy of social institutions of nearly every stripe, from every agency and branch of government to the press, business, and religious organizations.[25] The decline is a major liability for political organizations, which are increasingly understood as interest groups regardless of their aims and constituency.[26] This has an understandable direct effect on political participation, as citizens choose not to engage with structures they have little faith in being able to influence. But the detachment from nongovernmental social groups also plays a large role as younger citizens desert (more properly, never join to begin with) civic information sources, including the news and civil society organizations, that have been at the heart of civic engagement for a century and a half.[27]

THE PERSONALIZATION OF CIVIC IDENTITY

At the same time as existing social institutions appear decreasingly relevant in the face of power shifting into the global net, the expected response of the globalization of civic concern, identity, and organization is not materializing. Notwithstanding transnational activist networks, in fact "we observe the opposite trend throughout the world, namely, the increasing distance between globalization and identity, between the Net and the self."[28] The hyperconnectedness of the global network society has a paradoxically reductionist effect, increasing the salience of individual-level concerns at the expense of broader conceptions of self and public. The interconnectedness enabled by the web would seem to increase our capacity for identifying with one another on a global scale, but that is not the case: What are instead emphasized are individual, nationalistic, and local identities. Today, individuals are challenged to establish and maintain personal identities in the onslaught of uncontrollable information: it is a "crisis of the self, shaken by uncontrollable connectedness," in Castells's phrase.[29]

What Castells is pointing out is that each late modern individual still strives to develop a satisfying self-conception—or identity; the conditions of late modernity, however, make the creation of a satisfying and authentic identity all the more challenging. In the modern society, the social groupings with which one was associated offered an important identity anchor: one was a Teamster, or an Elk, or a member of a church, or of the Progressive Study Club of Henry, South Dakota.[30] With the declining relevance of these anchors, identity establishment and maintenance becomes a further individual-level responsibility. Anthony Giddens has described late modernity as a period of intense reflexivity, as institutions and individuals continually construct and update their practices and, most especially, their "narratives of the self."[31] These narratives are ongoing stories that must be maintained as a core source of identity in a world in which traditional identity sources have been removed or found lacking. An individual's actions and habits find their motivation, or at least justification, in their congruence with the ongoing narrative: an individual is inclined toward practices that bolster the positive aspects of the narrative, whatever those may be. In Giddens's words, "The narrative of self-identity has to be shaped, altered and reflexively sustained in relation to rapidly changing circumstances of social life, on a local and global scale."[32] As a result, what we see are a host of practices that help individuals to establish and maintain satisfying identifies. These include an obsession with fashion and taste and the nature of self-presentation that is possible through them—often known as lifestyle politics.[33]

Yet it would not be quite accurate to simply claim that individuals are suffering from isolation and atomization. This is not what is happening—because forms of association are coming into focus that are replacing, or at least taking some of the burden earlier shouldered by social groups. In particular, this is a shift from a society organized around groups and institutions to one constituted through networks. Late modern citizens are increasingly experiencing a form of social organization that Barry Wellman terms "networked individualism."[34] The dual nature of the term captures the sense of the idea: networked individuals are individuals in the sense that they stand independent from formal social groupings in a way distinct from members of the modern society. But they are not isolated or atomized: the nature of their connections with others tends to be through networks with the individual as the central node. As Wellman and his colleague Lee Rainie have pointed out, the networks have been there all along, though they may have been both less essential to individual well-being and less visible to scholarly attention; the decline of formal groups, the increasing reliance on individually maintained networks, and the widespread deployment of social technologies adept at managing those networks have all brought them into relief. [35]

In sum, these changes point to a social context in which individuals must be increasingly self-reliant for economic well-being, social support, political influence, and civic identity. Consequently, we see late modern citizens demanding: increasing *autonomy* from the official structures that are losing credibility and protective capacity in the globalized world; *flexibility* in the formation of connections and practices of civic life that fit busy lifestyles; and *opportunities for expression* necessary to create and maintain satisfying self-identities.[36] All of this is a considerable departure from the modern social order citizens experienced through the mid-twentieth century, in which economic, social, and political well-being were organized through hierarchical and clearly demarcated groups. Though criticized as conformist and prescriptive in the political and expressive roles available to citizens, such organizations did foster a high degree of stability and a reliable set of social roles, expectations, and identity goods,[37] as well as concrete resources in the form of social connectedness, outlets to public life and political influence, exposure to (some degree of) difference, leadership opportunities, and, as we will see in Chapter 3, opportunities to understand political communications and in some ways to participate in it.[38]

YOUTH CIVIC ENGAGEMENT: DECLINE OR CHANGE?

The impacts of these changes are evident, if not always clearly articulated, in recent discussions of the civic health of young people.[39] One variety of scholarly accounts has emphasized youth's shortcomings, often comparing them unfavorably with the Greatest or "long-civic" generation that came of age during the Great Depression and Second World War.[40] In comparison to that modern-era civic high point,[41] younger people are found wanting in their interest and knowledge of politics, following the news, sense of responsibility to participate in politics, and almost all forms of participation in electoral politics, especially voting.[42] A "generational displacement" has been posited to underlie why younger citizens—who by almost every measure enjoy more of the material and educational resources that should prepare them for civic and political participation—fall short of their grandparents. Younger people are somehow *different* from previous generations, in the sense that there is something wrong with them—perhaps the lack of salubrious experiences of adversity and cooperation such as the Great Depression or World War II. The prescription of this view is that new experiences must be constructed to offer young people the sorts of civic participation they are lacking.

A competing perspective, developed with increasing vigor in recent years, holds that far from being politically apathetic and ignorant, youth are poised to reinvigorate democracy with their tolerance, commitment to democratic values, and creative problem-solving.[43] Proponents of this optimistic view tend to discount data on declines, and caution against relying too much on outdated modes of participation such as serving in the military, voting, joining groups, and following the news. Russell Dalton, for instance, contends that more active forms of engagement are now taking their place in the action repertoires of younger citizens who seek opportunities to be more—not less—engaged and expressive on issues they care about. For such citizens, a mere vote once every couple of years is very meager citizenship indeed—and they consequently are more likely to turn to activities such as forming independent opinions, trying to understand others, self-expression, and participating in voluntary network actions: "as political skills and resources expand, citizens realize the limits of voting as a means of political influence . . . and participate through individualized, direct, and more policy-focused methods."[44]

Though this view may ascribe to young citizens more political consciousness and instrumental intention than many possess, there is a larger point here that is compelling and becoming widely shared: younger citizens appear to be adopting a civic mentality and action repertoire that is distinct from those of previous generations. Consequently, as scholars such as Dalton, Ronald Inglehart, Michael Schudson, Lance Bennett, and Cliff Zukin argue, nonconventional activities that are on the rise deserve attention as the civic practices adopted by young people faced with a changing social fabric. Considering the nature of those practices may help us to understand the world and life experience with which they are dealing.

Emerging forms of civic engagement popular among youth exhibit three characteristics, each of which leads away from conventional political participation: first, they tend to be civic rather than political in nature; second, they tend to be activities that can be organized on a private and flexible basis, as opposed to through sustained, institutional groups; and third, they tend to be activities that lend themselves to self-expression and the production and maintenance of identity through expression and communication.

What kinds of activities fit these characteristics—or constitute what we might call young citizens' engagement repertoire?[45] Perhaps the most widely noted trend is an increase in volunteering among young people. Zukin and colleagues report that volunteerism is one of relatively few civic behaviors for which young people do not trail their elders: they note that about 22% of young Americans can be considered regular volunteers, compared to about 23% of all adults.[46] Volunteering is one of a few civic behaviors that actually has increased over the last decade or two, a result partly of college admissions boards that look increasingly favorably on community service and increasingly prevalent service learning initiatives across the country.[47] What makes volunteering attractive to young people? In addition to not being overtly political, volunteering can also be engaged in and organized privately, or at least highly flexibly: regular participation in a large institutional group is usually not necessary to be a volunteer.

A further set of activities, at the intersection of a politics of the personal and postmaterialist values not well-expressed through conventional political participation, are lifestyle politics—the opportunity to act out one's concerns through everyday activities and on an individual basis.[48] One of the most prominent, and most easily conceptualized, set of activities that might fit under the rubric of lifestyle politics is consumer politics—enacting one's civic concerns through consumer behavior. Such activity is intuitive for young citizens immersed in a hyperconsumerist context and used to acting out identities in a consumer mode.[49] Research usually finds young citizens participating in lifestyle or consumer politics at rates comparable to those of older adults—notable as one of a few civic activities where youth do not significantly trail their elders.[50]

What lifestyle politics excel at is giving its participants the opportunity to *express* a civic identity: engaging in daily acts of conscious dressing, shopping, eating, and buying is rich way for a person to communicate to the world (and herself) who they are and what they care about. As noted above, the need to express and maintain a satisfying civic identity is one of the greatest deficits currently facing young citizens operating in the absence of large identity-anchoring institutions. The rise of lifestyle and consumer politics can be seen as a direct response to that "identity vacuum."

Further emphasizing the importance of expression in youth engagement, when Zukin and colleagues outline three categories of engagement focused on politics (electoral engagement, cognitive engagement, and public voice), public voice is the only kind of action that does not display a robust trend of increasing practice with age. Young people in their study were at least as likely or more likely than older citizens to report participating in a march or demonstration or signing an email petition. (On other measures they were less likely; in contacting a public official about an issue they were particularly far behind, doing so half as frequently as members of the baby boomer generation.)[51]

The existence of these activities implies that young citizens do have concern for their communities' problems, and the initiative to do something about them: each of these are activities that are either on the rise or at least not declining, and in which young citizens either lead their elders or are at least not far behind them. But what these activities clearly show is that young people do not see the civic world in the same way as older citizens; in particular, addressing problems through formal political processes, especially those structured through parties and interest groups, is not an obvious path for them.[52] As Zukin and colleagues note, "it appears that the members of the youngest cohort have not rejected the political system so much as they are indifferent to it."[53]

THE LIMITATIONS OF CIVIC STYLES

In attempting to theoretically sort out changes in the civic orientations of younger citizens, scholars have offered a number of typologies of civic life:

- Ronald Inglehart has contrasted the modern society's "materialist" concerns with "postmaterialist" ones that became widespread in the American context in the latter half of the twentieth century.
- Michael Schudson sees the "informed" citizen ideal of the early twentieth century giving way to a "rights-bearing" one.
- Lance Bennett argues that for many contemporary young citizens, civic identity and attachment is less about a "dutiful" orientation to civic life in which action is motivated by a sense of responsibility and more a "self-actualizing" one in which motivations are more personal.
- Russell Dalton sees "citizen duty" as decreasingly relevant to a new generation demanding the opportunity to be "engaged" in public life.[54]

Each of these frameworks offers an account of why we see the particular patterns of engagement and attachment among young people documented in the past several decades. And although they differ in their emphases, sources of evidence, and conclusions, the larger point should be that they share much in common. These scholars recognize that an emerging orientation to public life, most visible among the more recent generations, is distinguished by an inclination toward personally resonant forms of action organized through personalized networks rather than formal groups. Issues of personal relevance are especially important here, which are not necessarily the issues pursued in news and formal politics. Further, there appear to be preferences for a rather different set of civic activities to pursue those concerns, as just noted.

The framework of competing civic styles sheds light on the youth civic disconnect in a couple of ways. First, if the activities young citizens choose to engage in have changed, we will underestimate their participation if we continue to measure it in the terms of the older style. Measuring declines in the portion of citizens who turn out to vote is an inaccurate gauge of engagement if citizens' identities lead them to another form of action. Second, we should note that although there may be competing civic identities operating alongside each other, this does not mean that the playing field is level: for one thing, our society's civic institutions are structured to facilitate the participation of dutiful citizens. As a result, actualizing citizens may find many fewer productive outlets for their preferences than their dutiful peers. This is partly a historical legacy reflecting the fact that those institutions were designed by dutiful citizens to serve dutiful citizens. But it also is a result of the slowly changing nature of civic norms: as a society, we remain entranced by the norms and ideals of the modern, dutiful society even as many of our citizens are moving beyond it. This is a theme that will recur many times in the following chapters.

A couple of caveats are in order. First, as these scholars are quick to note, typologies of civic styles are necessarily simplifications of extremely complex phenomena. Cleanly sorting any individual, much less a generation of individuals, into any particular category is an impossible task: civic identities and practices are complicated and multifaceted, and any person likely engages in a range of diverse practices, some of which might take on, for example, materialist concerns as well as postmaterialist ones. We thus need to remain cognizant that each of the typologies represents ideal types that may correspond to general social trends aligned generationally, but that the actual social scene is much more complicated.

Second, while scholars have been understandably eager to theorize the emerging civic style—what is coming next for society—emerging evidence suggests this may be premature. In particular, recent work by Kjerstin Thorson has supported the notion that a reasonably unified and coherent set of civic norms existed in the modern society, but that the contours of the rising civic style are not nearly so well established.[55] In her reading, young people are moving away from the practices that constituted dutiful citizenship. But she is skeptical that this is well described by the lens of a shift in the norms of citizenship: for one thing, young people by and large continue to endorse the core ideals of previous democratic eras, even if that does not play out in conventional civic action. Perhaps more significantly, she shows the problem with the idea that what is emerging is a coherent set of *new* norms. The young people in her study did not express clear connections between their civic activities and norms that were guiding those activities. Instead, she found that contemporary youth engagement is often a hodgepodge of activities and expressions drawn from a variety of sources and opportunities and pieced together on an individual basis. As a result, Thorson proposes that we think of young civic practice as Do It Yourself (DIY)—increasingly the responsibility of individuals no longer reliant on experts or institutional affiliations.[56]

To this point, we have explained the civic disconnect in terms of changing *civic* styles, by which I mean especially the bases for civic identity and the expression of that identity through civic practice. Civic styles have received considerable attention from scholars, and yet Thorson aptly makes the point that there is more to the matter of changing civic practices than changing civic norms—and we could expand the critique to also suggest there is more at work here than civic styles or identities.

To develop better our theoretical understanding of young citizens, we should note the oft-made observation that there seems to be some concurrence between actualizing civic styles and innovative uses of digital media.[57] But why this is—or should be—the case has been underspecified: what has received little attention is the possibility that shifts in civic style are inherently related to the *information* styles that shape the civic experiences of young people, predominantly mediated as they are. Bimber, Flanagin, and Stohl make explicit the relationship between civic experience and media use, observing that the availability and ubiquity of new media tools reshapes the types of relationships they seek: "Living in a world in which two people wishing to communicate must choose among doing so in person, in writing, by phone, by e-mail, by text message, by Twitter, by wall post or message, by chat, or by video call, and in which most of these options are available on devices in their pockets, means that communicative practice and norms are undergoing great change, and with that social and political norms and practice will necessarily change as well."[58]

My intention in the remainder of this chapter is to offer a specification of those new norms, with an eye to imagining the types of communicative relationships that will be most amenable to young people considering civic involvement. What we will see is that it is no coincidence that actualizing citizens are often associated with, or found using, tools of digital media. The information environment in which many young actualizing citizens have come of age is one that both builds on and feeds larger cultural and civic shifts. What we are witnessing is much less than a wholesale abandonment of dutiful civic norms—and for this reason a focus on civic styles is incomplete at best, misleading at worst. I propose that it is more productive to consider how a shift in how younger citizens relate to civic information and the communication processes they engage in is reshaping their relationships to objects of civic involvement—and how that shift affects their inclinations for being engaged given the civic information practices of the democratic institutions around them. To complete our description of young citizens' preferences for civic information, we turn to changes in the structure of information, and how it is used and interpreted by young people with great familiarity with and reliance on digital media.

A Digital Culture?

A strong interest of theorists of communication and new media is describing the uniqueness of communicating online—what is essentially *new* about new media. This type of work has included analyses of how communicative practices have developed online, in differentiation to those offline—a sort of emergent behavior of online communication and studies of how people are changed by their exposure to and immersion in digital media.[59] For us, the question here is how immersion in a digital communication culture from a young age has influenced the instincts and expectations of civic information held by the youngest generation of adults—the "digital natives" of the early twenty-first century.

That regular exposure to digital media affects how people relate to information is the case made emphatically by John Palfrey and Urs Gasser, who describe how the members of the "first generation of digital natives" are coming to understand the incredible information world into which they have been born.[60] Drawing on numerous interviews and focus groups with youth, they claim that contemporary young people are markedly distinct from older generations in how they understand information, and especially communication online. Their respondents expressed a view of the coextension of reality and the web, such that the Internet is seen as a nearly exhaustive source of information about the world, and thus that information and people must be communicated online in order to have a legitimate reality.

More recently, sociologically grounded scholars have put this somewhat differently. As Sonia Livingstone shows, young people's uses of online media are less the result of early habituation to the media, and rather oriented to primary concerns of young people: managing social lives and enacting satisfying senses of self-identity. This takes different forms for different youth and at different stages of development. Online tools can be used both for enhancing the privacy of interactions with peers (for example, excluding parents' supervision by texting friends from home) and for revealing selected aspects of the self (for example, on social networking sites).[61]

There are several reasons that youth make the choice to use online media in these ways. The most obvious is that they are simply available, and that peers are using them. But this is not the whole story: the lived experiences of many young people are now relatively more constrained in terms of the geographic spaces available for gathering and hanging out, as dana boyd has observed. The combination of increased surveillance and regulation of previously available spaces for youth interaction (such as malls and parks), and increased concern of parents for the dangers of public areas leaves many young people in the home, and seeking to find spaces for peer interaction—for which they turn to online media.[62]

As a result, for many young people in the industrialized world, digital media have become primary sites for the interlinked processes of social life and identity development. Livingstone notes that "identity is constituted through interaction with others," and as more and more of that interaction occurs—at least some of the time—through online media, we see uses of those media becoming more elemental to young citizens' identity construction.[63]

Apart from a specific focus on young users of new media, theorists of digital culture have also argued that the processes of sharing and gathering information from digital sources engender a set of norms and expectations different from those of previous media eras. Mark Deuze has developed the concept of a "digital culture," a notion meant to describe the "set of values, norms, practices, and expectations shared by . . . those inhabitants of modern societies most directly affected by computerization, such as in going online regularly during the week at home or from work."[64] (It might be noted that those most directly affected by digital media are, in large part, the young people who use digital media so continually and for such a variety of purposes.) Deuze's perspective is not deterministic: he carefully notes that many of the celebrated characteristics of the online world are extensions of practices or aspirations borrowed from predigital eras, and he sees the online world's innovations as expressions of larger social changes such as those described above. But he does argue that those predigital aspirations and social changes, combined with the now-pervasive presence of computerization in industrial societies, has given rise to a digital culture with a distinctive set of values and expectations "expressed in the activities of news and information media makers and users online."[65] Building on Deuze's sense that a distinctive digital culture is emergent, below we trace three key elements of that culture: participation, bricolage, and communication power.[66]

PARTICIPATION

The single most powerful ethos of the digital culture may be participation: the notion that across many domains, from television to video gaming to politics, "people [are] increasingly claiming the right to be heard rather than be spoken to."[67] The aspiration to participate in communication processes, or public life more generally, well predates the digital era; it is one of the essential ideals of modern conceptions of democracy.[68] And it is heightened in late modernity: in the context of declining institutional faith, late modern citizens turn increasingly to themselves and peers to create goods, such as information goods, once provided by institutional actors.[69] The rise of DIY cultures is one manifestation of this trend.[70]

Digital communication makes possible participation in the communicative arena on an almost infinite scale. And with that new possibility is emerging a firmer *expectation* that communication will come with participatory opportunities—opportunities to contribute one's own ideas, meanings, and reactions to a given text. As Deuze puts it, "a sense of participation is what people have come to expect from those aspects of society they wish to engage in."[71]

Consequently, notions of participation and its applications have become a central theme in much of the writing about the new media era. Henry Jenkins's conception of "convergence culture" emphasizes that the lines between producer and consumer of information are blurring to the degree that they are often indecipherable. This is particularly the case for young citizens, who gravitate toward interactions in which they play a hybrid consumer/producer role. Jenkins attributes considerable civic significance to convergence culture: for him, the participation in cultural life made possible by digital media allows citizens to appropriate and reshape the cultural ideas surrounding them in all forms of media: it is an access point for cultural and political power.[72]

The upshot of all of this is that in contrast to the predominantly one-way communication that older generations experienced, when young people receive information it is natural for it to be commented on, rearranged, and shared across a friend (or other) network.[73] This daily experience of media that is rearrange-able, sharable, and interactive leads young people to expect those opportunities in all information contexts.[74]

BRICOLAGE

A second constitutive characteristic of digital culture involves individuals' patterns of gathering and evaluating information. Deuze's concept here, drawn from Lévi-Strauss, is "bricolage," alluding to the construction of a reality by piecing together elements from a variety of sources—much the same way an artist may make a single collage out of many disparate images and texts. In an obvious way, bricolage is the information-gathering pattern of a network logic—the equivalent of rigorously following one's preferred newspaper in the modern society. Deuze's point is that digital media facilitate and create a norm for gathering information from multiple sources to be collated.

Again we see here the specter of rising skepticism—or declining authority—of specific, authoritative sources of information, an instead patterns of testing reports across a variety of sources. Consequently, tools for evaluating information quality and credibility are changing. Older citizens operated in an information world in which it made sense, both socially and in terms of the structure of information, to evaluate information based on authoritative sources, such as trusted news channels and civic leaders. By contrast, younger citizens are more likely to rely on credibility standards based on reliability and replicability: drawing together the claims of many diverse sources to evaluate how well they support one another. Once again, digital media's multiple channels of information exchange and aggregation tools, including social networking sites, are peculiarly well suited to the changing dynamic.[75]

We see evidence of it on multiple levels: at the level of the individual, it is possible to design one's own communication environment by selectively choosing which content to access or using specific tools such as browser bookmarks and RSS feeds, and young people do this to a great extent.[76] But we also see a sort of bricolage occurring at the level of media portal: from major blogs to Google News, Huffington Post and (to a lesser but in some ways more significant extent) the *New York Times*, media sources are casting a wide net to aggregate content they think might appeal to readers. In this way, what were once information centers are becoming information nodes, connecting users to sources in a network much wider than a single institution.

COMMUNICATION POWER

A third aspect of digital culture is the increasing assumption of the power of communication itself. Most prominent among young people, this is a sort of intuitive sense of the possibilities inherent in digitally networked communication—to reach sometimes surprising numbers of people and audiences, to amplify beyond all reasonable expectation, and occasionally to have surprising effects on taste, politics, business, justice, and everything in between. This recognition of the power of communication is in evidence in many contexts. One is the drive for online self-presentation among young people that has been widely documented.[77] Another is the use of digital media to build political power, for example by developing large and sophisticated online petition drives or organize protests.[78] Perfect examples of the individual use of digital media to capture power are recent instances in which people have used Twitter or other social media to create a public relations problem for companies such as airlines, and in some cases have won substantial settlements as a result of their ability to cause embarrassment. In a famous case, a musician had an expensive guitar broken on a United Airlines flight. Although the company originally rejected his appeal for reimbursement, after he wrote a song titled "United Breaks Guitars," posted it to YouTube, and starting receiving hits, the airline contacted him to resolve the situation.[79] This is a new sort of public relations relationship for the airlines: "Calling or writing an airline is a private matter. Using social media is public. Should the response from the airline be different simply because of that difference?"[80] Whether or not it should be, it is evident that it is, with airlines becoming so conscious of the threat that they now take extraordinary measures to monitor what is being said about them in social media, and acting quickly to ameliorate situations that could become public relations disasters:

> Many airlines have operations dedicated to seeking out and resolving online complaints, also searching for their company name with words like "suck" and "bad" online . . . Delta . . . created a channel called @DeltaAssist and told workers in the social-media lab to offer customers quick fixes, such as rebookings and reimbursements. Sometimes that means even waiving rules that consumers typically find unbendable at airlines.[81]

What such cases illustrate is the power of digital communications communicated to a public—and the employment of that power by citizens. For many young people, what is clear is that the levers of power open to them may not so often be the formally political ones with which they can interact, but communication media themselves.

Late Modern Citizens and Digital Tools

The two perspectives we have just explored, one rooted in traditional social science and the other in new media studies, each point to a number of reasons that the civic identities and aptitudes for information of young citizens may lead them to a relationship to civic information distinct from that prescribed by the informed citizen model. But as much as these two bodies differ in origin and theoretical perspective, they share several core conclusions. At their convergence we can note several trends in how younger citizens' civic information styles are developing.

- *Antiauthoritarian.* In both literatures there is a marked antiauthoritarian streak, an abiding skepticism of received wisdom and expertise, and an urge to replace authoritative information structures with personally built ones. One of the most reliable longitudinal findings of research on public attitudes is the declining esteem in which formerly authoritative institutions are held, and the same trend is apparent in individuals' information-consumption choices, as people forego institutional sources of information for diversified, personalized choices.
- *Participatory and self-expressive.* The complement to the antiauthoritarian impulse is a participatory one. Further, participation in the communicative arena often—or perhaps necessarily—takes the form of self-expression. As we have seen, late modern citizens are responsible for personal identity projects to an unprecedented degree; it would seem no coincidence that younger generations have made such extensive use of the new technology for expressive purposes.
- *Participation is less structured, and organized through networks, not formal groups.* Combining rising institutional skepticism, demand for self-determination, and life politics also leads young people away from bureaucratically organized groups and toward network participation and action. Conveniently, digital media appear to be fortuitously suited to the coordination of flexible, network-based participation over which the individual has considerable control.[82]
- *Recognizing and deploying the power of communication:* The "mediatization" of society that occurred over the second half of the twentieth century meant that even before personal digital tools became widespread, citizens were aware, on some level, of the late modern locus of power: the media.[83] Media politics is the outcome of these conditions and represents the explicit contestation of power through society's communication processes.[84] Given this, it should be no surprise that young people's interactions with civic media display an intuitive understanding of the power of media and

information—evident in rising demands for meaningful self-expression across online spaces and the communicative nature of many of the rising forms of civic engagement.[85]

• *Youth-oriented*. Finally, though we have continually referred to and noted young citizens' aptitudes for innovative uses of digital media, it is worth making explicit the fact that both sets of literature have identified young people as uniquely important figures in contemporary social changes. The concerns of civic engagement scholars of the 1990s, first exploring the possibilities of a distinctive youth civic orientation, read in retrospect like a profile of a generation seeking ineffectually for a platform on which to build its (civic) future. The coming of the digital era represents, to some, just such an answer to a generation's needs: where expertise and authority have lost their credibility, digital media seem to engender participation; where social groups had lost their effectiveness and meaning, digital media seem to enable coordination along network logics; and where citizens were once shut out by elite driven media politics, digital media seem to offer a populist foot back in the door.

That there are common themes running through both work on civic identities and new forms of engagement and the literature on new media is no coincidence. Like any other innovation, digital media developed in a particular context—the 1980s and 1990s, a time rife with the civic displacements and shifts described earlier. It should not be surprising that the uses to which they have been put, and the uses for which their uses found resonance with a broad spectrum of users, complemented those users' desires for particular kinds of informational civic opportunities. As Lee Rainie and Barry Wellman put it, "the affordances of the technologies helped them fit beautifully into the lives that users were already leading."[86]

This is exactly the case made by Fred Turner in his account of the countercultural origins of digital media. Turner asserts that digital media have been imbued with a particular set of meanings and norms as a result of the early influence of a particular confluence of individuals, including software engineers, journalists, artists, and "communards" in San Francisco, Silicon Valley, and communes across the American west during the 1960s and 1970s. The common connecting point for these otherwise disparate networks was the node of Stewart Brand, the founder of the Whole Earth Catalog in the late 1960s, then a founder of the Whole Earth 'Lectronic Link (WELL) in the 1980s, and an early supporter of *Wired* magazine. According to Turner, conditions of technological innovation and social change fortuitously intersected in Brand's eclectic set of San Francisco Bay-area acquaintances: engineers were experimenting with the communicative possibilities of early digital tools, while a movement of countercultural New Communalists were contemplating postbureaucratic forms of life and interhuman connection. A heyday of both sets of experimentation was happening at the same time and within miles of one another.[87]

If we see the New Communalists as on the forefront, starting in the 1960s, of social values that were shifting in the direction of the antiauthoritarian, participatory, and self-expressive values just discussed, then the influence of those values on the development of digital media the New Communalists influenced would have been profound. Turner argues that they were: through early experimentations and innovations, and influence on the thought of early digital technologists,

> By the late 1990s, Brand and his Whole Earth colleagues had repeatedly linked these technological and cultural changes and in the process had helped turn the terms of their generational search into the key frames by which the American public understood the social possibilities of computers and computer networking.[88]

The argument here is that the norms of digital media most clearly express larger social changes that have been underway for some time; it is in digital media that those larger social changes are most completely played out—a point essential to the notion of civic information styles developed below. As Bruce Bimber put it, "digital media emerged from the corporate and academic labs at a time in history perfectly suited to accelerate . . . generational changes stemming back decades."[89]

What this discussion emphasizes is the need not to artificially separate the civic orientations of young citizens from their media use and experiences of digital communication: they are intertwined and inseparable. Not only have younger people's civic identities undergone major shifts as a result of social and economic changes—which themselves have shifted young people's inclinations for and patterns of engagement—but young people's lives have also become increasingly immersed in, dependent on, and shaped by interactions with digital media, which has developed a novel set of expectations about what information should offer and how one productively interacts with it. Bringing these sets of insights together into a framework for understanding what is notable about how young citizens interact with civic information is the purpose of this discussion.

Reconceptualizing Civic Information

I contend that what we are seeing with respect to young citizens' civic participation is a shift that is not a shift in civic identity, or a shift in communicative style, or a shift in media use: instead it is all three, at the same time, inextricably bound to one another. What we are seeing are changing *modes of interacting with civic information* that have profound consequences for whether and how younger citizens choose to participate in public life.

By modes of interacting with civic information, I mean to draw attention to the intuitions and preferences citizens bring to the communication processes they engage in. Only in rare cases do citizens process information with a conscious evaluation of "do I like this?'" or "does this resonate with my sense of who I am as a person?" More often, our information evaluations and practices—which quickly become habits—are casual ones: we react quickly and offhandedly, only haphazardly storing information for later retrieval. And yet matters of preference, interest, and resonance are essential to decisions about what kinds of content to consume and how to interact. What I wish to argue is that those practices and habits, or intuitions and preferences, are importantly shaped by the trends just described: those toward a networked individualistic orientation to public life and a digital era-sense of the nature of information.

Their product, I argue, is an emerging information style contrasted with that of the high modern era. As mentioned in Chapter 1, I refer to the good citizens of the modern society as *dutiful*, to emphasize that era's orientation to civic life and communication; and to the emerging civic information style as *actualizing*, to emphasize the personal engagement and information mutability of our era.[90]

The framework developed here thus builds on the dutiful and actualizing typology of citizenship and shifts its focus to informational styles: we will elaborate how the dutiful information ideals, which align closely with the informed citizen model and are embraced by older citizens and most institutions of the political world (the news, political parties, conventional interest groups, etc.) now differ from those of young actualizing people and digital/participatory culture. In line with previous conceptualizations of the dutiful-self-actualizing civic identity framework, it should also be noted that the types are meant to represent ideal types the ends of a spectrum that is in fact much more nuanced and complex than a simple either dutiful or actualizing.[91]

To illustrate the types, let us consider the implications of our above discussions for how dutiful and actualizing approaches to civic information differ on four critical dimensions: who is an appropriate creator, or *source*, of civic information; citizens' inclinations for how to *interact* with information; the processes by which citizens *interpret and assess* information; and citizens' preferences for the *kinds of civic action* made possible by interacting with civic information. These key dimensions are sketched in Table 2.1 and described in detail below.

Table 2.1 **Contrasting Dutiful and Actualizing Civic Information Styles**

	Older/Dutiful Style	*Younger/Actualizing Style*
Appropriate sources	***Experts authenticated*** through civic institutions: ***news, political leaders, officials*** of civic organizations	***Varied*** and ***diverse***; ***news, organizations,*** and ***movements*** of interest, ***social contacts***
Modes of interacting with information	Centered on ***reception of information*** from news and key leaders	Expectation of ***participation*** in production and sharing of information
Information interpretation and assessment	Guided by membership/ identification with ***social groups, parties***; ***authoritative sources*** key to credibility	Driven by individual interests and ***trusted networks***; credibility based on ***relevance*** and ***reliability***
Action outcomes	***Targeted,*** often ***official*** actions that place the ***actor as secondary*** to the organization's maintenance and strategic objectives	***Expressive*** actions communicated through ***networked publics***; ***actor is at the center***, both influencing peers and expressing own views

APPROPRIATE SOURCES

Differences between dutiful and actualizing civic information styles begin with the sources of that information itself. The modern-era dutiful style, as we have seen, was committed to a vision of civic information that could be reliably produced by expert newsmen and communicated to citizens. Authentication by institutional norms was the key here: Cronkite was Cronkite first and foremost because CBS had put its backing behind him, and as an institution CBS had staked its reputation on a vision of public service that demanded first rate journalism.[92]

What the secularization we discussed earlier means here is that such authenticated sources of information are losing their special appeal. Consequently, the actualizing style is seeing a great diversification of potentially legitimate sources of information. This is partly a result of the fragmentation of media and increasing abundance fostered by digital technology; but the trends in audience skepticism of institutional communications is an equally important factor. This does not mean that citizens wholesale abandon or reject traditional formats; those formats continue to play important roles in the emerging civic information landscape. But it does mean that they increasingly contend with other information sources, which may include civic organizations (the focus of the next chapters) and social contacts. And it means that establishment news organizations can no longer claim the kind of monopoly on legitimacy and credibility—or proximity to events, often—that they once could. Indeed, as Pew has found, it is now very common for individuals to come across pieces of information from one of information source and turn to others to check them. This is a process of replication and reliability, new practices for establishing credibility that we will explore below.

MODES OF INTERACTING WITH INFORMATION

We have seen the significance of what we may call the *participatory impulse* in accounts of late modern civic identity and uses to which digital media are put. To briefly summarize, what we are seeing is an increasing inclination on the part of younger citizens to play an active, autonomous role in defining and personalizing the terms of the activities in which they take part. Following Deuze, we have suggested that participation is now a strong enough ethos among younger citizens that we might describe it as an *expectation* of communications and communication platforms: younger people are most comfortable and engaged in contexts that allow participation and make peers' participation visible. Those features lend authenticity to the ideas promoted, and allow young actualizing citizens the opportunity to express complex civic identities. As a recent Pew survey found, news consumers are increasingly taking advantage of digital tools that can shape their own communication environment and that of the people around them, including information selection tools such as RSS, and sharing tools such as comment features and social media.[93]

   We should not pretend that the urge to participate emerged sui generis with the late modern period or digital media. Movements toward engaging previously latent or disenfranchised publics and engaging them in both governance and knowledge coproduction has become a staple of the literature on local empowerment and urban studies.[94] And yet the social context and media possibilities of the dutiful era simply could not emphasize autonomous participation of the sort we see in demand today. Instead, in that model of citizenship citizens' interactions with civic information are targeted toward following information produced by authoritative sources, particularly news channels and trusted leaders. The communications of those authorities are assumed to be of interest because of their expertise, and without reference to other sources. Thus, while dutiful citizens certainly are expected to be active—actively following civic affairs, and putting their accumulated information to use at prescribed moments of action—when it comes to civic information there is not the sense in which dutifuls should actively be contributing to the construction of the information itself. In the specialization and separation that is a hallmark of modernity, those tasks are assigned to professional experts; it is the duty of the good citizen to attend to what they have to say.

INTERPRETATION AND ASSESSMENT

A second dimension of difference between younger and older citizens' information styles arises from the different ways in which they interpret civic information. The civic information produced in the news of high modernism was seen as a reasonable depiction of reality, and in order to find out about that reality, a citizen simply needed to tune in to the program of a credible journalist. Much of the interpretation of the information was already taken care of there, by a certified news expert. Individuals supplemented this interpretation of news with interpersonal discussion, of course, as well as membership in and identification with social institutions such as churches, professional associations, and social clubs. Those social groups lent members contexts for understanding key events and players in the news, as well as direct communication with other members and group leaders. In short, interpretation of information was largely performed by the dual functions of expert sources and rich social fabric.

Both resources are now in short supply, as we have seen.[95] With the decline of membership-based groups and identification, many citizens now lack the conventional contexts for interpreting and understanding news, as well as faith in the credibility of that news—circumstances that have led many to turn away from conventional politics. The result is an era of some confusion in patterns of obtaining and interpreting civic information, though the situation is not quite as dire as simplistic assertions that people believe everything they read on the Internet. Rather, new practices for ascertaining credibility are emerging. Especially, we seem to be seeing new patterns of information interpretation and assessment based on reliability and relevance rather than authoritativeness: where citizens of the high modern era looked to one or two trusted news figures for credible information, citizens of the digital era are able to look to many sources to verify stories of interest.[96] Social networks of trusted and interesting friends can further lend credibility to information and give it context through sharing and commenting.[97] We might summarize this as a preference for *networked information seeking*, in which citizens seek out multiple sources of information from both official and peer sources and compare them for reliability and relevance rather than authoritativeness.

ACTION PREFERENCES

Whatever one's model of citizenship, the culmination of one's interactions with civic information is taking civic action—the activities that constitute civic engagement. However, our depiction of the actualizing civic information style suggests that how younger citizens understand civic action, too, may be undergoing change—another source of disconnect and frequent criticism. The heritage of high modernity encourages us to understand informing and acting as separate constructs that require separate, if related, skill sets and occur in separate times and contexts. For the informed citizen informing happens regularly, every day; the media structure of the mid-twentieth century lent itself nicely to time structured around becoming informed, with morning and evening papers and daily news broadcasts on television. Action happened in its own, separate sphere at designated moments such as elections and associational meetings. Consequently, the dutiful sense of information is restricted to the informing role, stimulating and guiding, *but not a part of,* real forms of civic activity.

For young actualizing citizens, the lines demarcating informing and acting are much less clear. They inhabit an environment of constant flows of information in which the news hour is potentially every hour, have the opportunity to participate in this flow, and sense the power of communication inherent in media politics. This type of action sometimes takes the form of low-effort communications such as Facebook "likes" and Twitter retweets—lending itself to criticisms of "slacktivism";[98] we should be judicious in our application of the word "civic" to every activity anyone undertakes, online or elsewhere. But we also should not allow examples of low-effort distract us from the reality that actualizing citizens have an intuitive grasp of the power of communication and treat what modern citizens might understand as informative or communicative activities as action.

The inclusion of communicative activities in the accepted canon of political participation is not wholly foreign to the dutiful mindset. For example, forms of public voice such as contacting public officials and writing to media outlets have long been recognized as important in American civic life,[99] and in recent years they have been digitized for ease and speed.[100] But young actualizing citizens now also have access to a new set of expressive activities that may be qualitatively different—and different rates of participation across these two types of activities may be further indicative of the civic information divide we are delineating.

One of the best studies of public voice across generations concluded that younger and older citizens are roughly equally likely to engage in some forms of political self-expression, such as signing petitions. But the youngest cohort markedly trails their elders when it comes to several key kinds of communication, such as contacting a public official or writing to the media. In short, these conventional manifestations of public voice look very much like conventional civic engagement when we look at their distribution across the generations.[101] Pew data from the 2008 US presidential campaign, widely cited as a watershed both for youth participation, show the same pattern: forms of online communication that enabled digital versions of older forms of offline communication, such as contacting officials and signing petitions, followed the pattern of conventional political engagement (like voting), with older citizens showing a comfortable advantage.[102]

But activities involved the use of digital media to produce new content, share content, and connection with candidates in publicly visible networked spaces shows exactly the opposite pattern. Among social networking site users, those 18- to 24–year- old were more likely than any other age group to have engaged in each of five forms of political action through social networking sites—such as friending a candidate or looking for friends' political preferences.[103] Younger citizens similarly outmatched their counterparts in posting original content online during the campaign: 40% of 18- to 24-year-olds who used the Internet for any political purpose chose to post their own thoughts, compared to half that portion (21%) of 30- to 49-year-olds and smaller slices of the older demographics.[104] The patterns held in 2012, as young people exceeded their parents on nearly every political use of social media the Pew Research Center asked about: most striking were findings that 44% of 18- to 29-year-old social media users liked or otherwise promoted political information; 42% posted their own thoughts on political issues; and one in four even followed a public official or candidate.[105] Though older citizens' political uses of social media generally increased as well, the fact that young people, generally less politically engaged, still exceeded them is notable.

These results suggest that there are profound differences in how younger and older citizens see communication's relationship to politics. For their part, the actions preferred by older, dutiful citizens tend to represent communicative extensions of the other modes of conventional engagement. Actions such as emailing a public official, signing petitions, and writing to media outlets are directly linked to formal political processes, and operate in the context of groups representing citizens' interests and interacting in an institutional political sphere. (Though not usually conceptualized as a communicative act, voting could similarly be seen as a targeted act of formal and institutionalized political expression.)

In contrast, the communication acts preferred by actualizing citizens are less likely to be oriented toward influencing an element of institutional politics, or reliant on strong affiliation with a particular membership group. Instead, activities such as sharing political media with friends or a network, posting political information to social networking sites, or establishing a connection to a candidate in such sites are oriented toward opportunities for self-expression, information-sharing, and informing or influencing a network. Connections to formal, institutional politics can certainly occur, and this was one of the most exciting stories about Obama's campaign in 2008. But rather than subordinating the interests and views of the individual to the service of a larger group strategy, what sets these kinds of actions apart is that they are first and fore-most opportunities for the individual to define their own political identity to some public or network—for example, by friending a candidate in Facebook, in which case the candidate appears as a friend on the user's profile, and the friending would be posted to friends' news feeds.[106]

In sum, what we have established are two quite different notions of the role in communication in civic action: for the dutiful style, communication is largely a precursor to civic action that takes place separately; when communicative activity takes place, it tends to be officially *targeted* and *strategically directed*. In contrast, for the actualizing style, civic actions are always permeated with communication practices, and the distinction between the two is impossible to draw. Further, civic communicative activities frequently have important expressive components, allowing the communicator to express aspects of their identity alongside what may be instrumental attempts to influence the opinion of networked publics.

Conclusion

The civic roles and capabilities of young citizens have been debated intensely over recent decades. This chapter proposed a novel way of thinking about young citizens' engagement that highlights the fact that older and younger citizens may relate to civic information quite differently. We saw how generational dif-ferences in civic styles and citizen identity are related to different approaches to the civic world under changing social and political circumstances. And we considered the norms of communication and information exchange that have arisen in digital media contexts—norms that appear to simultaneously originate, contribute to, and complement younger citizens' civic orientations. Synthesizing these perspectives, we developed two ideal types of civic infor-mation style, one relating to the information paradigm of the modern society, which we have termed a dutiful civic information style, the other depicting an emerging paradigm, which we called actualizing. And we argued that members of the contemporary young generation holding actualizing preferences tend, more so than their elders, to look for civic information experiences in which participation, networked information seeking and sharing, and expressive opportunities for action are present.

A last point to be emphasized is that in contrasting the youth civic infor-mation style with that of older citizens, we are not simply comparing gen-erations and observing their turnover. It is essential to understand that possessing a distinctive civic information style not only separates young people from their elders; it also places them in a peculiar position with respect to the dominant institutions of political life. Specifically, the major news organizations, politicians, parties, and interest groups are for the most part organized along dutiful lines. Furthermore, they are almost exclusively run—and funded—by older citizens likely to be dutifully inclined. Not surprisingly, this is a divergence in perspective with the potential to cause disconnect between civic communicators and the youthful publics they are trying to reach. In the following chapters we take up this problem, and attempt to develop an idea of what sort of civic communication environment young people experience.

3

Civic Organizations in the New Media Environment

The civic information styles described in Chapter 2 illustrate a shift occurring within the publics of Western societies. In the wake of declining roles for group-based social institutions, increasing volume and complexity of the communication environment, and the rise of personalized, networked digital media, citizens—and especially younger citizens—are displaying a set of preferences for interacting with civic information that we have termed *actualizing*. Further, because of generationally different experiences of both social change and technological adoption and use, citizens of different ages are likely, by and large, to hold distinct preference sets. This raises the possibility that an important source of the ambivalence many young people feel toward formal politics may originate with a clash of information preferences: if younger citizens tend to prefer a civic information style different from that of their elders, and civic institutions tend to reflect older, dutiful, styles because of institutional legacies and current (older) leadership, this could produce a *disconnect in civic information style* that alienates many young people from essential structures of political life.

Having explored the citizen side of civic information preferences, in this chapter we develop the other side of the theoretical logic, building a rationale for how and why the institutions of civic life communicate as they do. We focus on a particular category of civic institution: organizations aiming to engage young citizens in civic life. Voluntary civic associations have been essential to citizen participation in the United States for many years, and widely understood as mediators between members of the public and formal political processes in government and policymaking.[1] As such, their communications at a time of social and technological change potentially shed light on the possibilities and limitations of communicating with young citizens with actualizing preferences for civic information.

Analyzing those communications begins with the problem of defining what, exactly, is a civic organization today. The set of organizations and other collective forms captured by terms such as "voluntary association" and "civic organization" is large and diverse, and social, political and technological changes have altered the composition of the voluntary association population. The operational definition we offer aims for both parsimony and completeness in capturing the sorts of civic formations most likely to be appealing to young citizens for engagement.

We next discuss the position of civic organizations as prominent civic communicators. In the traditions of political science and sociology, we are accustomed to thinking of civic information as almost exclusively the province of news producers. In the rationalized and differentiated high modern information paradigm, information was produced by authoritative news producers; action was the domain of parties and other civic groups, which aggregated the contributions of citizens informed by the news. As a result, the primary frames of analysis of civic organizations considered their work in the context of the larger political system, their structural elements, or the degree of democratic characteristics of their internal government.[2] Of course, this specialization of civic tasks was never so complete or neat, but our analytic frames have long underrecognized civic groups as conveyors of civic information. We correct that underemphasis in this chapter. What I wish to highlight is that the communicative role is becoming especially prominent in the era of networked digital media: whereas in the mass media era civic organizations did rely to a significant extent on news media to communicate with publics, the networked media environment is making that decreasingly true. Civic groups now communicate directly with innumerable individuals at every level of commitment to the cause, at frequencies limited only by organizations' perceptions of supporters' tolerance for emails, texts, and status updates.

Combined with the analysis of the previous chapter, this makes the question of *how* civic groups communicate with supporters a highly consequential one. To address it with the richness required in a time of multichannel, multidirectional message flow, we will work from the notion that communications through digital media constitute a *communicative relationship* between organizations and citizens. This allows us to think productively about why organizations present the sorts of communications they do, and how those communications are received by citizens with the potential to be mobilized. We will develop the idea in a reconsideration of three periods in organization-communicative history: the "classic" era of the federated associations, the late twentieth century "check-writing" era, and the era of voluntary networked associations now emerging. In the existing literature, scholars have tended to emphasize how social conditions and "political opportunity structures" have influenced how organizations orient themselves to their supporters.[3] Our recognition of the role of civic organizations as providers of civic information enables us to consider how communicative relationships have evolved over time, helping us to draw links between changing dynamics of citizen participation and organizational communicative behavior.

In particular, one aspect of late-twentieth-century civic life often overlooked by organizational scholars coming from fields such as political science and sociology is that this was also the era of media politics, a time in which organizations and their professional staffs learned to zealously protect and control their communications. The continuation of basic conditions of this period, and the habits and routines developed over several decades, are likely to significantly inhibit many organizations' inclinations to substantially open their communications to citizens who may welcome opportunities for contribution and self-expression.

Yet we shall also see that the early twenty-first century is a moment in which new organizations coming on to the scene are experimenting with new modes of involving communicatively active supporters—and are sometimes punished for it—while more staid organizations tend to resist interactive opportunities, with costs for their support in active young publics. These observations raise the essential questions of how readily organizations will adapt to the new circumstances, which organizations will adapt relatively more and less readily, and what forms those adaptations will take. It is the task of this chapter to account for the challenges facing established civic organizations and develop expectations about how they will respond.

The Civic Organization: Defining a Domain of Study

The rise of the network society and accompanying research attention to political networks, social movements, and hybrid organization has made apparent the myriad of ways in which citizens can connect with one another—can *associate*—for civic purposes.[4] The increased visibility of nonformalized relationships between individuals heightens our awareness that the associational forms of a particular time are just that—particular to a given set of conditions and incentives, and likewise conducive to certain sets of outcomes. Changes in a societies prevailing conditions—of social structure, of technology, of the distribution of power—give rise to changes in the associational logics of society, and consequently the composition of group and organizational forms.[5] Among the associational entities subject to is the population of groups of primary interest here: organizations dedicated to involving young citizens in civic life.

Being in the midst of ongoing changes makes the problem of how to define the contours of a population for study especially difficult. This is not to say the problem was ever a simple one: there are vast literatures in political science, sociology, and communication on various conceptualizations of the forms that coordinated civic-political activity can take. These go by names as varied as interest groups, civic organizations, advocacy organizations, nongovernmental organizations, social movements, social movement organizations, protest movements, voluntary associations, collective actions, and more.[6] And all of those examples were in existence before the development of digitally mediated communication platforms; we could now add a variant of most with the term "networked" preceding it.

It is important not to be led astray by definitional silos that have arisen as a result of the particular emphases of different disciplines; at a time of sharp change in organizational form and practice, this would be especially unproductive.[7] Thus here I conceptualize our domain of interest functionally, based on the role civic groups play in the lives of the citizens they interact with, rather than borrowing an established literature based on perception of structure or purpose. Our interest here will be focused on organizations that *promote civic or political involvement or the development of citizenship among youth and young adults between the ages of fifteen and twenty-four*. This is an intentionally broad definition, potentially encompassing representatives of many of the forms just listed: it certainly includes political parties and campaigns, some government agencies, interest groups, and social movements that wish to involve young citizens as supporters of their work. It also includes more civic-minded organizations that take less political, and more civic or service approaches, to community improvement or individual empowerment. An organization such as the Boy Scouts, for example, aims to improve communities and individuals' citizenship, but outside of contentious political processes. Its vision statement makes this mission explicit: "The Boy Scouts of America will prepare every eligible youth in America to become a responsible, participating citizen and leader who is guided by the Scout Oath and Law."[8]

At the edge of the changing landscape of civic organizations just described, the definition also includes a diverse set of organizations that have formed online and cross some of the boundaries previously established. Organizations such as MoveOn, Avaaz, Care2, and others have created online spaces in which participants connect; learn about civic issues; communicate interests, concerns, and identities; and potentially take action. (More youth-focused, if lesser-known organizations, that appear in the samples of Chapters 4 and 5 include groups such as DoSomething.org, YouthNoise, and TakingITGlobal.) And yet such online groups often do not have some of the key structural characteristics typical of previous eras of civic organization, fitting in this way somewhere between classic civic organizations and activist networks largely free of bureaucratic structure.[9]

As we will see in this and following chapters, this conceptualization of what I will call in general *civic organizations* allows for a broad survey of the communication practices of American civic groups, as well as comparisons between different types of groups and communications across different web media.

Civic Organizations as Sources of Civic Information

Considerable work is ongoing to understand the current state of American civic organizations, for several reasons. One strand originates with the observation of the connection between civic groups and individual-level measures of engagement, and the corresponding fear that civic organizations are in decline. Robert Putnam's famous work on social capital is primarily about the type of social capital formed and exercised in the particular social formations of civic groups.[10] Another is that civic organizations are undergoing a transformation as the result of new social and technological challenges and opportunities, and that their changes herald a new era in political association and participation.[11]

One important product of accounts that concern themselves with change in civic groups' constitution or behavior is a helpful attention to historical precedents to current conditions. It is widely accepted that since the mid-nineteenth century, civic institutions from political parties and interest groups to good-government watchdogs and community associations have provided essential resources connecting individual citizens to political processes. Those resources have included, at the most basic, coordination of collective efforts, as well as perspective, mobilization, social capital, camaraderie, and, increasingly in the later twentieth century, strategic expertise and resources necessary to navigate complex and expensive political processes.[12] Debates over civic organizations and collective action in the contemporary period typically concern some aspect of whether and how emerging formations will be able to offer these resources.

Curiously, however, what has been less well recognized are the communication processes that make the conduct of these organizational activities possible and vital to civic life: In truth, relationships between organizations and constituents have always been constituted through a variety of communication modes, as civic groups work to communicate with citizens to inform them about the organization and its actions, current events likely to be of interest to members, mobilizations that the organization is attempting in the pursuit of its goals, and so forth.[13] As such, they have, to varying degrees across the history of American civic organizing, been important—sometimes primary—sources of the information connecting citizens to politics. Referring to perhaps their most widely known communicative resource, Jack Walker noted, "publications are provided by groups of all types and universally thought of as among their most important benefits."[14] Yet little work has considered the styles and outcomes of civic organizations' communications systematically over time.

The point here is that organizations have been sources of civic information beyond and as part of the organizational and mobilizing activities for which they are most often recognized. Further, what we draw attention to in this chapter is the fact that the communication dynamics of a particular organizational form matter: they surely reflect structures and strategies, but do not derive inexorably from them—they have logics, and consequences, of their own. Most of all, what the last chapter showed is that the nature of how a young citizen is able to interact with a civic entity may affect his or her inclinations about whether to continue doing so. In short, whereas as substantial recent work has attempted to make sense of the implications of change in communication processes (brought on in particular by digital technology) for organizational structure and function, here we train our lens on how organizations shape the communicative relationships they offer young supporters.

Of course, voluntary associations are far from the only sources of civic information young citizens encounter, and some notes are in order to situate the communications of civic organizations in the diversity of civic information flows young citizens encounter. The best-recognized source of civic information in most advanced industrialized democracies is journalism, from newspapers, television, and radio news to cable news, blogs, and other public affairs media. But journalism as the default source of civic information is a product of a particular information era, the high modern period, in which it was spun off as a special locale for civic information. At least in the United States, since the Progressive Era, the journalistic profession has worked hard to develop itself and its reputation around the task of providing a great quantity of information to enable citizens to be informed.[15] But in fact it is civic groups that have the longer history of providing civic information, especially civic information of the mobilizing variety. It is notable that it was civic groups that created many of the first newspapers, which only later were spun off independently. Tocqueville's famous quip reveals the entwined relationship between the two in the first half of the nineteenth century: "newspapers make associations, and associations make newspapers."[16]

This historical fact might be of limited import were it not for our need to rethink the sources of flows of civic information experienced by contemporary citizens. And in fact there are some intriguing reasons to suppose that our civic communication environment may bear similarities to the pre-high modern period of civic information provision, as we will see. The world of digital, networked media exchange is characterized by the drastic weakening of modern-era news organizations' claims to credibility, authoritativeness, and objectivity; the simultaneous convergence of content and formats across media actors; and the much-heralded ability of even relatively marginalized groups to reach large audiences. This means that some organizations may return to a position of prominence in the communication experiences of their supporters—and this is exactly what we are seeing in the practices of a new wave of online organizations such as MoveOn: what these groups are more than anything is not networked or (often) genuinely crowd-sourced. On the contrary, MoveOn is quite strategically run by a small group of staffers. What is most distinctive about these groups is that they so innovatively constitute their relationships to constituents through communication.[17] These are not quarterly newsletter organizations: they are email (and now social media) groups that attentively monitor the communication environment and pass news, opinion, and interpretation along to supporters on a daily basis. (There is a notable echo here of Jeffrey Pasley's observation that membership in American opinion movements of the early nineteenth centuries was not defined through dues-paying and meeting attendance, but through subscription to the newspaper supporting discourse on the topic.[18]) A result is that for many contemporary citizens, especially those most attentive to at least one civic group—but also, in networked social spaces, those one and perhaps more networked links out from such people—civic information may come as often through the channel of a civic organization as through a traditional news channel.

Also in contrast to the communications of civic groups, the civic information provided by journalism is rarely the kind of civic information that aims specifically to mobilize citizens to civic action. In the United States, journalism's decisive reformulation in the Progressive Era led it to focus on providing impartial information about public affairs, but only offer mobilizing information in very specific circumstances, such as when providing information about elections or community meetings, or, very occasionally, when editorializing. By contrast, civic associations have provided civic information with mobilizing frames aimed to both inform citizens and move them to engagement: whether they are providing knowledge about the issues facing the organization, or notices about action opportunities, such organizations' intents are always, directly or indirectly, to build a base of knowledgeable and inspired supporters ready and willing to be engaged in politics and public life. Once again, here we may be seeing a return to a form of information provision by agenda-driven civic groups.

The claim is not that the communications of these organizations constitute all or even most of the information of potentially civic relevance that a young person experiences in a day; it would be reasonable to argue that in the contemporary information environment, no single study could do that. What is more, the role of journalism in providing civic information is very far from over: on the contrary, much of the information provided over digital networks by civic organizations is journalistic content reframed with mobilizing intent. A recent study pegged the portion of news content originating with daily newspapers at a remarkable 85%.[19]

As such, the place of journalistic contributions to the stock of circulating information is still critically important to the overall civic ecology. Nonetheless, the communications of civic organizations online do represent an important and underrecognized measure of the way that engagement is being communicated to young citizens at this particular point in history. So how are the communication-based relationships between organizations and their supporters changing? How ready are the high-modern mobilizers of political activity to adapt to the identity and communication preferences of digital-era citizens?

Communicative Relationships

To answer these questions, I propose that we need refined tools for thinking about how citizens' membership in organizations is constituted through communication. We have seen that communication has always played a critical role in associational life, but the communications from organizations to their members have received comparatively little attention in organizational scholarship. Even the slightly broader topic of individuals' experiences of membership in organizations has often been downplayed in favor of analyses of organizational structure, interorganizational relationships, and organizational ecological studies.[20] And yet we are making the case that in digitally networked media organizations may have the opportunity to reassert their significance in civic communication, even as they struggle with redefining memberships based on that communication.

Some tangential attention has been paid to intraorganizational communication dynamics in studies of the democratic quality of organizations' structures and practices, and how participants' experiences of membership are affected by relatively more and less democratic contexts.[21] The problem has long been recognized as central to collective organizing: work on organizational processes are replete with references to the "iron law of oligarchy," stipulating that individuals in positions of power in organizations will tend to try to consolidate power, both for the purpose of more efficiently advancing the organization's goals and for personal ends.[22] It is quite clear that organizational elites, armed with resources and access to policymaking levers, and unhampered by cumbersome and time-consuming consultations with a widespread and diverse constituency, may often have an advantage in policy work over others heading more democratic organizations.[23]

At the same time, oligarchic tendencies are at odds with the inclinations of many organizational members, who would prefer to have more control over the direction of the organization to which they contribute. In fact, the evidence from a body of work on the outcomes of democratic process within organizations suggests that involving members in organizational governance can be quite consequential to mobilizing and sustaining participation: studies in contexts as diverse as industrial labor, teaching associations, and nonprofit organizations have documented the greater commitment and involvement displayed by individuals in contexts in which they experienced some degree of control over decision-making and self-determination.[24] We should keep these findings in mind as we consider the implications of how organizations construct their communications with followers: one way of reading the democratic qualities of an organization is as responsiveness to the concerns voiced by members through available communication channels.[25] Nonetheless, even in these studies, communication dynamics are subsumed into discussions focused primarily on governance and organizational process: the actual communication modes of organizations receive little attention.

This is an omission we correct in this chapter. The vantage point from which we operate is that for many young citizen members, a—and often, in today's media environment, *the*—primary experience of an organization's work is through communications over networked digital media. The possibilities of those communicative dynamics are multidimensional, necessitating choices on the part of organizations as to how to interact with supporters. To capture these dynamics, we employ the notion of a *communicative relationship* to describe the organization–citizen tie in the new media environment. The idea of a communicative relationship highlights the possibility that the sorts of communication an organization offers to supporters are consequential to young citizens used to interacting with a variety of entities through digital communication media. We might see the communicative relationship as a parallel to the question of the democratic qualities of an organization: just as a particular organization's governance processes might be measured in terms of how many mechanisms of democratic responsiveness it employs, so an organization's communications might also be assessed in evaluating the sort of communicative relationship fostered with members. To give the notion a bit more shape, we could define a communicative relationship as the *nature of reception and (possible) interactions that constitute the information exchanges between an organization and its individual supporters.*

It follows that the characteristics of organization-supporter communicative relationship may take a variety of forms, and change over the course of time, particularly with shifts in political and social circumstances and the available communication technology. Naturally, in line with the theoretical concerns introduced in Chapter 2, we will soon be concerned with identifying more actualizing, and more dutiful qualities in communication relationships fostered in organizational communications. But first, to lend some illustration to the notion of communicative relationship, let us consider the forms those relationships have taken over the major periods of associational activity in the United States.

This step is necessary to this analysis for two reasons: first, following existing work on political organizational behavior, a historical perspective offers the advantage of laying out clear points of comparison and change. Though communicative dynamics have rarely been a focus of the literature on the history of associational life, that work can be productively reconsidered in the service of a discussion of how the communicative relationships available to citizen members have shifted over time—and what we can say about their possible future. Specifically, here we articulate the evolution of communicative relationships across civic eras and across forms of organization. Three eras stand out: the classic era of civic formation and practice that we can trace from the 1880s to the mid-twentieth century, the check-writing era that came to dominate from the latter half of the twentieth century, and the digital era emergent today.

Second, in addition to broader historical trends reaching back across the last century and a half, many of the most important civic organizations still in operation themselves originated in the specific historical periods just mentioned. This makes the historical perspective not an obscure history lesson, but a recognition of the specific contexts that gave rise to the very organizations we deal with today—and that appear in the samples of the studies in Chapters 4 and 5. We could add that many of the individuals who continue to work in, lead, and make consequential choices for contemporary civic organizations experienced their formative years in the height of the last era. This is not a claim of strict path dependence, as though organizations' and individuals' histories years are all-defining and unchanging over decades. Nonetheless, I do intend to highlight organizations' origins and the opportunities and concerns that gave rise to their forms and practices—and the habits and inclinations of the people who work within them. This purpose gives the following discussion the added value of highlighting for us factors that may, indeed, influence organizational responses to opportunities and threats in the digital media environment, to which we turn at chapter's end.

The Classic Era of Civic Association

Alexis de Tocqueville's famous observations of American political life were nowhere more awestruck than in his descriptions of Americans' capacity for creating structures for collective action, or "associations."

Americans of all ages, all conditions, and all dispositions, constantly form associations. They have not only commercial and manufacturing companies, in which all take part, but associations of a thousand other kinds,—religious, moral, serious, futile, general or restricted, enormous or diminutive. The Americans make associations to give entertainments, to found seminaries, to build inns, to construct churches, to diffuse books, to send missionaries to the Antipodes; they found in this manner hospitals, prisons, and schools. If it be proposed to inculcate some truth, or to foster some feeling, by the encouragement of a great example, they form a society. Wherever, at the head of some new undertaking, you see the government in France, or a man of rank in England, in the United States you will be sure to find an association.[26]

What is even more impressive was that Tocqueville was recognizing only the beginnings of a long stretch of associational activity in the United States that in important ways was merely in its infancy at the time of his visit in 1831. Today the period between the Civil War and the 1920s is regarded as the heyday of the formation of major new civic organizations.[27] As Theda Skocpol has noted, "disproportionate numbers of eventually very large membership associations were created in the decades right after the Civil War" such that by the 1920s there were some twenty-five organizations whose memberships *each* amounted to more than 1% of the US adult population.[28]

The structure of these organizations is highly significant: a great many were "membership federations," with local branches across regions of the country and leadership structures from local to national levels. This structure mirrored that of American government, a fact that facilitated the organizations' abilities to harness their members for effective civic action, even as participation in formal political parties was in decline.[29] At the same time, such organizations were built into the fabric of local communities: discrete organizations did not emerge sui generis, but were formed out of the interactions and conversations, and concerns arising as citizens engaged one another in community meetings, artistic groups, religious gatherings and informal talk. As such, local chapters of federated organizations were much less local outposts of a larger institution than active community members who coordinated with a larger structure for the purposes of enhanced informational resources and connections to larger systems of power.[30]

And as relatively inclusive organizations, at least in terms of including members from diverse backgrounds and professions (generally *not* in terms of including members of diverse ethnicities), the organizations of the late nineteenth and early twentieth centuries also served to integrate society and encourage some degree of interaction and identification across social classes.[31] It is fair to say that this classic era of associational activity forms the bedrock of how Americans and scholars think about citizen involvement in politics, and current narratives of decline can be traced to some form of reminiscence—justified or not—for this formative period.[32]

For our purposes, the key question is what sort of communicative relationship existed in this era of participation. Interpersonal interaction was far and away the dominant mode of communicative experience, for civic and other purposes, for citizens. Before radio monopolized the communication of information and entertainment in the 1930s, it was a host of local and traveling meetings, preachers, speakers, and performances that offered those functions.[33] Local organizational meetings were one of the most habitual formats, of course, and were crucially important. Scholarship on civic organizations of the day makes clear the variety of regularly meeting groups that undergirded civic participation. In addition to groups formally organized to a particular cause, these included standing community groups that might be roused to interest in an issue, including women's, youth, and religious groups. An illustrative example comes from a 1914 letter from a Superindentent Holsaple of the South Dakota Anti-Saloon League, who exhorts concerned citizens in his state to "Get the folks to singing local option songs in your campaign meetings, Sunday School and young people's societies," indicating the diverse set of interpersonal networks to which activists could appeal.[34]

Another peculiarly fascinating manifestation of interpersonal communication for public civic education, entertainment, and organizing was the Chautauqua movement. Chautauquas were large public gatherings roughly comparable with carnivals or fairs today. They took both permanent forms, such as the original, the Lake Chautauqua Institute, which took place on Lake Chautauqua in western New York state in the summer of 1874, and rotating circuit chautauquas that made their way from place to place.[35] In the spirit of the age, a great deal of what chautauquas offered was self-improvement of various sorts, including religious instruction, education, and discussion of public affairs. Some of chautauquas' most prominent offerings were lectures by well-known educators, writers, politicians, and activists, many of whom are still highly familiar to us today, such as Susan B. Anthony, Henry Ward Beecher, William Jennings Bryan, and Mark Twain.[36] The names make clear that such lectures dealt with matters of importance to their times, and not infrequently exhorted citizens to action.

We should not downplay the significance of the interpersonal nature of these communicative experiences. Receiving information as a copresent collective, rather than on an individual basis, meant that even in the moment in which a speech was being given or a policy proposed, listeners were gauging one another's reactions and beginning to articulate responses. In the wake of a public meeting or speech, or between events at a chautauqua, citizens had the opportunity to immediately compare notes, discuss, and digest: as Tapia puts it, "the information and issues presented in . . . public forums were subsequently discussed and argued in countless farmhouse kitchens, dry goods stores, and barber shops."[37] These qualities made speeches, meetings, and presentations less discrete, neatly bounded individual performances and more elements in a discursive exchange that was going to continue, and be celebrated, criticized, and amended by members of the community.

It also meant that civic information was never far removed from civic action. Not only were speakers often intending to arouse listeners to action; listeners had immediate access to others who had just experienced the same communicative event and were similarly moved. It was precisely in response to events and discussions at the first chautauqua, in 1874, that women from various local Women's Temperance Leagues decided to form the national-level organization that would become the Women's Christian Temperance Union (WCTU).[38] And as Holsaple's quote above indicates, average participants were quite empowered to make choices about the civic actions taken and their participation in them. The opportunity to be engaged in discursive reflection and reframing, or to spur a local group to sing a particular antisaloon hymn, gave citizens a sense of empowerment and determination over the work of the group.

In addition to the interpersonal communications that took place at organizational meetings, rallies, chatauquas, and informally, organizations benefited from an impressive web of mediated communication that traveled from national-level organizational offices to local chapters, between chapters, and from all levels of organization to individual members by way of personal letters, chapter newsletters, "newspapers . . . pamphlets and petitions."[39] The creation of newspapers were primary ways social reformers of the nineteenth century sought to enter larger conversations and connect with publics who might join action on their issues: John Nerone shows the immense efforts—though often limited lasting success—of activist publishers such as Samuel E. Cornish and John B. Russwurm, who founded *Freedom's Journal*, an African American antislavery paper based in New York City; Elias Boudinot, who ran the *Cherokee Phoenix* from North Carolina; and white abolitionist William Lloyd Garrison's *Liberator*.[40] As Pasley puts it, "new political groupings founded or secured control of newspapers before they did almost anything else, and in many cases a newspaper originated a movement nearly on its own."[41]

Similarly, as Peter Odegard showed in his early study, the Anti-Saloon League of the early twentieth century stood out for its prolific publications on the issues of prohibition and the political processes surrounding it, as first individual towns and counties, then states and the American federal government were won over to alcohol prohibition. The league published both national publications, including its flagship magazine, *The American Issue*, of which some 14 million copies were printed at its peak in 1920.[42] Alongside thirty-one state-specific editions of the *American Issue*, other league magazines, books, pamphlets, and other media, Odegard concludes, "one might almost say that the liquor business was drowned in a deluge of temperance literature."[43]

Clearly, these movements made providing civic information central parts of their missions. And though—to be sure—their publishing served in large part to make their own cases and mobilize supporters, they also carried the kinds of contextual information citizens need for more general participation in politics: the rules and processes for making and changing laws, the roles of key political actors, the interplay of interest groups. Though a particularly prolific group, the Anti-Saloon League was not atypical in its use of multiple mediated communication channels to inform its members and connect them to civic action. The mediated communication promoted by organizations thus often mirrored organizational structure in its federated nature, which meant that members could expect to be regularly informed about the events and actions being taken at his or her local level, as well as goings-on at other local chapters, and about the interactions state and national-level officers might be having with other elements of the political or social structure. All of this added up to a richly configured opportunity for members to understand and participate in multiple levels of politics through the lens of a highly integrated organization.

These communication characteristics were critical for associations' abilities to foster participation. Although hierarchical in every sense of the word, organizations at the turn of the twentieth century also existed in a society in which such formality and hierarchy were endemic and thus were no different from most other aspects of participants' lived experiences. Further, the federated nature of organizations meant that individuals experienced frequent opportunity for active participation and local autonomy, as people took up roles as officers and decision-makers in their chapters. From a communication perspective, we could imagine the sense of give-and-take, self-determination, and meaningful membership experienced by person who spoke and felt him or herself heard in a meeting, contributed to a local newsletter, and read bulletins from the national council.

This local and participatory nature of voluntary civic associations has been recognized as a key site for learning the skills of organizing and politics: scholars have characterized smaller associations as generally more democratic and inviting of participation than those that are larger.[44] It also raises the intriguing question of the degree to which personal interaction itself fostered the beneficial outcomes of civic participation and to what degree it was the sense of being listened to and making decisions that was the key ingredient. As we move to a civic-communication environment that may provide the latter, but less so the former, this is a critical question to which we will return.

At the same time, regular participation in a local organization working in tandem with a federated structure that offered clear connections to the major levers of power also gave participants a great deal of context for understanding politics even at levels beyond which citizens were likely to directly experience: national politics would surely have been a topic of conversation at local chapter meetings, and on an individual basis group members would have had a context for understanding events and news.[45] Elisabeth Clemens's analysis of women's groups at the turn of the century illustrates this combination of localism and greater political influence nicely: "Since a typical club program consisted of one member presenting a paper on which others commented, women were forced both to speak in public and to voice their own opinions on a wide array of topics . . . clubs provided a haven in which new skills and dispositions could be cultivated," while also operating in large bureaucratic organizations that could effectively generate pressure in the formal political realm.[46] It was this combination of personal active and communicative engagement, of learning and development, and of the confidence that one's contributions aggregated to something at a larger level that formed the bedrock of civic organization–based engagement through the middle of the twentieth century.

Late-Twentieth-Century Media Politics and Check-Writing Engagement

By the end of the century substantial changes in the dynamics of civic associational life had taken place that are often characterized as a move from federated membership associations to nationalized, professionalized, and highly strategic organizations that had jettisoned many of the participatory features of the earlier groups. The results of this shift, it has been argued, have included consistently documented diminished levels of engagement in civic and associational life.[47]

The question of why this discordant state of affairs arose is an obvious one, and a number of factors have been implicated. As American politics became increasingly bureaucratized, a matter of competition over government attention and resources focused in Washington, DC and mediated by the logics of mass media, the foundations of how political interest organizations created political leverage changed.[48] Especially important from the perspective of the organization–citizen relationship, where once organizations were primarily directed at building and connecting large and locally engaged bases of supporters and mobilizing them, beginning in the 1960s they increasingly relied on professional expertise in lobbying and image management to achieve political goals.[49] A range of factors may have hastened the decline of mass voluntary membership organizations, including changing racial attitudes, which undermined the racial exclusiveness of many fraternal organizations, women professionalizing and entering the workforce, and changing attitudes toward war and the military. Changes in the "political opportunity structures" surrounding the federal government were also monumental. In Skocpol's words:

> Determined to take advantage of new opportunities, staff-heavy research and lobbying associations . . . took much of the action away from more cumbersome popularly based voluntary federations that had previously served as important conduits between the federal government and citizens in the states and districts. Where once it made sense to try to get things done in Washington by first gauging the opinions of grassroots association members and influencing officials and representatives in the localities and states, now it made much more sense for civic activists to aim their efforts at national media and intervene with staffs or agencies in Washington.[50]

As a result, the relationship between the organization and the citizen underwent a profound change. Where, as we saw above, earlier organizations' relationships to citizens were underpinned with interpersonal contacts at the local level and a web of communications connecting citizens within their communities to larger levels of organizations and politics, organizations in the late twentieth century saw their supporters as peripheral to political activities taking place primarily in Washington. Supporters were relegated to much more minor roles—no longer the officers and day-to-day operators of the grassroots of organizations, but now primarily sources of funds and, occasionally, points of highly scripted political leverage—for example, in petition drives or calls to legislators. For the supporter, the effect was participation that was discontinuous and over which one had minimal control and marginal personal impact. This shift has been described as one "from membership to management": to groups that no longer operate from committed participation by supporters, but increasingly from the top and aim to aggregate individuals' resources in a strategic and efficient manner.[51]

While this has been an effective method for achieving political goals in the political circumstances of the late twentieth century, at the level of citizen participation it was a corruption of the membership model of the beginning of the twentieth century. Many old institutions remain in place, but have moved away from work that fostered the kinds of activity among members that once formed the bedrock of civil society and citizen experience; hundreds more have come to life since the 1960s with no history of federated participatory organizing. The widespread declarations that we are observing a "democracy without citizens" and a politics of spectacle in which most citizens can hardly expect to meaningfully participate are in large part the product of this change.[52]

Extant scholarship has told this story from the vantage points of organizational, structural, and strategic transformations, but changes in the political communication environment were equally important. Because this is also the era of *media politics*.[53] What media politics means to actors attempting to stake a claim on the political process is that there is a new sector of society that must be constantly handled and mollified: the press. By the latter stages of media politics, it has become clear to many that communication concerns have infected the strategic considerations of all political actors to such a degree that it has virtually become a part of their DNA.[54] As Jay Blumler and Dennis Kavanagh put it in reference to political parties, one set of those actors, "major parties have thoroughly absorbed what may be termed the imperatives of the professionalization of political publicity . . . 'How will it play in the media?' is a question asked at an early stage in decision-making."[55]

This documents the other side of the coin of political opportunity structures. Though latter twentieth century organizations certainly were responsive to opportunities to pursue their agendas through new policymaking channels, they also were substantially constrained by a communication environment that demanded constant attention and management. The results of these circumstances for our discussion is an emphasis on message control and what we might call *communicative risk aversion*—the abiding fear in managers of political effort from the latter twentieth century that any informational misstep will be, within a news cycle, repeatedly played and replayed, rapidly diminishing the organization's credibility and support. While the implications of communicative risk aversion for how organizations manage their official communications are obvious and have been dealt with, what has been less recognized is how significant the trend is for organizations with members they may wish to involve in political mobilization—and communication. Put succinctly, an organization feeling the pressure of a communication environment poised to attack may forego offering members opportunities for public expressions of identity and opinion in favor of the communications of professionals who can be counted on to placate the media beast.[56]

What did conditions of changing political opportunity structures and media politics mean for organizational communications as experienced by citizen members—for the communicative relationships fostered by organizations? We see in the period the communication relationship largely reduced to carefully strategized newsletters, frequent appeals for financial contributions, and targeted uses of mass media. A couple of features of this communicative relationship are worth highlighting. First, interpersonal connections between citizens were greatly removed from the equation. This was the product of converging factors: first, social changes such as those detailed in Chapter 2 undermined the group substrate on which larger civic structures were built. Second, organizations seized upon new opportunities to more efficiently communicate with and mobilize supporters. Technology played a crucial role here, not only in the mass media through which organizations increasingly sought to communicate themselves, but also in the techniques being invented for appealing to supporters, such as computerized direct mail, which greatly reduced the cost of addressing a mass of potential supporters and tracking support.[57] Consequently, though a few major civic organizations continue to have a genuinely federated structure in which local, small group participation is paired with bureaucratic organization at a national scale, this is no longer the norm.[58] In communicative terms, this means that most supporters experience communications as an individual, not a member of a public in which reception, evaluation and response take place collectively.

Third, the valence of communication became very much unidirectional: organizations produce strategic communications meant to elicit response from a sufficient portion of potential supporters to continue their work and generate public pressure, and citizens' options are primarily the dichotomy between contributing money and being a member or opting out.[59] This reflects an underlying transformation in the membership mobilization strategy pursued by civic groups. Whereas small groups had no choice but to be responsive to members' concerns and complaints—what Albert Hirschman referred to as the option of exercising *voice*—large postmembership organizations appealed in reality not to individual members, but to an identified sector of the mass public—a market sector—that could be counted on to care about a given issue at a given time. Among such a market, voice becomes essentially irrelevant, as members make their complaints known almost exclusively with their feet (Hirschman's *exit*). In Hirschman's terms, signs of the threat of significant exit can spur an institution to rethink its operations, and even increase spaces for voice.[60] But because subjects in a market are interchangeable, this does not result in a change in organizational policy so much as additional appeals to members of the mass public to take the places of departing members.

The result of all this is that whereas once civic participants experienced a rich and varied set of communications through a variety of interpersonal interactions and media, as well as opportunities to respond to and be recognized by the group, in later twentieth-century organizational communications individuals' roles became much more strategically defined, individually targeted, and unidirectional. Such communications undoubtedly provide some contexts for understanding politics and participating: interest organizations carefully advertised their positions on candidates and issues and attempted to mobilize publics in certain ways for key events. And some group members may want little more than the sense that they are contributing to a worthy cause and some information about how that cause is progressing. But in comparison to the rich civic communicative experience of members participating in earlier civic groups, it is indeed a thin one. The irony, of course, is that this very same period was one in which many citizens were increasingly rejecting systems of hierarchical authority and aspiring for opportunities to participate and express themselves more directly, as detailed in Chapter 2. But many of the groups organizing political life, for genuine and legitimate strategic reasons, were in moving the opposite direction. Many remained nominally federated, but most dropped the local centers of citizen participation for an increasing focus on fundraising, lobbying, and mass communication through elite media. These organizations, and the communication relationships they allowed with supporters, fit least well with citizens' preferences but survived (arguably, thrived) because they had tailored themselves to the conditions of late-twentieth-century media politics. One consequence has been the period of disengagement from political life and civic information experiences by many citizens, especially the young.[61]

Voluntary Association and the Digital Era

It is against the backdrop of late-twentieth-century check-writing media politics that the digital revolution stands out. Because amidst this dysfunctional civic order has emerged a communication technology that many see as peculiarly suited to reforming its dynamics. The multichannel, multidirectional communication system and the cultural priorities developing alongside it, as described in Chapter 2, herald a possible revision of the previous era's intense focus on top-down, command-and-control strategic communication. This is an exciting moment in which we are observing organizations, individuals, networks, and other collectivities experimenting with new ways to communicate engagement to citizens.

Naturally, great interest surrounds the question of how citizens will associate, and order politics, as the digital era becomes more firmly entrenched. A prominent answer receiving some of the greatest attention in recent years is that civic involvement will happen outside the structures of organizations as we have known them. This argument has developed out of analyses of case studies in which the rules of collective action—and even economic modes of production—appeared to be broken by the possibilities created out of the unlimited many-to-many communications enabled by digital media.[62] The movements at the opening of Chapter 1, or at least narratives surrounding them, are examples of the enthusiasm for this line of thought. So are descriptions of novel forms of collective organizing, ranging from transnational activist movements to youth-driven movements across the web and from communities emergent among players of multiplayer games to not-for-profit productions of knowledge and culture.[63]

Underlying the interpretation of these examples as evidence for a paradigm-breaking shift in coordinating rules is the notion that the contemporary media environment offers something so startlingly new that what were once fundamental rules of the game of human collective endeavor no longer apply. Exactly what this new is varies from somewhat from author to author, but the common thread is something along the lines of the diminishing costs of creating and exchanging information. Yochai Benkler has set the larger argument on some of its firmest theoretical footing by contending that the logics of communication and the production of informational goods have always been different from those of other industrial products. For centuries, informational and material goods were artificially coupled by the simple fact that information was predominantly conveyed over material objects such as books and newspapers. It is when information creation, storage, and distribution are freed from those industrial-material bases that the alternative logic underlying the economics of information becomes consequential.[64] Then, as costs of communication and coordination fall to near zero, things change decisively: individuals enter the marketplace of cultural and intellectual creation who previously would not have; forms of collaboration in pursuit of ends as varied as superhero fandom, marijuana legalization, and white supremacy arise and quickly spread around the globe.[65]

As a result of the very recent decoupling of the material and informational economies, these forms of collaboration often display characteristics once thought to be unsustainable in collective endeavor. Before the advent of rapid digital communication, communication with a public of any size was expensive enough that it could only be accomplished through an organized collective action that could structure individuals' contributions and overcome the obstacle of rational free-riding.[66] Digital communication technologies have profoundly changed this equation, because they have made the key elements of collective action—communication with and within a large group of people—almost trivially inexpensive.[67]

There are significant qualifications to these arguments, however, and many of the more hyperbolic accounts of how spontaneous collective action takes place under conditions of information abundance show cracks upon closer analysis.[68] One point of crucial importance is that it is not at all clear how well self-directed collectives are able to aggregate their contributions in contexts that required highly focused, time-sensitive collaboration. Autonomous, opt-in, opt-out interaction has great potential for the accomplishment of some tasks, such as aggregating the world's knowledge or building open-source software—no small feats, to be sure—but less so for others, such as winning legislative battles. It would be a mistake to force the false dichotomy that either everything we know about organizational activity is obsolete or that nothing has changed.

Recognizing that this means that many of the major civic organizations will not simply vanish but will, indeed, soon inhabit a greatly changed communication and civic landscape, recent scholarship has looked for guidance to some of the oldest questions about collective action and organization.[69] The challenges of collective action have always been in identifying a common interest among members of the public, communicating with and between those individuals, and coordinating their engagement in pursuit of their interests—fundamentally problems of communication.[70] As a result, changes in the possibilities of communicative connectedness, and their costs, are likely to reconfigure the possibilities for collective action. This is the point made by Bruce Bimber, Andrew Flanagin, and Cynthia Stohl in their call for a reconsideration of Mancur Olson's foundational *Logic of Collective Action*. What they show is that reduced communication costs mean a reduced barrier between private and public action on the part of participants, and thus a falling need for organizations to formalize the process of private-to-public transition or create mechanisms to overcome problems of free-ridership, which Olson saw as defining to the problem of collective action. As he saw it in the predigital age, collectives of individuals had significant incentives to organize hierarchically into an organization that could accomplish tasks and to which all could formally contribute; correspondingly, organizations had great incentives to bureaucratize, formalize, and offer members selective benefits. Only through these means could collectives and organizations extract great enough participation from (rational, instrumental) members to meet the costs of coordination.[71]

But as organizations' costs of coordination fall and members' personal costs of crossing the boundary into public action similarly diminish, organizational processes are changing; we are seeing the emergence of "postbureaucratic political organization," the weakening of the formerly great need for highly structured organizations to facilitate collective political action.[72] In place of the development of hierarchical structures that can dictate and coordinate actions, organizations appear to be more free to sustain themselves on continuous flows of communications with and between networked members. These connections "stress complementarity and informal relations based on trust . . . [and are] built around short-term material flows that link people together."[73] Crucial for the current discussion, they also shift the center of gravity of decision-making, and sometimes even strategy, in the direction of many increasingly autonomous supporters. Flanagin and colleagues have characterized this pattern of empowering supporters with the agency to choose their own entry points and manners of engagement as an entrepreneurial mode, contrasted to an institutional one more dominant in earlier periods. In brief, individuals coordinating in an entrepreneurial mode give up little in their personal agency of how to engage with a collective action or when: they retain great latitude in choice of what sorts of actions to take or expressions to make.

This description of the possibilities of postbureaucratic entrepreneurial engagement is an exciting echo of the actualizing civic information style developed in the last chapter. Because it is precisely the informational preferences of actualizing citizens—for expression, autonomy, peer sharing—that appear alongside the entrepreneurial engagement mode in many emerging associational forms. This is why it should not be terribly surprising that many of the most successful and striking collective action networks emerging today, such as the examples that opened the book, have embraced more entrepreneurial forms, exhibited highly actualizing styles of communication, and attracted disproportionately engaged young publics. Many have been either resistant to or unable to centralize and institutionalize, and have remained able to offer participants points of identification and expression without demanding rigidly prescribed participation modes. (A few conventional civic organizations also successfully created entrepreneurial arms, such as Howard Dean's 2004 presidential run, which married institutional campaign structures to far-flung networks of bloggers and supporters who connected through MeetUps, but such an example is exciting mainly because it occurred in an arena typically so resistant to those forms of organizing.)[74]

So what is the relationship between mode of engagement and the actualizing civic information style? Is there any value in keeping them conceptually distinct—in continuing to separate Flanagin and colleagues' mode of engagement from our modes of civic information? There is, for three reasons. First, the distinction is conceptually valid. How we engage is different from how we communicate about how we engage. Varying degrees of individual latitude in what sorts of actions to take, and when, and under what conditions (mode of engagement) is not the same as the set of factors related to our modes of civic information. This is illuminated by the second reason, which is that our historical look at previous eras of civic organizing demonstrated that many supporters experienced a high degree of agency and autonomy in their communications within membership organizations: they had the opportunity to speak, be heard, respond to others, and so forth. It would not be correct to say, however, that the nature of engagement of these members was entrepreneurial. Members were not free to choose, on an individual basis, the nature of the actions they were to take. To be sure, communications and leadership positions offered the opportunity to shape the organizations' choices of what activities it sanctioned and promoted, but that is a far cry from individually autonomous choices of involvement—it is the difference between a membership mode of participation and an entrepreneurial one.

This leads to the third reason, which is that we are not entering wholesale a brave new world, a renaissance of new organizations free to reinvent institutional forms, practices, routines, and structures. Older, bureaucratic institutions, with histories and norms, invested leaders and members, and ties and influence within formal political spheres, also are exposed to new forms of engagement and communication. For existing organizations, there is nothing simple about amending rooted processes of decision-making and authority delegation—successful bureaucratization serves to inhibit rapid change in those areas. What is more, as we shall shortly see, the era of media politics is still very much alive and well, a fact with substantial implications for the behavior of civic communicators who must be most protective of their image in the public sphere. Nonetheless, existing organizations now exist alongside both cultural changes that have shifted the information preferences of their youngest supporters and emergent networks, movements, and organizations that have embraced more fully postbureaucratic political organizing. These are now potential competitors for civic energy in which more entrepreneurial and actualizing experiences are being made available to young potential constituents.[75] This is exactly the nature of an inflection point in organizational ecology: one set of "legacy" organizations must contend with the intrusions of a new variety, which comes bearing potentially paradigm-shifting new characteristics.[76]

An intriguing question in this context is to what degree modes of engagement and styles of communication are separable for such established organizations. Bureaucratic institutions structuring involvement for citizens may have few chances to offer genuinely entrepreneurial engagement to their supporters. But is that so for actualizing patterns of communication? Or—like their predecessors the interpersonal membership organizations—might contemporary civic institutions have an opportunity to combine relatively bureaucratized, institutional engagement with communication patterns that offer members more autonomy?

This discussion suggests the possible utility of a term to capture what we are talking about. We might refer to this new positioning of the participant within civic life as affording an increased degree of *communicative autonomy*. The term describes an individual's experience in an organization or movement that is larger than him or herself, and the extent to which the individual is invited, or has the opportunity, to express herself and develop an independent civic identity, yet also potentially have the sense that her contributions affect the meaning of the larger group.[77]

Communicative autonomy is a concept at one level of abstraction higher than the actualizing civic style. The actualizing style would thus be the twenty-first century manifestation of a larger set of citizens' inclinations for communicative autonomy: as we observed, the desire for members to have a say in their organizations' decision-making and meaning construction did not suddenly emerge with the ascent of actualizing preferences. On the contrary, we saw how civic organizations of the classic era of civic organizing, though built with classically bureaucratic structures, also rested on social substrates that were highly local, and that together gave organizations their characteristically participatory form.[78] For the citizen in these contexts self-expressive opportunities were many, and even if these were not free-form expressions of self-identity, they represented moments in which members could genuinely feel that their contributions made a difference to the meaning of the community of which they were a part. This is communicative autonomy's value: its generalizability across quite different contexts, allowing us to consider the extent to which forms of organizing and organizational communications of very different periods bear resemblance to one another.

In sum, the communicative relationship between citizens and the movements in which they take part may be transforming once again. At the organizational level, ease of communication and coordination are freeing organizing structures from the hierarchy and bureaucracy necessary in earlier eras. New patterns of coordination make possible organizing forms open to an increased degree of member agency, or entrepreneurialism. At the same time, citizens' inclinations have moved strongly toward greater opportunity for self-expression and self-definition in political engagement—at an individual level especially, though we might add that some movements have explicitly connected their form of organizing with more comprehensive ideology.[79]

Anticipating the Emergence of Actualizing Communications

This discussion returns us to the book's core questions: To what extent are young actualizing citizens able to find civic communication experiences in line with their preferences? Where are those experiences appearing? The studies presented in the next two chapters offer answers to these questions along two dimensions. First, drawing on our concern for how the established members of American civil society are reacting to changed communication conditions, we will look across the landscape of civic groups to investigate how different members of that population are using digital media to communicate with youth. Second, by looking at two different new media forms—websites and social media—we can gauge the extent to which norms and practices built into a communication platform affect organizations' practices within it.

To guide these investigations, we can draw on the preceding discussion to identify three factors that suggest themselves as primary reasons encouraging or discouraging organizations from adopting actualizing features of communications. The first is the general cultural shift toward more autonomy on the part of individuals as participants in larger structures. The second are how organizational workers and leaders respond to the larger cultural shift with

changes in communication habits and patterns, and what organizational members are demanding of them. And the third is the question of how pressures
of media politics continue to affect organizational communication in digital
media. As we will see, these factors are complex, differentially important for
different types of organizations, and often in tension.

CULTURAL CHANGE

The rise of the actualizing civic information style described in the last chapter was not an emergence sui generis among young citizens surfing the web.
Rather, we described the actualizing style as one particular manifestation of
the confluence of much larger social-cultural trends and particular but related
developments of digital media. The late modern society described by social theorists has undergone, and continues to undergo, fundamental changes toward
individualization and de-institutionalization. Though we argued that these
often affect youngest generations most acutely, they are much broader, and
have reflections at all levels of society.

What this means for our current concerns is that we should expect late
modern cultural changes to push organizations to at least grapple with contemporary discourses about increasing member participation and interactivity.[80] As we will see, the outcome of this grappling may not often result in a
fully-fledged commitment to communicate in a way resonant to young actualizing citizens, but nonetheless there is little doubt that most organizations
experience cultural pressures in this direction. This particular pressure is likely
to be experienced by all civic organizations, though the degree to which it is
felt, and acted upon, may vary greatly. But based on what? The larger cultural
trend toward interactivity and participation should be strongest in organizations most invested in the norms of digital culture: we should anticipate that
organizations most comfortable with digital culture norms, and accustomed to
them, will be relatively more inclined to promote an actualizing communication experience for members. But which organizations will be most invested in
norms of digital culture?

INFLUENCES OF ORGANIZATIONAL LEADERSHIP, HABIT, AND EXPERTISE NETWORKS

One simple answer to this question lies in the growing set of organizations
that have been created specifically for the purpose of engaging young people
online—organizations that did not exist before the Internet, and that do not
operate offline programs. These organizations' creators clearly see a potential in using digital media to engage youth since, after all, they have chosen
exactly that medium for their youth engagement project. Leaders of such

organizations tend to be younger, though much more importantly, tend to have experience and a degree of comfort and expertise with digital media that sets them apart from the leaders of conventional civic groups. Such faith in digital media, and the choice to create an organization online specifically to take advantage of digital media's possibilities is likely to be reflected in a communication style that emphasizes digital norms, and their close cousin, an actualizing communication style.

On the other side, organizations that did exist before the Internet, or that invest heavily in offline programs, are likely to be different. All else equal, these organizations are likely to have older leaders who are more firmly rooted in a mode of engaging supporters developed before youth civic styles and the norms of digital culture. The result is likely to be an organizational inertia—heritage and memory in a past social and communication era that is likely to make them highly protective of messages and resistant to sharing their message-making with supporters.

Further, established organizations are likely to be much more firmly rooted in structures of leadership, funding and alliance networks that inhibit fundamental changes to organizational vision, practice, and branding. Many organizations rely to a major extent on a few big-ticket donors and foundations, who exert considerable pressure on organizational processes and decision-making. Such funders, many of whom have long personal experiences in organizational work and funding, may not see the possibilities presented by adapting an organization's work and communication to the norms of digital media. Similarly, civic organizations are not well understood as purely independent entities free to reconstruct relationships with members at will. Within any given field of civic activity, there tend to be close ties between organizations, and between organizations and governmental bodies, that are dependent on trust and reliability on the part of all actors. This is a crucial element of the shift to the management style Skocpol sees in contemporary civic organizations: many organizations' focus has shifted to technocratic, expert deliberation over matters of science and policy. Such professionalized groups, who justify themselves to both the public and working partners on the basis of their expertise, may have too much to lose to open their communications to lay member input.[81]

The intuitions supporting this prediction are hinted at by previous studies. When Flanagin et al. place organizations in their collective action space, it is online-only organizations and networks that conspicuously fill the entrepreneurial half of that space: MeetUp, Care2Connect, the WTO Protest network and MoveOn are all present—all started, and continue to do most of their work, online. Although two organizations with significant offline components (Grameen Bank and Howard Dean's campaign) also make appearances there, they are notable cases for that reason. And no online-only organization appears in the institutional half of the chart.[82] Additionally, it is quite well known that as organizations age, their leaderships become more entrenched in established practices.[83] Similarly, funders are likely to want to stick with processes and leaders that have worked in the past.[84]

There is a corollary to the inclinations and intuitions of organizational leaders on the part of organizations' members. We should remain mindful that not all members are likely to expect or demand the same experience from all organizations. The landscape of civic groups is vast and diverse enough that it is unrealistic to assume that even actualizing citizens will want active, expressive opportunities with all of them. There may be certain types of organizations, that is, that are not expected to offer particularly interactive, rich experiences, just as there are likely to be some citizens who are not often seeking them. Bimber, Flanagin, and Stohl have argued that expectations of how one's involvement with an organization will be can significantly affect individuals' assessment of their participation. Particularly where an organization's brand would lead members to expect a relatively staid, dutiful experience, members are typically not disappointed by that experience. It is where an organization's brand would seem to offer a richer, more interactive and personal experience that members who do not find the experience lose affinity for the organization.[85]

Thus it is possible that some groups will be granted greater leeway to maintain a dutiful style of communicating because it complements their brand identity; others may have greater need to respond to young citizens' actualizing preferences with correspondingly interactive and participatory communications. But which groups are which? Presumably, parallel to our expectations of leaders' inclinations for their organizations' communications, supporters of newly created, online only groups are likely to demand higher levels of actualizing communications than supporters of other sorts of groups. The fact that they have joined online only groups to begin with suggests that they see a unique potential in the kind of work those groups can do. In sum, these considerations point us to a simple bifurcation of organizations: between those that have been created in the last twenty years, and exist only in digital media, and those that have existed for longer, and were founded—and likely continue to operate—brick-and-mortar services and actions.

THE CONSEQUENCES OF MEDIA POLITICS

Finally, we must not lose sight of the fact that contemporary organizations and their members continue to reside in a period of brutal media politics, which will continue to exert its influence even where structural limitations to ease of communication and coordination have eased. Put more bluntly, there are still good reasons for organizations to wish to constrain their members' communicative participation. We should expect this to constitute a considerable constraint on the extent to which organizations respond to larger cultural shifts and offer communicative autonomy to their supporters. The key question becomes, what sorts of organizations are most likely to be concerned with protecting organizational messages in the agonistic public sphere?

One answer is that institutional resistance to changing communication styles may be most pronounced within groups with the closest proximity to formal political processes. It is organizations combatting in the formal political sphere who have the most to lose from communications that escape their control, and the most enemies tracking messages ready to publicize missteps. Bimber recognizes this factor in broader organizational terms:

> Like firms, but not parties and especially not like government institutions, collective action organizations are largely free to reorganize and adapt themselves independently to changing conditions in their environment without the necessity of agreement by other institutions, public support, or legislative or constitutional action.[86]

But there is great variance within collective action organizations. Even when we refer to Tocquevillian associations or Skocpolian organizations, we are referring to a great number and variety of organizations and organizing forms. We might especially observe that among these organizations are both formal political interest groups and nonpolitical community and service organizations. The former, while not parties, clearly do have much closer ties to parties and governmental processes, and the latter have little direct affiliation with those things.

We might consequently argue that it is not only parties and government groups likely to suffer from a reticence to adjust to postbureaucratic organizing and communicating styles. Interest groups doing political work also must carefully manage their communications in a fraught environment—witness the attacks suffered by MoveOn in the wake of their crowd-sourced video contest.[87] It may thus be that more political organizations feel pressures of media politics to a greater extent than service-oriented ones—because the formers' work is so dependent on the reputation it constructs and presents to the public and to officials. Along the same lines, more political organizations naturally have more enemies, and thus feel greater constant scrutiny of every communication that bears their brand. The Girl Scouts, for example, though certainly feeling a great need to maintain a healthy brand, have little to fear compared to the Human Rights Campaign should a wayward supporter make the news by doing something embarrassing or publishing something inflammatory. All of this suggests that we might productively predict that organizations' proximity to formal politics will predict their willingness to embrace communicative autonomy for supporters, including actualizing communications.

Stephen Coleman's work aligns with this assessment. His study suggests a stark divide between the conventional politics of government-oriented and political organizations and the activities of activist groups—and that the more autonomous communication style is somewhat anathema to organizations trying to communicate conventional political engagement. In his view, governmental organizations, and other organizations operating in the formal political world, simply have too much to lose by opening real debates and participatory opportunities to youth who may either create communications that are embarrassing or otherwise find their way into compromising situations.[88]

There is, however, an alternative account that rebuts these presumptions. A handful of recent political campaigns, most notably Howard Dean's campaign of 2004 and Barack Obama's 2008 victory, suggest that some political organizations can embrace the possibilities of actualizing communication. Such examples suggest that political parties and politicians experience may in fact experience such fierce competition that they are relatively more willing to innovate in general, including to experiment with modes of engagement and communication that nonprofit civic groups not facing such brutal imperatives never attempt. The relatively more frequent turnover of parties and politicians—owing to quick cycles of success and failure—may also favor the emergence of individual leaders more willing to try out new forms of organizing.

Nonetheless, the bulk of the theory on how an organization's agenda affects their communications with supporters suggests that being close to the workings of politics will tend to inhibit an organization's willingness to present an actualizing communication environment. The consequence of this is that governmental organizations, political parties and political interest groups may be most set on dutiful communications, while less overtly political groups may be relatively more inclined toward actualizing patterns.

These three factors ground our investigations of organizational communicative behavior in detail in Chapters 4 and 5. Before moving on those analyses let us conclude by taking note of a crucial contextual variable also playing a significant role: the particular digital media contexts through which organizations communicate.

Communicating Engagement Online

Studies of communicative behavior on the web have always faced a set of challenges peculiar to that remarkable environment: first, Internet communications afford a great variety of types of exchange. Unlike television, or the telephone, Internet communications include one-to-one media and broadcast potential. They include text, video, and audio. And each of these affordances can be employed in a variety of ways. It becomes deeply problematic to compare two entities' Internet communications the way we once compared uses of television or print media: online, one may produce a multimedia website with social media tie-ins and a great deal of video while another is primarily sending emails. Relatedly, Internet communications and their possibilities change so quickly that it is extremely difficult to develop sustained empirical impressions of online behavior: unlike questions on a survey, these measures are never quite the same.

One of the most important solutions to these challenges has been the development of the notion of *affordances* in Internet study.[89] This emphasis has allowed researchers to focus on *characteristics* of technological platforms rather than their specific identities. In this way, a blog becomes not a blog per se, but a communication technology that includes the affordances of regular posting capability, syndication (RSS), and interactivity (commenting).

The approach taken here builds on the notion of affordances, but takes it to a further level of parsimony. Rather than examine specific affordances, in the following chapters we will examine two of the most common web platforms that we can think of as *affordance packages*—that is, they are online communication media so common that all organizations will likely know of them and be familiar with the general set of affordances they come with. Specifically, in the following two chapters we will examine organizations' communications through their own websites (Chapter 4) and Facebook (Chapter 5).

WEBSITE ANALYSIS: CHAPTER 4

Websites are an obvious initial choice for analyzing an organization's patterns of communication with potential participants. Over the last two decades websites have become the default online presence of any entity aiming to communicate online: they are organizations' official presences in the digital realm, and as such are the online medium through which organizations are most formally presenting themselves.[90] Further, websites are digital environments over which organizations exercise maximal control, and a relatively great deal of control over the kinds of communication that take place. Because they are customizable, and impose no particular structure or pattern to organizations' interactions with supporters, websites should show us how the organizations are preferring to communicate. Further, because of young citizens' strong reputation as "digital natives," organizations are likely to see the web as a key medium through which to reach young people.[91] Websites thus suggest themselves as a critical starting point for evaluating the communications of organizations of different types. We should expect organizations' communications there to starkly display their responses to the factors noted above.

FACEBOOK ANALYSIS: CHAPTER 5

While a focus on websites is a critical test of organizations' communications, in the Web 2.0 era such a focus has limitations that can be improved upon by adding an analysis of communication patterns in a major social networking environment. First, it is not clear that many young people experience civic communication through the sites of youth civic organizations. A few such sites boast tens of thousands of active users, and total accounts occasionally reaching into the hundreds of thousands.[92] One somewhat exceptional case is my.barackobama.com, the social networking environment created by Obama's innovative new media team, which boasted 2 million profiles—by no means all or even mostly youth—by election day 2008.[93] But most have many fewer, and what we do know about those participants suggests that they are relatively more advantaged and politically interested than the youth population at large.[94] In contrast, social networking sites are exactly the place where the youth are. In surveys of Americans, the portion of online young people (those 18–24) with social networking profiles is regularly placed between 70 and 80%, with around half of those reporting daily use.[95] The numbers are similar for teens.[96]

A second limitation of an exclusive focus on websites is that such a view offers a restricted impression of the kinds of communication relationships organizations are creating. Because organizations now have so many options for communicating with supporters, even within the web domain, drawing strong conclusions based on an organization's communication in one medium could give an unrepresentative or distorted view of that organization's practices because it may not devote significant resources to that form of communication, or it may focus its communication energy (and budget) elsewhere. In short, although an organization may maintain a website for certain kinds of communication, it may not intend its website to be the primary portal with which to interact with young supporters.

To address these limitations, this book's analyses are not limited to organizations' communications through websites, but also analyzes their communications through the massive social networking site Facebook. As noted above, the point here is not to simply describe communications in this particular online environment—though if that were the case, Facebook would also be a first choice owing to its size and universality. Rather, Facebook here represents an *affordance package* in that its functionalities represent the major affordances offered by what might be described as a class of platforms that make up Web 2.0: person-to-person online networking; identity expression, including through the use of profiles; and media and information sharing. What further sets such an environment apart from websites is that unlike the unlimited control an entity has when creating a website, the functionalities of Facebook are very much written in to the experience. As described in Chapter 5, analyzing these communications gives an indication of how organizations communicate when they choose to enter into a web medium that is *already* strongly steeped in norms of digital culture.

Analyzing both websites and social networking presences gives us relatively greater confidence that we are capturing the essence of an organization's online communication strategy—whether it is occurring in a long-standing form of web communication of the Web 1.0 era or in a more contemporary Web 2.0 form. And just as significantly, the possibility of comparing organizations' communication practices in the two media give us an impression of what impact the presence of digital culture norms in Facebook might have on organizations' orientations to supporters.

Conclusion

This chapter has added to the conceptualization of civic information developed in Chapter 1, and the modes of civic information preference developed in Chapter 2, by exploring possible sources of civic communications with which young people are likely to interact. Specifically, it has interrogated the communication that makes up the relationship between young citizens and civic organizations—a relationship, it has been argued, that has been an essential component of American political involvement for a hundred and fifty years, and is likely to continue to be critical.

This is a new contribution to a field that has so far separately developed accounts of youth citizenship and digital communication practices and notions of how organizations are responding to the challenges and possibilities of the new media environment. One outcome of the existing focus is that many scholars interested in the transformation of organizations and social movements under new media conditions have concerned themselves with structure: it is, after all, in terms of organizational structure—authority relations, coordination—where some of the most exciting change is taking place. The shift from hierarchical, bureaucratic organization to a network form of some type is the general form of change most often described. But the typical participant in an organization or movement never sees the underlying structure. What they do see are the communications that make up their relationship with the entity—whatever that relationship is, and it surely varies a great deal between different members.[97] This is especially true for young citizens in the social media environment, who are very likely to encounter a particular movement or effort in mediated form—as shared by a peer on Facebook, or advertised directly to them through a targeted ad buy, or recommended by Facebook's algorithm. For these people, communicative relationships with civic organizations may be their entry point into civic action. Structures may well be important—they surely are reflected in communication styles. But to the extent that changed structural forms encourage greater involvement by younger, actualizing citizens, this pathway should be visible through different communicative patterns.

Considering the last century's history of civic organizations from this perspective, what we noticed is that that communicative relationship between individuals and structures of civic action are likely going through a new period of change. A new era of civic organization and their relationships to supporters is emerging; what is yet unseen is what that relationship will consist of, and especially whether it will consist of communications more amenable to young citizens preferences than the set of communication practices honed by many civic organizations toward the end of the twentieth century. And from our discussion we have developed a set of expectations: that many of the newer, online-only organizations emerging may offer relatively more actualizing communications than traditional organizations rooted primarily offline, and that the an organization's ties to formal politics may particularly inhibit its ability to offer information in an actualizing mode. It is to testing those propositions that we now turn.

4

Civic Organizations' Communications on the Web

For many twenty-first-century young citizens, communications via digital media are now primary entry points into multiple spheres of life. These include the social, often mediated by social and other interactive media; the economic, mediated by bank, credit card, and other online financial transactions; and even the romantic, mediated by both social media platforms and specialty dating websites.[1] As we saw in the last chapter, the mediation of civic life by digital media has implications for organizations aspiring to inform and engage young people in civic life. This point emphasizes the need to understand the nature of communications offered to young people in digitally networked spaces, and this chapter offers a primary exploration toward that end.

Both citizens and organizations come to their new communicative relationship with certain needs, preferences, and habits concerning meanings and uses of civic information. The story emerging from the past two chapters implies that changes in young citizens' lives, organizational practices, and dynamics of public communication over the course of the last half century has driven these relationships out of alignment, with substantial consequences for the participatory inclinations of citizens, especially younger citizens. In the early twentieth century, citizens and organizations were more or less in line in terms of what they expected from one another and from their communicative relationship. Toward the end of the century, however, that harmony was disrupted as organizations sought to exploit political opportunities and contend with the communication imperatives of late-twentieth-century media politics, and citizens grew frustrated with increasingly prescribed, contrived, and manipulated communication experiences. The opening of the twenty-first century is a time of transition, and this chapter begins to trace the extent to which the organization–citizen relationship is being reinvented in a new and still developing communication paradigm. We address the question empirically, by examining how youth civic organizations communicate in a single but central component of their online presences: their websites.

Websites

Since the inventions of the World Wide Web in 1989 and the first graphical browsers shortly thereafter, websites have been essential components of online communication.[2] Because of the web's accessibility to great numbers of people, it has been the primary experience of the Internet for the vast majority of users. As a result, websites have come to represent the unique address for individuals and organizations on the web.[3] They were the fundamental building blocks of so-called Web 1.0, and though their direct influence has been moderated by the ability of people and organizations to represent themselves through social media platforms such as Facebook (explored in Chapter 5), they remain indispensable resources for communicators of all sorts.

As such, the websites of organizations wishing to engage young people in civic life are an obvious place to begin exploring their presentation of civic information. They literally contain organizations' homepages, are entirely under the organizations' control, and often are the first result of a web search for a given organization. Websites' content represents what organizations choose to present to users: it reflects intentional choices on the part of organizations about who they are, who their imagined audience is, and how they want to present themselves to that audience. They are the core of an organization's online self-representation and embody what sorts of civic or political relationships they are seeking to establish with supportive publics.

Recognizing their central role in organizations' communications with supporters, in this chapter we examine the presentation of civic information on civic organizations' websites. Several steps lead us through this exploration. We begin by more closely defining the sort of organizations we are concerned about, and describing the specific organizations that make up the study. Next, we consider several ways of looking at organizations' website communications: in terms of two varieties of civic information, in terms of more dutiful and more actualizing modes of interaction, and in terms of the specific activities in which organizations ask supporters to engage. In each, our analyses test the proposition that a communicative disconnect exists between civic organizations and young citizens, and explores the nature and origins of the disconnect by examining how different types of organizations respond differently to online communication possibilities.

Organizational Categories and Sample Selection

Chapter 3 ended with three factors consequential to the communicative relationships fostered by civic groups. These included cultural changes; an organization's history, leadership, and brand identity as older and primarily offline, or as one that had recently started, and was still exclusively online; and media politics as a contextual variable constraining some organizations' willingness to adopt actualizing features in public communication.

With these, we were able to make some predictions about the relative likelihood of an organization of a particular variety to offer dutiful versus actualizing communications. In particular, we concluded that it was reasonable to expect that organizations that are exclusively online will be relatively more attuned to the norms of digital culture, and thus more likely to offer their supporters actualizing communication experiences. In contrast, organizations with clear offline roots and missions would be more likely to be committed to a more traditional, dutiful conception of citizenship and information.

The second expectation developed in Chapter 3 was that groups' proximity to formal politics would make a difference in the kind of information experience they offered supporters. We presumed that organizations with formal political agendas and missions would be relatively more reluctant to embrace actualizing styles of communication, and thus remain more wedded to dutiful communications. This gives way to the expectation that overtly political organizations will offer relatively more dutiful communications when compared to organizations without clear political agendas.

To test these expectations, we must distinguish specific varieties of organizations, especially whether they are primarily online or not, and whether or not they are formally oriented to politics. A sample for examination was designed with these concerns in mind.[4] First, we identified *online only* organizations, in contrast to those that we loosely term *offline*. Here we are identifying a set of organizations that have been created since the Internet's popularization, and base all or nearly all their work online from those that have existed since before the Internet or conduct extensive offline work. Organizations such as YouthNoise, TakingITGlobal, and DoSomething are examples of online only organizations.[5]

Next, among offline organizations, we can distinguish formally political and nonformally political organizations. One set of organizations that clearly fits into the overtly political category are governmental agencies, the organizations affiliated with formal political parties, and specific political campaigns and candidates: the likes of the United States Environmental Protection Agency, presidential campaigns, and the Young Democrats of America. These kinds of organizations have obvious—and usually legal—connections to the state, and must contend with media politics on its most direct level: these organizations are almost by definition in the public eye, and receive constant and intense scrutiny for their policies, actions, and communications.[6] What is more, in the face of changes in the role played by organizations in engagement described in the previous chapter, some scholars are arguing for increased attention to what government can do to foster positive civic opportunities.[7] Here we will explicitly identify this category of organizations as *government/party* groups.

Another set of organizations that must be included in the set of formally political groups but are not agencies, candidates or parties, are elements of civil society that have established themselves as advocates for particular kinds of legislation and other government action. As argued in Chapter 3, these kinds of organizations are likely to resemble parties and government in the kinds of communication they present because they operate in an overlapping arena: they must also organize and mobilize a constituency, and strategically bring that constituency's influence to bear on the operations of the state. The Sierra Club, NAACP, and NRA are all representatives of this category. As a result, those organizations, which I call *interest* groups, experience many of the same pressures that come with operating in the formal political sphere.

This differentiation leaves a final category of organizations: offline groups oriented toward civic engagement that do not exhibit clear political agendas. These organizations, such as the Boy Scouts, Girl Scouts, and Boys and Girls' Clubs, are oriented to providing citizens with services or developmental programs, and tend not to advocate for a specific interest groups or—often—lobby for specific legislation; in the terms favored by Cliff Zukin and colleagues, they are not *political*, but *civic* in the sense that they aim to build community and foster the development of good citizenship.[8] Here we denote such organizations as *community* groups.

This discussion yields four categories of organization whose communications might be compared. Using traffic counts as a rough metric of popularity, 90 organizations were drawn as a sample: thirty-five from the online only category, fifteen from the government/party category, and twenty each from the interest and community category.[9] The four categories, with organizations representative of each, are arrayed in Table 4.1.

Table 4.1 **Four Types of Organization and Examples**

Online Only	Government/Party	Interest	Community
DoSomething.org	Barack Obama	NAACP	4-H
Idealist.org	College Republicans	NRA	Boy Scouts
ThinkMTV.org	Young Democrats of America	Sierra Club	Channel One News
YouthNoise.org	Hillblazers	Gay-Straight Alliance Network	Youth With a Mission

Research Context

Although the aim of this analysis was to identify general communication patterns offered by organizations, and not their communications about specific events, some notes on the particular research context in which data were gathered are in order. The organizational communications presented in this chapter were observed in the spring of 2008, a notable time for political communication in general, and political communication online especially. Even as Hillary Clinton continued an energetic attempt to challenge him for the Democratic nomination for president, Barack Obama was building a massive following, buttressed by unprecedented success at reaching people online, raising money, and receiving support from across the Internet.[10]

For their part, many nonparty and noncandidate activists and organizations were also gearing up to be heavily involved, working both for their own agendas and in auxiliary forms in the campaign. Interest organizations were working hard to raise the profile of their issues of concern and their positions, and some were actively mobilizing to support a favored candidate. And nonpartisan organizations were actively reaching out in a bid to increase turnout among younger people. All in all, this was already an election season that would receive great acclaim for the engagement of young people and for the role of digital media in facilitating that engagement.[11]

At the same time, one advantage of observing the communications of organizations in the early months of 2008 is that individual events, and especially the election, did not yet dominate organizations' communications—as they surely would in October and early November. There were still several months to go to the final days, and so we might presume that organizations were not deviating completely from their usual strategies for reaching out to young people.

Two Categories of Civic Information: Knowledge and Action

The digital media environment pushes us to reconsider civic organizations not only as structures of community and organizing but also—and here perhaps returning to a role more dominant in an earlier era—as communicators in the diverse information networks of young citizens: in the terms of Chapter 1, as purveyors of civic information. There, we offered a definition of civic information as *the continuous flow of facts, opinions, and ideas that help citizens understand matters of potentially public concern and identify opportunities for action.* This purposefully broad notion was meant to offer a more general sense of the information that passes between citizens and the political world around them, and allow us to rethink the relationships that the information constitutes. As we move toward an examination of those relationships, however, a somewhat more precise conceptualization may be helpful. To that end, in what follows we will think of civic organizations as involving essentially two sorts of stuff. The first is information that informs supporters of issues, events, and perspectives of which they should be aware. These are the facts, opinions, and ideas that help citizens understand matters of potentially public concern from our definition. In short, it is the information that organizations want citizens to *know*, and for that reason we will refer to it as *knowledge*.

While the informing variety of information may be our generic, default way of thinking about civic information, the information conveyed by civic organizations also has another crucial component: the sort of message that helps a citizen identify opportunities for action. Once again, drawing on Chapter 1, this has not typically been how we think of civic information, especially in the patterns of the high modern period in which informing communications were largely siloed from mobilizing communications, with the former flowing over news channels and the latter over civic organizations and action networks. But the civic information patterns of the contemporary period suggest the possible reuniting of these information modes, and for that reason we will also explore this other form—the actionable information describing activities that organizations would like citizens to *do*, which we can refer to as *action*.[12] In this and subsequent chapters, those terms are capitalized when they refer specifically to these measures to distinguish them from more general discussions of civic knowledge and action.

We were able to reliably identify sections of civic organizations' websites largely dedicated to communicating knowledge and action. A team of three coders identified webpages within each website primarily dedicated to communicating either knowledge or action.[13] Across the 90 websites, 196 unique pages were dedicated to either knowledge or action: ninety seven of these were offerings of knowledge and 123 were offerings of action, meaning that on 24 pages organizations offered both knowledge and action. These relatively large numbers do disguise that fact that some organizations were not found to have pages primarily dedicated to either knowledge or action, while others offered multiple of them: across the ninety websites, 58 (64.4%) of the sites offering one or more page for knowledge, and 73 (81.1%) offering one or more page for action. (In no case was a website determined to offer no knowledge and no action.)

Figure 4.1 displays these percentages across the four categories of organizations. The general story is clearly that most organizations of all types presented pages dedicated to knowledge and action—hardly surprising given our sample's focus on organizations aiming to engage young citizens.

The one exception is among community sites, where only 35% (7 out of 20) dedicated pages to knowledge. This may be product of the goals of sites

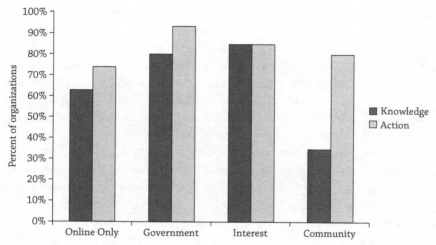

Figure 4.1 Percent of Organizations Within Each Category Dedicating at Least One Page to Knowledge and Action.

within that category: whereas interest sites, for example, dedicate considerable website space to explaining issues to supporters and developing appeals for engagement, community sites' strong emphasis on turning out citizens to community events means that they focus much more on action.

Modes of Interaction in Civic Communication

Having established that civic organizations indeed use their websites for conveying civic information, can we identify relatively more dutiful and actualizing ways of presenting that information? How would we do that? Let us return to the conceptualization of dutiful and actualizing civic information styles offered in Chapter 2. Specifically, Table 2.1 displayed several concrete ways in which information preferences varied across the two styles. One of these described differences in the *mode of interaction* experienced by citizens in civic communication. Mode of interaction differentiates information styles based on the nature of the information exchange: the dutiful civic information style is essentially one-directional, with an authoritative leader or organization calling supporters' attention to what the leader has deemed important information. The actualizing style, by contrast, prizes bidirectional, expressive participation—opportunities for young citizens to contribute to an information experience, rather than simply being addressed.

The logic of this bifurcation is derived from the two civic information patterns conceptualized in Chapter 2. For the dutiful citizen—or organizations presuming to communicate with dutiful citizens—a sort of organization-driven model of communication makes the most sense. These citizens' identities are rooted in organizational memberships, and those organizations' messages thus form a backbone to citizen engagement. Dutiful citizens feel a sense of responsibility to stay in touch with those messages to hear about engagement opportunities and stay generally informed about the civic world around them. And they especially value information that is produced by authoritative sources like major organizations. As a result, these citizens are comfortable with receiving information produced and broadcast by organizations they trust.

Actualizing citizens, by contrast, are likely to be less wedded to the organizations they encounter in the course of more personally motivated engagement. Rather than formally committed to organizations and using them as key identity reference points, these citizens are continually creating and refining a network of sources of information they find useful. Further, their values for information are not based on production by authoritative sources, but on validation by a network of peers and other sources. The kind of civic communication environment that resonates with actualizing citizens is thus one in which peers can share and evaluate information, and their own self-expressive tendencies can be exercised in contributing to information.

Both knowledge and action, as we have defined them, might appear in a more dutiful or actualizing form. When it comes to knowledge, organizations are creating a platform for distributing useful information to supporters. The content of this communication may include recent news about topics of interest to supporters, intraorganizational news, or an organization's position on an issue. That information may be communicated in a dutiful mode, with the organization producing information and posting it for supporters to consume; or in an actualizing mode, with users encouraged to contribute their own information and read content produced by peers.

As for action, the category of civic information that includes all the ideas what supporters should be *doing* as citizens or to contribute to the organization's mission, those ideas might come directly from an organization, which dictates the kinds of actions that should happen (dutiful), or they might come from supporters themselves, who relate what kinds of things they have been doing or raise suggestions for things to be done (actualizing).

The notion that knowledge and action might be presented in more dutiful or more actualizing forms gives rise to four basic communication patterns: dutiful knowledge, actualizing knowledge, dutiful action, and actualizing action. These are displayed in Table 4.2.

To systematically assess the appearance of these modes of communication on organizations' websites, we applied a coding scheme to the knowledge and action pages just described. This resulted in judgments over whether knowledge or action on a particular page was being offered in a dutiful or actualizing form, or in a few cases with multiple, rich content offerings, both.

Table 4.2 **Dutiful and Actualizing Forms of Knowledge and Action**

	Conceptual Definition	*Dutiful Form*	*Actualizing Form*
Knowledge	Information that supporters should *know*	News about an issue, or what organization is doing; appeals to fans to learn about something by clicking a link	Appeals to supporters to share information, knowledge or opinion; appeals for feedback from supporters
Action	Things that supporters should *do*	Encouragement to take a particular action	Appeals to supporters to share action ideas

It was immediately evident that the dutiful mode of interaction is the more common. When it came to presenting knowledge, every page except one (96 of 97, 99%) was coded as containing at least some dutiful conveyance of civic information. Sites regularly presented pages dedicated to delivering basic information to supporters, often under headings titled "Get Informed," "Learn More," or "FAQ." And they delivered: the sites were nothing if not littered with inspiring stories, policy descriptions, facts and statistics with which organizations made their case.

Figure 4.2 offers an illustration. Battlecry.com is a website for youth that offers a Christian perspective on why and how young Christians might get involved in their communities. On this page, titled "The Crisis," BattleCry presents information about what the organization views as a cultural crisis, suggesting that users explore the page to understand it better. A viewer can see from the available menu options and links that the site also includes pages with which it hopes to mobilize youth for action ("Fight Back," "Your Battle," "Enlist in the Coalition"). But this page is clearly dedicated to conveying to supporters what the organization views as the problem: its main appeal is to "Understand the Crisis." In this way, the site was presenting information (knowledge) it wished supporters to consume—a dutiful form of information presentation.

This manner of providing civic information stood in comparison to only 21 pages (22% of all knowledge pages) that offered an actualizing invitation for supporters to contribute their own information or view information that peers had posted. Such invitations occurred less consistently, and in varying style. Some sites encouraged the sharing of relatively formal forms of self-expression, as Girls, Inc., an organization catering to young women, did on one page: "Do you have a great idea for a book? Whether it is for a picture book, middle grade chapter book, or young adult novel. . . turn your idea into

Figure 4.2 BattleCry's The Crisis Page as an Example of Knowledge in a Dutiful Form.

a story that people will enjoy reading!" Others, such as Campus Activism and Razoo, provided what were essentially databases of ongoing youth-led projects that provided information about world problems and what participants were doing to stop them.

High School Journalism is an initiative of the American Society of Newspaper Editors dedicated to improving journalism education for young people. In Figure 4.3, on the site's "Ask a Pro" page, users are asked to post a question for a journalist to answer. Visitors can also visit an archive of past responses to users' queries. These qualities meet the definition of offering information in an actualizing form—because user content is being requested and displayed.

The imbalance between dutiful and actualizing communication styles is even more striking when it comes to action. Of 123 pages identified as presenting some form of action, fully 120 (98%) offered dutiful instruction in the sort of activity that should be carried out. Predictably for organizations dedicated to engaging youth, sites regularly provided a page or multiple pages dedicated to elaborating action opportunities—often with the ubiquitous page title "Take Action." The Register to Vote page of the youth activism program Rock the Vote is a case in point (Figure 4.4). As is evident from the page, the website gives a specific suggestion for how a user can become involved: by registering to vote. There is no indication that suggestions from site visitors are sought or displayed by the website, which would

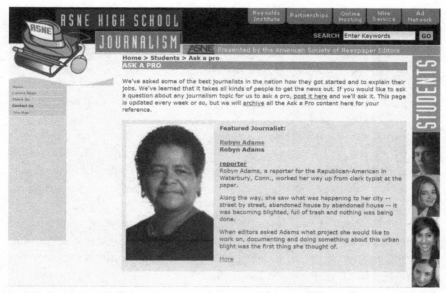

Figure 4.3 High School Journalism's Ask a Pro Page as an Example of Knowledge in an Actualizing Form.

Figure 4.4 Rock the Vote's Register to Vote page as an Example of Action in a Dutiful Form.

reflect an actualizing approach to communicating action. Instead, Rock the Vote is simply instructing young people that they should register, a dutiful way of conveying action.

By contrast, only 7 (6%) action pages offered any actualizing invitations to contribute action ideas. One of these came from DoSomething.org, a now-well known website fostering community and civic engagement among young people. Figure 4.5 is its "Projects" page, on which users are encouraged to post their own actions, or view the actions that other users have posted—a clear demonstration of actualizing action. What Do Something is offering is a database of users' projects; they specifically advertise it as a place both for young people to post action ideas, and potentially learn about others' actions.

The initial answer to our research question must therefore be that there are few opportunities to experience actualizing interactions with civic information in this sector of the civic web. The dearth of actualizing presentations of action pages is particularly striking, perhaps reflecting deep reticence on the part of organizations to open questions of appropriate or necessary engagement to young people; but even on pages designed primarily to inform, organizations chose to offer only dutiful instruction in what citizens should know on 76 of the 97 pages analyzed (78%).

Figure 4.5 DoSomething.org's Projects Page as an Example of Action in an Actualizing Form.

MODE OF INTERACTION ACROSS DIFFERENT TYPES OF ORGANIZATION

The analyses to this point have aggregated together pages from the websites of very different organizations. In addition to our interest in these overall levels of dutiful and actualizing information style in the civic web, we also anticipated that different kinds of organizations would respond differently to the pressures of early twenty-first-century communication, with online only organizations leading the field in actualizing offerings, and government/party and interest groups bringing up the rear. To examine these predictions, and present a more refined impression of the data, we can break down the overall findings by the organizational categories laid out above.

Figure 4.6 does so. It displays the percentage of organizations within each category that presented knowledge and action exclusively in a dutiful way, and the percentage of organizations that offered at least one page with knowledge or action in an actualizing style.

The figure reveals significant differences in the presentation of civic information across organizational types. *Online only* sites were considerably more likely than others to present information in an actualizing form. This was particularly striking for knowledge, where fully half of the 22 online only sites that dedicated one or more page to knowledge offered at least one page offering

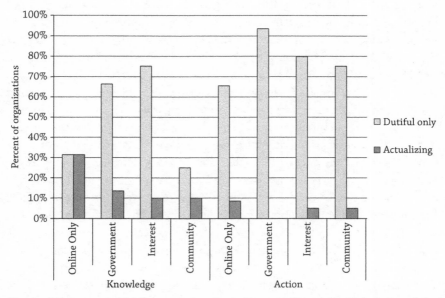

Figure 4.6 Percent of Websites Within Each Category That Offered Only Dutiful, or at Least One Actualizing Form of Knowledge and Action. *Note:* bars do not add to 100% because not all organizations within a category offered a particular type of information (e.g., 91% of government organizations offered action, all in a dutiful form).

that information in an actualizing mode. (The other half offered knowledge only in a dutiful form.) Sites from the category with the next most actualizing knowledge—the community category—offered that form of content 28.6% of the time that any knowledge was offered, though websites in this category were most striking for offering few spaces specifically oriented to delivering inform-ing civic information to followers. And clearly, actualizing knowledge was quite rare among sites in the government/party and interest categories.

The story is similar with respect to action, with the overriding caveat that across all site categories actualizing action was quite rare. Among sites that offered at least one page dedicated to action, online only sites again led the field, but there are only three of twenty-six sites (11.5%) offered actualizing action. Nonetheless, the community and interest sites achieved only about half of that modest number (only one site in each category offering any actualiz-ing action), and within the government/party category, not a single instance of actualizing action was recorded—this despite government/party being the category that most regularly offered action pages. The emphasis on dutiful con-veyance of information about being engaged is clear.

Thus, exploring the distribution of knowledge across the site categories reveals that the overall low levels of actualizing knowledge disguise significant variation. Online only organizations in fact offered this form of communica-tion a great deal—a given online only organization that offered knowledge had a 50% chance of offering an actualizing version of it. This is in line with our expectation that such organizations will be relatively more inclined to adopt an actualizing sort of relationship with supporters. Similarly, though they did not prioritize conveying knowledge on their websites, community organiza-tions offered an actualizing knowledge experience a quarter of the time. With interest and government/party organizations at very low levels, our general expectations about differences between site categories is supported here.

There is a more muted version of this story when it comes to action. There, online only organizations offered actualizing action more often than other types of groups, but only because those other groups offered it hardly at all, and government/party groups not once in our sample. But even online only organizations did so rarely, highlighting that organizations seem markedly hesitant to invite young supporters to suggest avenues of action—a consider-able constraint on the entrepreneurial style of engagement noted in Chapter 3. Notably, when it comes to action offerings we see no evidence that community organizations are more willingly embrace actualizing communication modes with supporters than government/party or interest groups. In the terms of the factors introduced in Chapter 3, this finding strongly suggests that differences between organizations is being driven much more by different responses to cultural change, and the particular inclinations of organization leaders than by any specific response to media politics.

The Activities Organizations Promote

The mode of interaction fostered by an organization when communicating knowledge and action offers an important impression of their communication styles and the kind of relationship they seek with supporters. Yet it is a limited one: this impression tells us only the degree to which organizations choose to dictate knowledge and action, or allow supporters to guide the knowledge and action that appear among an organization's communications. There are several reasons we may want to consider other aspects of the information styles favored by organizations. First, as we have just seen, different organizations face different degrees of interest, opportunity, and risk, in offering communications with an actualizing mode of interaction. Organizations working on contentious issues, for example, may be loath to create public spaces that could become a public relations liability if extreme supporters, or disruptive opponents, chose to make a scene.[14] Such organizations experience much more risk than broader-spectrum engagement organizations in opening their knowledge and action to supporter contributions.

Similarly, some organizations have strategic reasons for dictating what they present to supporters in a strongly dutiful style. They may have specific actions they want supporters to take to achieve a policy or public opinion goal; encouraging supporter-driven action suggestions in the midst of a campaign could undermine the goal of motivating supporters to commit to strategic organization-driven action. Before an election, for example, an organization is highly likely to want to forego invitations to supporters to suggest ways they can be active citizens, in favor of highly specified and strategic voter turnout appeals.

On the other side of the communicative relationship, even young citizens with highly actualizing information preferences may not be looking for civic experiences in which the burden of providing civic knowledge and action always falls on them and their peers. Many may be looking for attractive suggestions that help them express themselves and contribute positively to work on an issue they care about. After all, the reason they have come to a site to begin with is to see what it has to offer—both its organization-driven communications and, probably, the content offered by peer others.

Any operationalization of a theoretical framework as rich as dutiful and actualizing civic information styles necessarily involves simplification and parsimony. But these observations raise two important points. The first is that although the above framework dichotomizes dutiful and actualizing modes of interaction, in reality a purely actualizing set of communications may be unlikely, even undesirable. What we are likely to see are organizations that offer a mix of communications, some more clearly dutiful in style, others more actualizing. This in no way precludes our ability to detect meaningful variation in how organizations choose to offer their communications, and draw inferences from those differences. But it does raise the question of what an ideal degree of actualizing communication offerings would be—a question we are not prepared to answer at this point. Without more investigation and cases for comparison, this fact leaves us is with comparative analyses that pit different kinds of organizations against one another—a further reason for expanding our measurement of dutiful and actualizing communication.

The second is that beyond the manner in which information is presented—the mode of interaction—the very content of that information, or the substance of the action recommended, may be relatively more or less in line with actualizing information preferences. This recalls another of the elements of the depiction of the two civic information styles in Table 2.1, the "action outcomes" favored by relatively more dutiful and actualizing citizens. Alongside the facts that in every site category the more common type of information offered by organizations was action, and that the action pages maintained by organizations were overwhelmingly dutiful in the mode of interaction they offered, this suggests that it may be productive to explore what sort of action, exactly, is being promoted on those pages.

REPERTOIRES OF ACTION

There is considerable discussion ongoing among scholars of digital politics and social movements over what digital media portend for the practice of activism. Jennifer Earl and Katrina Kimport are proponents of a view that the magnitude of change is very great. They argue that the activism possibilities enabled by digital media are transformative enough to constitute a new era in how activists go about their work. Specifically, the possibility of noncopresence of member activity, the possible absence of coordinating organizations for ongoing sustainability of movements, and the broad categories of claims that may be subject to what was once a relatively narrow political sphere all contribute to change in the very basis of what constitutes civic action.[15]

This analysis leads Earl and Kimport to propose that a new era of contentious action is emerging, characterized by massive online petition drives and other movement activities that are able to take place online and sustain themselves in the absence of formal organizing. And intriguingly, their description of newer forms of contentious activity intersects with the shift in action preferences we noted in Chapter 2: that young citizens with actualizing preferences for civic information are increasingly inclined to see communications through digital media as sites for the building and exercise of political power. This is very much in line with Earl and Kimport's argument, which highlights the role of online petition drives and how a multitude of concerns and policies can be propagated through them.[16]

But somewhat peculiarly, those authors do not go so far as to suggest that a new *kind* of action is emerging—only that the underlying dynamics of already existing action possibilities are transforming. Their "new digital repertoire of contention" is made up not of new action possibilities, but of online applications and extensions of existing tactics such as petitioning and protesting. Their points are valuable and well taken, yet the "action outcomes" row of Table 2.1 suggests that we may, in fact, be able to conceptualize and measure a particular, emergent form of action: in the table, we depicted a preference among young actualizing citizens for "expressive actions communicated through networked publics," with the "actor at the center, both influencing peers and expressing own views." The actions of digital communication embraced by younger, actualizing citizens attempt to leverage the power of communication and information sharing to influence a network—of friends or otherwise—about a problem, issue, or idea. An essential characteristic of these activities is that the individual identity of the actor is not subordinate to the action, but expressed through it: such expressions have the twin features of informing and (potentially) persuading a networked audience, while simultaneously constructing or maintaining the actor's identity as someone who pays attention to, knows and cares about the topic.[17]

We thus have Earl and Kimport's contention that a new repertoire of contention is emerging among digital activists, the proposition that the actualizing civic information style favors communicative, expressive online actions, and our ongoing question of how best to gauge civic organizations' online offerings to youth. To productively combine these insights, let us take a step back to Tilly's work on the *repertoires of contention* employed by social movements, which informs Earl and Kimport's analysis. For Tilly, a repertoire of contention is the set of strategies and tactics employed by a movement in attempting to achieve its goals. Crucially, movements do not all employ the same repertoires: they don't all have the same repertoires available to them, for various reasons, and they do not make use of all the repertoires that could potentially be available. Rather, the repertoire of which a movement makes use is dependent upon the context in which a movement operates, and its own particular characteristics—such as whether it has a leadership able to envision and implement particular tactics.

Adapting Tilly's social movement-oriented concept to our specific organizational context, we might conceptualize the *repertoires of action* of civic organizations as the particular set of actions in which they ask supporters to engage. Combining Tilly's insights with this book's core concerns, a particular organization's repertoire of action might be seen as a reflection of that organization's perceptions of its relationship with supporters and what its supporters are capable of achieving. And following Earl and Kimport, we can define separate categories of action corresponding to time periods in activist history: but rather than identify them with the "traditional," "modern," and "digital," as they and Tilly do, let us align ours with the major periods of organization-supporter relationship developed in the last chapter. These correspond to the shift in organization-supporter relationship over the course of the twentieth century that led from a "membership" relationship to a "management" one, and that today is turning—unevenly—toward what we will refer to as a "network-expressive" one. We can identify a set of activities corresponding to each.

In the membership era, participation in large, federated membership organizations was largely constituted through interpersonal communications. Members attended meetings, speeches, and community events, and were rewarded with formal membership and group-joining, and admission to groups' particular programs. Putting aside the wealth of civic communications produced by organizations in this era, the essence of participation for typical citizen members was showing up. This description lends itself to a set of activities that we might describe as membership-oriented: attendance at offline events and meetings, participation in formal (offline) programs, and the like. We might also include in this category efforts to participate by engaging in particular behavior, such as purchasing patterns and lifestyle choices.

The shift to the management era of member participation introduced a new category of activity. As organizations centralized and moved the focus of their work to Capitol Hill, and shifted increasing resources to competing in a media-saturated communication environment, their needs for interpersonal participation on the part of members declined. Correspondingly, organizations' orientations to membership moved from one of many rich interpersonal interactions at the local level aggregated into political influence—an arduous and administratively expensive process—to one of directly reaching many potential supporters for financial support and, occasionally, appealing to supporters to communicate their views to officeholders or media figures via letter or petition. Activities we might identify here would thus include efforts to influence public official or media companies, and, certainly, to contribute money to the organization's mission—the check-writing aspect noted and decried of this citizenship era.

The growing digitally driven sector of the civic organizational economy portends further shifts in the nature of what organizations ask citizens to do. Though evidence is still accumulating as to the sorts of action enabled, and the extent to which organizations encourage them—here we offer some of the first evidence of this sort—we can sketch its basic contours. Networked organizations are likely to engage more fully with individual supporters' communication networks, encouraging supporters to play an active role in conveying a movement's message and action appeals. They may also request that supporters become involved with forming networks for activism, or contribute personal testimonials of commitment and action. Activities of these sorts might include attempts to share information and meanings over supporters' own digital social networks, to subscribe to networked information through online groups, or create and contribute digital media artifacts to an organization's archive.

This discussion offers some conceptual rationale for identifying and categorizing the activities recommended by organizations. Table 4.3 illustrates a breakdown of the catalog of activities we found on our civic organizations' websites and Facebook pages into the "membership," "management," and "network-expressive" categories.

Notably, we are not claiming here that the management action category wholly supplanted the membership one, nor that new varieties of network-expressive actions are cleanly displacing both of the older versions. We have good evidence that contemporary organizations' action repertoires are made up of a variety of sorts of activity.[18] Instead, what we are looking for are differences in the aggregate profile of organizations' action repertoires, which may indicate differences in how organizations understand their relationship to supporters, and supporters' relationships to the digital media they encounter.

It is also important to recall that all of the activities displayed in Table 4.3 occur on pages presenting action with a dutiful mode of interaction—in which an organization is dictating the kinds of actions that supporters should take. The notion is that just because an organization is prescribing the actions to be taken, it does not follow that all of those actions will be necessarily unattractive to actualizing citizens; on the contrary, an organization that crafts a mix of activities, some of them of the network-expressive variety, may have a good chance of appealing to actualizing citizens.

MEMBERSHIP, MANAGEMENT, AND NETWORK-EXPRESSIVE ACTIVITY RECOMMENDATIONS

Among the 90 websites in the sample, 114 pages were identified as presenting action with a dutiful mode of interaction.[19] When we looked at those 114 pages for the specific activities listed in Table 4.3, we recorded 171 total activities: 85 (50%) were of the membership type, including regular appeals to attend a group's meeting or events. Another 59 (34%) were management activities such as appeals to vote, donate, or help raise money, or target a communication at an official via petition or email. The remaining 27 (16%) were of the network-expressive variety. There, supporters were encouraged to join or start an online group, share information via a social networking site, or more generally to spread the word online.[20]

These findings fall mainly in line with our mode of interaction analysis of how engagement is being communicated by youth civic organizations. Half of all activities were membership ones, suggesting that most organizations are encouraging young people to meet them in their (offline) spheres, rather than

Table 4.3 **Categorization of Activities Encouraged By Youth Civic Organizations**

Membership activities	Management activities	Network-expressive activities
• **Attend an event**: Attend an offline event, meeting, protest, service, volunteering, or other offline organizational business and activities.	• **Contact officials**: Email, phone, petition or other message to *politician or government agency, a corporation or nonprofit organization, or a newspaper, broadcaster or other media outlet.*	• **Email friends**: Email, text message or otherwise contact friends or other social contacts.
• **Join an offline group**: Start or join an offline group or organization.	• **Petition**: Sign a petition not directed at a specific person or entity, online or offline.	• **Share via social media**: Share, post or tag an item to a social media space.
• **Participate in a program**: Apply for a job, internship, student program, scholarship or similar.	• **Vote**: Vote, either offline or online, in a formal political process or in organizational business, or register to vote.	• **Spread the word**: Share information with others. Includes general calls to "spread the word," "let others know," "pass it on," etc.
• **Conscious consumption**: Shape your consumption habits in support of a goal (i.e., by buying or not buying a particular thing).	• **Donate**: Donate money to an organization or candidate.	• **Create new media**: Create your own digital media (music, videos, artwork, photos) and submit it to an online space.
• **Lifestyle**: Maintain a certain lifestyle (such as not eating meat, planting a garden, being "green," etc.).	• **Fill out a survey**: Take a survey or quiz for the organization.	• **Join an online group**: Start, join or encourage others to join an online program, such as an online campaign, or FB group, page, cause, or application, or create an online presence for your own group.

reaching out to young people online. A further third of activities fit our characterization of a management relationship between organizations and citizens. This left a mere 16% of activities that we categorized as network-expressive.

Figure 4.7 breaks down the findings from the activities analysis by organizational type. What we see there is a consistent pattern across offline organizations: membership activities were offered quite consistently, management activities somewhat less often, and network-expressive activities infrequently. Community organizations were in general less rich than government/party and interest groups in activity offerings, and focused their supporter appeals on attending events and meetings and, as we shall see, contributing money. They offered not a single network-expressive activity in our study.

For their part, online only organizations offered network-expressive activities more frequently than organizations of the other types, and membership activities less frequently—in line with our general understanding of what those organizations are about, and our previous findings concerning those organizations' relative alignment with the actualizing civic information style. But they also offered a great number of both membership and management activities, and in fact did so more frequently than they offered network-expressive ones.

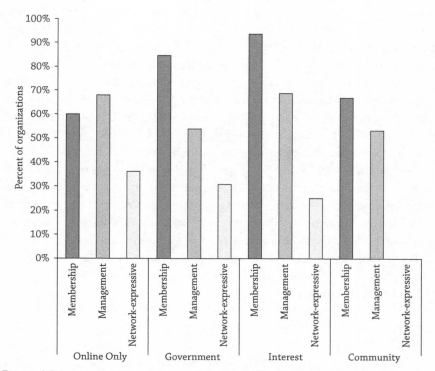

Figure 4.7 Percent of Organizations From Each Site Category Offering at Least One Instance of Each Type of Activity.

MEMBERSHIP AND MANAGEMENT ACTIVITIES

What was happening there? Somewhat against our understanding of these groups, online only organizations offered no shortage of suggestions to attend offline events and activities. The online activist community Idealist.org, for example, offered a wide array of community-building activity suggestions, including gathering community members together in "a local organization, school, community center, or house of worship, or in a coffeeshop, store or library." The youth-driven climate change activist website ItsGettingHotInHere similarly provided a list of summer activities that supporters might be inclined to engage in. These included a host of events, workshops, camps, and summer programs such as Mountain Justice Summer and the Northwest Institute for Community Energy. In a similar vein, several organizations also recommended joining local membership organizations as a way to effect change. The antibullying site Bullying.org, for example, suggested to youths being bullied that they might: "join a club, a team, or a group. This is a great way to make new friends. This really helps when you are new to school." Such examples offer a counterpoint to a view of these groups as attempting to entirely engage youth in online contexts.

When it came to management activities, online only groups offered a variety of suggestions for supporters to exercise the formal, targeted political voice. Several urged supporters to contact public officials, sometimes alongside recommendations to contact "the media" about issues. These included the "Advocacy" page of Youth Resource, a website with multifaceted information and resources for GLBTQ youth, which recommended: "Send letters to Congress, write the media and learn about your Representatives!" MySistahs, a support site for young women of color, similarly suggested that readers "find out who your elected officials are and write them a latter [sic], send a letter to President Bush and contact national and local media."

Two recommended contacting corporations, including a page from Peta2 that offered campaigns against Donna Karan's use of fur and one called "Kentucky Fried Cruelty." Several offered general, nontargeted petitions that supporters could sign, and surveys to submit opinions. And ThinkMTV, Declare Yourself, and Rock the Vote (on two separate pages) all offered information about registering to vote. Figure 4.8 displays a portion of ThinkMTV's rich "Take Action" page, which offers the opportunity to sign a petition, register to vote, and contact officials, all from a single page.

All of this demonstrates that online only sites were rich in opportunities for supporters to express themselves through managed varieties of action. From recommendations to contact Congress or the media, to suggestions to sign petitions or register to vote, followers of these organizations had no shortage of opportunities to contribute to formal political and communication processes.

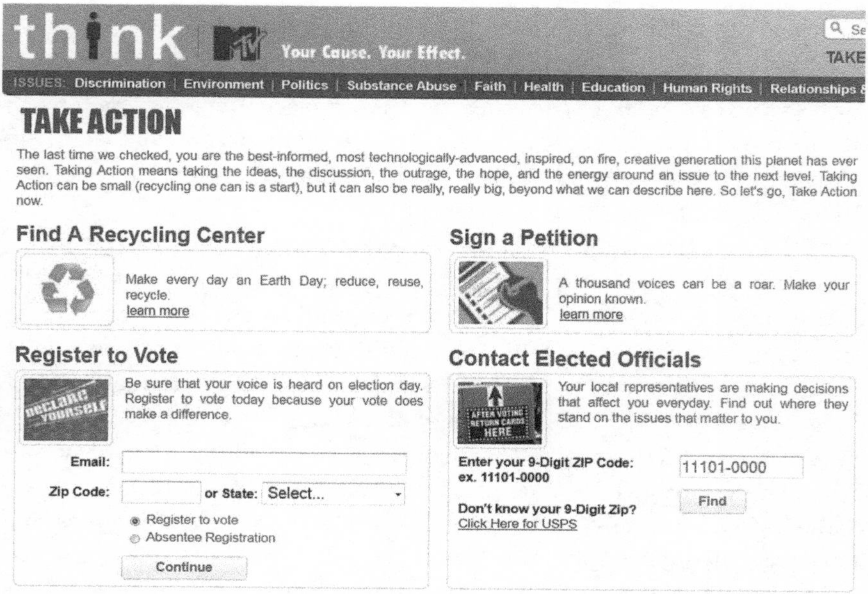

Figure 4.8 Clipping from ThinkMTV's Take Action Page.

In this way, online only organizations were very much in line with offline groups. *Government/party* sites similarly asked supporters to contact officials and vote, and interest sites offered recommendations to contact officials, sign petitions, and complete surveys. For example, the Democratic Party website presented several petitions on its site intended both to engage supporters—and, surely, acquire their contact information—and send a political message. And the College Democrats and John McCain both prompted supporters to register to vote.

But notably, what both government/party, interest and, for that matter, community, sites offered more than any other management activity was ask for money. Among government/party websites, fully 64% of management activity offerings were requests to donate or help raise money. Among interest sites the number was 50%. And community organizations offered no other management-style activity than requests for contributions, though this is not entirely surprising given those groups' nonpolitical aims: they would have little need to ask supporters to contact a representative or express their view in the media. Online only organizations, by contrast, asked for funds with 23% of their management activity offerings, instead offering the considerably wider array of options described above. Such a heavy volume of requests for donations from offline organizations emphasizes a checkbook-oriented relationship being communicated to supporters by many groups.

NETWORK-EXPRESSIVE ACTIVITIES

As for the network-expressive category, over a third (36%) of online only organizations offered at least one such activity recommendation. For comparison, 31% of government/party organizations and 25% of interest organizations did so, while community organizations offered not a single instance. These deserve further comment.

Of the activities that made up the network-expressive category, presenting online spaces in which supporters could join or start groups was one of the most popular, followed by admonitions to "spread the word" and invitations to produce multimedia. An illuminating example comes from a page from John McCain's website, called "Volunteer Action Center," which led the government category of sites with four instances of actualizing activities. As Figure 4.9 shows, McCain invited supporters to participate in the information environment of his campaign by contacting friends and family, joining an online association (McCain Space), promoting his message on social networking sites, and more generally spreading the word.

As a point of comparison, a comparable page from Barack Obama's campaign, his "Action Center" (Figure 4.10), offers only one of these network-expressive activities: contacting friends. Instead, the page—from a

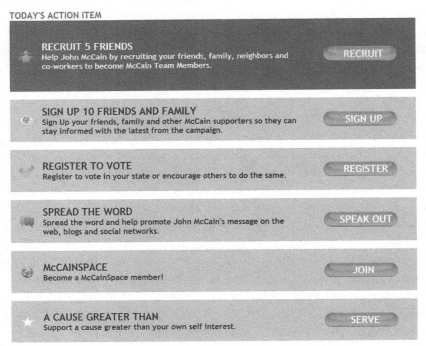

Figure 4.9 Clipping from John McCain's Volunteer Action Center.

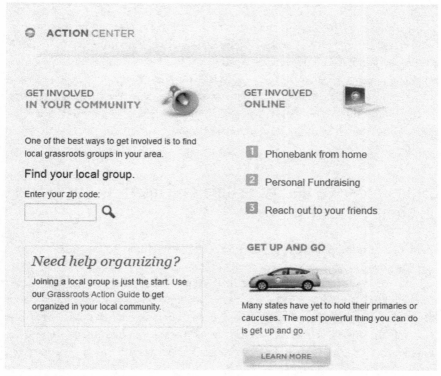

Figure 4.10 Clipping from Barack Obama's Action Center Page.

site that became famous for its innovative use of networking and grassroots communication—was mainly dedicated to using online tools to get people to engage in offline activities—such as finding community groups, phonebanking, fundraising, and going to events.

The other notable network-expressive activity, seen primarily in the online only category, but also observed on pages of two interest websites, was the invitation to create digital media. YouthNoise, an online only youth civic site, offered some of the richest examples of suggestions for producing digital media on its "Toolkit" page. Activities recommended there include: "Tell a story through visual arts," "Host a speaker, show a film," "Video content shooting for dummies," and "Use audio to tell a story." Each of these illuminate the dual personal-civic nature of the network-expressive category of activity: with these action suggestions, supporters are invited (and, in fact, offered tools) to develop their own voice about an issue and project it to a public connected through the organization's website. It is an opportunity, on the one hand, to say something about oneself, in the story that one might tell, or video one might shoot, but also to use that opportunity to tell a story with potentially civic or political consequence. In this way, they are actions that sit right at the edge of public and private, and of communication and action.

But such actions, though notable for their very existence, were not commonly occurring. The bigger conclusion to be drawn here is that most organizations were using their websites largely to drive behavior intended to happen offline—organizations were attempting to shuttle young citizens quickly from their websites into offline programs. We saw this least on the sites of online only organizations—and there saw more network-expressive activity recommendations—but even those sites had a surprisingly generous share of calls for membership and management-style action.

Communicative Relationships of Organizations on their Websites

From this book's opening pages, we have explored the possibility that young citizens' disaffection for politics stems, in part, from a generational and institutional disconnect in styles of civic information. The evidence of this chapter supports that conclusion. Whereas many young citizens are looking for civic information experiences that invite a degree of personal expression, contribution, and sharing to a collective action's work, what organizations presented on their websites were overwhelmingly dutiful instructions in what supporters were should know and do.

Especially if we narrow our focus to non-online only organizations, what emerged is a picture of strikingly dutiful information provision. We have characterized these organizations as among the most civically important, both historically and because of their continuing important position in American politics and civic life. They are the political parties; the websites of candidates when they run for office; the interest groups that bring citizens' concerns to the formal instruments of power; the community organizations that build civic skill, concern, and solidarity. Their ability to connect with citizens, and help to aggregate citizens' contributions into effective collaborative action has been widely cited and theorized to be a core element of American democracy. Yet the websites they used to communicate with publics—young publics most of all—were a far cry from engaging with the participatory potential of digital media. When organizations offered knowledge and action they did so in a remarkably rote, pedantic fashion: they stated what supporters should know, what they should do, and how to do it. Instances in which supporters were asked to do anything but follow the directions provided by the organization through the sites few and very far between. It is not overstepping the evidence to state that as of this study's data collection, in 2008, it appears as though the sharing and interactive norms of digital culture had hardly reached the heart of American civil society.

Our examination of the sorts of action in which they asked site users to engage told an only modestly different story. Appeals to engage in what we characterized as membership activities—attending meetings, joining offline groups, coming to events, and so on—were most common. What this means for a digital young citizen, we may surmise, is that many were faced with repertoires of possible activity that not only offered few attractive possibilities for action online, but insisted that they engage in the most effortful and potentially intimidating of actions. These organizations are ignoring activities that make private-to-public boundary crossing easy and convenient, instead maintaining expensive and formal boundary crossing procedures of predigital politics.[21]

The next most common set of activities recommended, management activities such as addressing public officials, voting, and donating money, are no more likely to appeal to young actualizing citizens. They are, after all, precisely the sorts of measures of youth engagement on which we base our concerns over decline. And they represent efforts on the part of organizations to define supporter contributions in precisely the sort of prescribed and instrumental but constrained way that we characterized as appealing to a citizen with a dutiful orientation to civic life and information. Further, as we noted, when organizations presented these activities, more often than not supporters were simply being asked to send a check.

Still, alongside these dutifully oriented forms of civic action, we did identify a small but intriguing set of activities in which organizations cast supporters in a different role: as individuals with personal networks and potential influence as people who could express views in those networks. These network-expressive activities were not common, but their very presence—including on the websites of presidential candidates John McCain and Barack Obama—may hint at a slightly evolving conception of how organizations may interact with young citizens online. We will have much more to say on this topic in the next chapter.

THE CASE OF OBAMA 2008

In light of this generally gloomy view of the nature of civic information provision by civic websites in 2008, one website that may deserve further attention is that of Barack Obama, who at the time of data-gathering was conducting a presidential campaign that would become renowned for the high levels of engagement engendered, including among young citizens. As Daniel Kreiss, among others, has noted, what Obama achieved was a successful combination of inspired grassroots activism with a terrifically focused campaign that was able to direct activists' energy into a tangible political goal.[22] In the spring of 2008, that goal was still the attainment of the Democratic nomination, though Obama was already looking forward to the general election; by midsummer, the campaign had pivoted to turning out the voters that would be required to defeat John McCain.

What does our analytic snapshot of the Obama campaign say about its communications with young citizens? First, we should begin by noting that it was, indeed, a snapshot. The limitation to a research design that enables the comparison of 90 separate websites is that the level of depth and detail gathered about any one is reduced; more detailed accounts of Obama's online campaigning can be found elsewhere. Nevertheless, an inspection of the impression that barackobama.com did make on this study's results is worth noting.

Obama's campaign website offered a number of pages dedicated to both informing supporters (knowledge) and mobilizing them (action). The two pages dedicated primarily to knowledge were titled "Learn" and "Issues." These pages constitute the essentials of what candidates must convey to voters: "Learn" was a twelve-paragraph biography of the candidate, describing the journey from his early years to his political career. The page also offered links to a video titled "Meet Barack," a page of "Obama Speeches," and news items. On this page, there were no invitations to supporters to add information, or to read the information posted by others users. This was no wiki: it was a strategic statement by the campaign putting forward a specific, selective view of the candidate. A dutiful conveyance of knowledge if there ever was one.

The "Issues" page was similarly strategically defined. There, the campaign laid out Obama's "Blueprint for Change," a comprehensive platform document, as well as a brief description and links to information on Obama's positions on twenty-one issue areas such as "Economy," "Education," "Family," "Iraq," and "Technology." Once again, there was no opportunity for supporter input on this page: the positions were explicitly those Obama was taking, and supporters were encouraged to learn about them, but nothing more. Thus, both "Learn" and "Issues" were identified as offering a dutiful form of knowledge and nothing more.

The story was similar when it came to action. Three principal pages advertised action as recommended by Obama's campaign: they were titled "Action," "Donate," and "Fundraising." The latter two, clearly, were appeals to give money directly, or to help the candidate raise it from other people—very typical concerns of any political campaign in the United States. The "Action" page is displayed above (Figure 4.10). There, the campaign is opening its participatory doors, but primarily in the direction of strategically calculated actions entirely dictated by the campaign. Requests to supporters to share inspiration and action appeals over personal digital networks—a network-expressive activity described above—did represent a modest deviation from a strictly dutiful communicative relationship, but on the whole the communications offered by Obama's campaign was far from an actualizing one.

How did Obama win such admiration for the participatory quality of his campaign, while his website was as staid and dutiful as we documented? Several factors contributed. First, as Kreiss has noted, Obama's campaign engaged in consistent and careful management of Obama's brand as one of interactivity and openness to citizen participation.[23] His well-known statements that "We are the ones we have been waiting for" and "I'm asking you to believe. Not just in my ability to bring about change in Washington . . . I'm asking you to believe in yours" (ellipsis in original), the latter of which appeared at the top of his campaign website throughout the spring of 2008, served to position Obama as a representative of a movement that was genuinely grassroots. To some extent, then, the impression that Obama's was a truly participatory and exceptionally democratic structure was the product of highly successful branding—part of core his message.

Obama also benefited from a wide array of supportive media that occurred outside the confines of his campaign. Massive hit videos such as Barely Political's famous "I've got a crush on Obama," which was posted to YouTube in June 2007—six months before primary voting would begin—and will.i.am's February 2008 "Yes We Can," built from Obama's New Hampshire primary concession speech and presenting a dozen A-list celebrities offered Obama a visibility and cool while also allowing the campaign to (truthfully) deny involvement. As a result, Obama Girl's mildly suggestive dances at locations around New York City, which could have been a disastrous scandal had the video come from within the nascent campaign, gave the campaign an air of whimsy, a youthful coolness, and a sense of being crowd-sourced, as though a couple of college students had come up with a clever idea for supporting the hippest candidate.[24] Indeed, in the month following the release of "Yes We Can," the front page of Obama's website featured it, branding it "a supporter-created video." And in addition to the blockbusters, Obama also benefited from a vast array of genuinely citizen-created media, from YouTube raps and folk songs to Facebook groups and events.

Alongside this genuine citizen (and celebrity) support, Obama and his advisers were able to craft a brilliantly strategic campaign, all the while building in citizen participation as part of his ethos—but also keeping it at arm's length. Kreiss characterizes this sort of relationship between a campaign and its supporters "structured interactivity," the process of "provid[ing] supporters with some ways to participate in the campaign (such as donating money) while not supporting others (such as formally contributing to the campaign's policy statement)."[25] Our examination of Obama's overall 2008 campaign website revealed this dual quality built into its very structure. The website has two central parts. One is a very typical Web 1.0-style site; it is to this content and style that the main navigation menu directs to, with links to pages with names such as

"Learn," "Issues," "Media," and "Action." There, the site presents a highly managed, strategic presentation of the candidate and his positions as just described.

This is the website to which visitors originally were directed, and as a result received the bulk of our analytic attention; further, this portion of the website was open to anyone, and required no login. It was the other mission of barackobama.com, however, that ultimately attracted more popular attention. This was my.barackobama.com, the social connection and expression portion of the site, wherein a user had access to a fully developed social networking platform, enabling connections between friends, the creation of groups and events, a personal fundraising tracker, and a personal blog. It was within my.barackobama.com that was the only location within the site where genuine supporter discourse took place.

From the perspective of presidential campaigns operations, my.barackobama.com was a revelation. But from the perspective of the communicative relationship between a civic entity and its supporters, the website did not foster a primarily actualizing information experience. Rather, the bulk of informing content (knowledge) was heavily dictated by the campaign on official pages where typical visitors were most likely to go, and action was entirely campaign-driven. A more open-ended expressive space did exist, but it was tucked away in a carefully separated platform: to reach it from the main page, one would need to follow the far-right column of information and action items to the sixth item—after being asked to donate, volunteer, learn about upcoming primary contests, read the campaign's factcheck section, and watch videos from barack.tv. Upon reaching my.barackobama.com, the user had to, for the first time, create an account and login with which all further activity within the site would be associated and tracked.

In this context, Kreiss's notion of structured interactivity might be better described as "sequestered interactivity." Supporters of Obama could indeed have an interactive experience with the website. They could create a blog and write whatever they pleased about the candidate's issue positions and what they should be. But that blog had virtually no chance of ever becoming a part of the meaning of the campaign—except, perhaps, for the individual herself and her network contacts.

The truth is that Obama's campaign was of exactly the sort that we would expect to have difficulty embracing an actualizing civic information style. No entity is as much at the mercy of media politics as the highest profile of presidential campaigns, and what is more, such a campaign has such a short timeframe (even in American politics) to achieve a very specific outcome that it makes more sense for them than any other organization to carefully structure what supporters do. Moreover, in such a campaign supporters may be more likely to acquiesce to such a communication style. In light of this, much of what Obama's campaign did *was* revelatory; some almost revolutionary. But when placed against other sorts of organizations in the present framework, it does not appear remarkably actualizing.

ONLINE ONLY ORGANIZATIONS

Those other sorts of organizations were online only ones, which did in fact belong to a special category. Their uniqueness was particularly evident when it came to presenting the particular form of civic information we termed knowledge: half of online only organizations presented an actualizing knowledge experience on at least one page, in contrast to what were essentially trace amounts among the other types of group. The reasonable interpretation here is that such groups designed their websites with an attitude that supporters may have something useful to contribute to the information store on a given website, and that they may be attracted by the opportunity to contribute something and see what peers had contributed. Online only organizations were similarly more likely to offer supporters recommendations for network-expressive activities: they asked young people to become involved in online groups, and participate through networked social spaces.

We should be careful not to overstate the overall actualizing quality of online only websites. For one thing, though they offered actualizing knowledge to a high degree, their offerings of action were surprisingly dutiful. It is somewhat puzzling why this should be the case—why one sort of information provision should take an actualizing form but the other remain resolutely dutiful. One interpretation would hold that despite the interests of organizational leaders in engaging supporters in an actualizing way, when it comes to the actual actions supporters are going to take, the sense of concern over what young supporters might recommend simply becomes too much. Drawing from the theory of Chapter 3, this interpretation would hold that there are limits to what even the most innovative leaders are able to offer in terms of actualizing communications.

Online only organizations' activity offerings also did not achieve the level of actualizing communications we might have expected. Though they were offered somewhat more often on online only sites than on the sites of other sorts of organizations, network-expressive activities were not more common than membership activities or even management ones. In fact, 76% of online only activities were either membership or management actions—a surprisingly high number, even if lower than those of other site types. What we seem to be seeing here are the early stages of a move toward Web 2.0 practices—this will become evident in the next chapters—but at this point, even among those organizations most committed to norms and practices of digital culture, such activities have made only modest inroads.

Nonetheless, the overall place identified for online only organizations in this study comports with the findings of others working in this area. Karpf, in particular, suggests that there is a novel class of organizations entering the American civic scene—one that brings with it a refreshed perspective on civic practices and ways of interacting with supporters.[26] Whereas he characterized that class largely in terms of its structure and the meaning of membership, here we have fleshed out what it means in terms of the communicative relationship between organizations and supporters. We detected among online only organizations a distinct shift toward opening communications to supporter contributions—to seeing supporters more as autonomous actors with views and ideas (knowledge) to be expressed, and with personal networks to be activated and mobilized (via network-expressive action appeals).

By contrast, offline organizations' communications proved markedly resistant to what we described in Chapter 3 as overarching cultural shifts toward interactivity and exchange. Despite the established importance of Web 2.0 by this period—and exhortations to civic website creators to create participatory and interactive opportunities much earlier[27]—the digital cultural features of participation and networked information sharing here were highly differential, favoring organizations that had primarily online components. Why so? Returning to that discussion, several factors are likely at work. First, the influence of organizational habit and the assumptions of organizational leaders may have played a large role. Online only organizations are likely to have the advantage of being directed by younger citizens, and at the least by citizens who have been drawn to online only projects by their own interest in the possibilities of digital media to reach and engage youth. The fact that the greatest differences were found between online only organizations and the three categories of offline groups suggests that this was playing a large role. Somewhat less so, hesitancy to invite controversy because of media politics may also have been a factor. It was the case that community organizations differed from government/party and interest groups in terms of their willingness to offer actualizing knowledge and action, but these differences were relatively very small compared to the difference between online only groups and those offline. And when it came to activity repertoires, community organizations offered not a single network-expressive activity. The patterns we observed are thus perhaps best categorized as the result of different organizations existing at different points along a curve of civic-cultural change: online only groups were relatively out ahead, with leaders and institutional norms that favored inviting supporters contributions to knowledge and the expression of citizenship through network-expressive action, other organizations clung to online manifestations of what were essentially twentieth-century civic practices.

Conclusion

This chapter took as its starting point the notion that organizations' websites embody choices about the sorts of communicative relationships organizations offer young citizens. Its analyses have not been about the structure of organizations or their internal decision-making processes—which are hardly visible from the surface of an organization's website. But what are visible are organizations' communications to young citizen supporters. We have conceptualized the organization–citizen relationship as one that embodies an organization's understanding of who their supporters are, and what they can be expected to do: how organizations imagine their supporters to contribute to civic or political work, whether they are seen as potentially productive sources of information and meaning, and in what kinds of activities they are expected to engage. In terms of the theoretical framework offered in earlier chapters, we were especially interested in examining whether—and where—young citizens are likely to find satisfying experiences of civic information, which we have described with the actualizing style of civic information.

Drawing out two components of the actualizing civic information styles from the framework of dutiful and actualizing civic information styles, we first examined the degree of participation invited as the site presented knowledge and action to supporters. It was posited that more supporter-driven, participatory invitations would be more in line with an actualizing style of civic information, while consistently organization-driven, pedantic communication aligned more with the dutiful mode. We then looked at the kinds of activities the site encouraged, distinguishing online activities that held the potential for expression, self-definition, and the use of networked communication as a civic tool in itself, from those that were more targeted, official, and prescribed, and those that simply directed site visitors to find and participate in offline events.

What we found supported our overall suspicion that a disconnect in civic information styles underlies youth disaffection from politics—and should temper optimism that civic organizations will easily adapt themselves to a changing communication and information environment. The websites in our samples exhibited highly dutiful communicative characteristics: most of the time, websites prescribed both types of information that we looked at—knowledge and action—in a way we might expect to inspire the classically minded dutiful citizen: one committed to a particular organizations' work, and interested in logging on to a website to see what the organization was doing and how he or she could help. Actualizing invitations, in which visitors were encouraged to express themselves or become involved in information coproduction with the organization, were very much the minority. Similarly, when we looked at the specific activities organizations promoted to supporters, the bulk of these we characterized as either membership activities or management ones: most of the time supporters were asked either to connect with the organization at an offline event or meeting, or were instructed to execute a specific, highly directed action, such as contacting a politician or—most commonly—to give money.

These patterns were notably weaker among online only organizations. There, we found near-parity between dutiful and actualizing approaches to presenting knowledge—suggesting that organizations of this type were pioneering a different relationship with supporters. However, this relationship did not extend to pages that offered action, perhaps suggesting residual hesitancy on the part of even online only organizations to open conversations about appropriate actions to supporters.

The pattern of these findings fell in line with our expectation that recently created, online only organizations may take a different approach to creating online civic spaces for young people than older organizations with significant offline work. What we seem to be seeing are norms, embedded at some level in organizational attitudes and culture, that privilege—or allow—a changing attitude toward organizational supporters.

These findings thus offer a baseline evaluation of our expectations in line with the theory developed in Chapters 2 and 3. But the website analyses just performed are only one way of viewing organizations' online communications, and one with significant limitations, which we address in Chapter 5.

5

Civic Organizations' Communications Through Facebook

A decade ago, an analysis of the engagement opportunities presented by civic organizations on their websites, such as those of Chapter 4, would have provided an accurate and quite comprehensive picture of the groups' online public communications.[1] But major innovations in Internet platforms during that time mean that an exclusive focus on organizations' websites is now too narrow an impression of how organizations are attempting to communicate online.

The most important of these innovations fall under the contested but descriptive rubric of Web 2.0, which describes an explosion of interactive and networking affordances developed in roughly the 2003 through 2008 period. These include the introduction of a host of media sharing sites such as YouTube and Flickr; the rise of social networking, starting with Friendster in 2002 and followed quickly by MySpace, which exploded in 2004, and Facebook, which came onto the scene in 2005;[2] a boom in blogging and other content sharing opportunities; a variety of tools for socially aggregating and commenting on content, such as Digg and Technorati; and the increasing use of similar features on established sites throughout the World Wide Web.

What these changes mean is that an entity's platforms for creating and disseminating online messages—indeed, their very online presences—are no longer resident on a single website: individuals and organizations' online manifestations are now networks of online communication that reach across the affordances of multiple platforms and media modalities. While a political candidate's online outreach between 1996 and 2000 was likely to rely predominantly on a central website and email lists,[3] today a comparable candidate would be remiss not to maintain presences on several social networking sites, post regularly to Twitter and Facebook, maintain a YouTube channel with campaign-produced and fan-produced videos, adapt content to mobile devices, and perhaps share a collection of campaign-trail photos on a photo-sharing site such as Flickr—all in addition to a main website, which itself might offer regular blog posts and even an in-house social networking platform.[4] What all this means is that the findings from Chapter 4 shed light on only one part of the picture of the engagement being communicated by civic organizations, albeit an important one for reasons already discussed.

Substantial depth can be added to our understanding of civic organizations' communication by considering their use of a major social networking site—not only because of those sites' meteoric rise in popularity over the last several years, but also because they are competing to become a centralized location for users' experiences of the web.[5] One element of the increasing sophistication of such sites is that they are making themselves a one-stop platform for connecting to a variety of kinds of content and platforms. For instance, many individuals and organizations connect their Twitter accounts to their Facebook profile, so that posts to one automatically appear on the other; Facebook's liking and commenting features are now found on websites across the web, from the New York Times to Levi's to Doctors without Borders, offering viewers the opportunity to share their opinions on topics ranging from politics to jeans and beyond, all while continuing the connect-and-communicate uses of the original social networking site platform. The proliferation of web tools beyond websites, and the functionalities of social networking sites, make them an essential location for examining organizations' communication modes.

Facebook

If we are looking for a social networking environment in which to explore organizations' overtures to young people, Facebook is an—even *the*—obvious choice. The global leader in social networking worldwide since 2009, Facebook continues to work hard to position itself as users' habitual and comprehensive Internet experience.[6] And Facebook's rapid growth and features tailored to politicians, nonprofits, and companies has made it an attractive communication platform for organizations and companies hoping to reach and develop communication relationships with people online.[7]

Facebook also continues to have a reputation, and an image, as a youth-oriented site, though its user base has grown considerably among older demographics in recent years.[8] At the time of the collection of the data collected below, younger adults were still the dominant Facebook user group: 29% of users were between 18 and 25, and another 23% were 26 to 34; though news stories in this period were beginning to point to the growing use of Facebook and other social media by older citizens, Pew studies showed continuing growth—almost to saturation among American youth.[9] This does not mean, of course, that young people spend all their Facebook time seeking out civic organizations, but it does mean that unlike websites they are unlikely ever to seek out, they may often be only a click away, as they browse friends' profiles or see acquaintances' connections to an organization. And once they are affiliated with a civic organization through a social networking site, their connection is maintained through the sorts of communication described below. For these reasons, Facebook offers the kind of social networking environment to serve as a perfect foil to organizations' websites: while not a fully representative or egalitarian space or exclusively youth site, Facebook does represent a much more prevalent youth experience than any particular website.

This leads us to one of the biggest reasons for examining communications on Facebook. As we shall see shortly, the norms of digital culture described in Chapter 2 may have a greater impact on organizations' Facebook communications than on websites. The notion here is that because websites are stand-alone, independent sites, their functionalities bring with them little by way of assumptions and norms about how communication should occur—site creators are free to translate their established habits and preferred communication modes directly onto their websites.[10] Facebook, by contrast, comes with most of its affordances built in; what is more, those affordances tend to reflect the essence of digital culture. Facebook's whole ethos is the assumption that people want to participate and interact with one another, and actively express themselves through communication.

Theoretical Expectations

Then what *do* we expect from organizations communicating within Facebook? Let us take a moment to revisit our core theoretical concerns. We continue to be interested in what sorts of communications young citizens find in the contemporary civic web. Or, as we have framed this question in the theoretical terms of dutiful and actualizing civic information style: how often are communications by major civic organizations offered forms likely to resonate with young people with actualizing preferences? How often do they remain resolutely dutiful?

Chapter 4 offered answers to these questions, and they were not encouraging from the standpoint of renewed youth involvement through digital communication. Most organizations' communications were heavily dutiful, with the communications of classic interest group communications—those we looked to with most interest for their importance in American civic life—almost exclusively dutiful. These patterns held both for modes of interaction and for the kinds of activities that organizations promoted. The question of how these organizations adjust to a different communication environment—potentially one more encouraging of personal expression and peer exchange—is thus a vital one.

The previous chapter also demonstrated that different kinds of organizations have taken different approaches to the communication styles they offer youth—approaches that aligned reasonably well with the factors outlined in Chapter 3: especially, we found that social changes in the direction of open communications and interactivity were largely muted by organizations' habits for essentially broadcasting communications to supporters. This was manifested by the fact that whereas online only organizations offered a (relatively) ecumenical mix of dutiful and actualizing communication, it was offline groups that hewed most resolutely dutiful. That is, on websites we saw scant evidence of a widespread cultural shift in the presentation of civic communications to young people. As for our concern that those hallmarks of late-twentieth-century communication, the paranoia of media politics and insistence on message control, we saw only weak evidence that less overtly partisan offline groups—those we termed community—would more readily adapt to actualizing preferences than government/party and interest groups. Here in Chapter 5, we have a new opportunity to assess those dynamics on a platform that may offer a quite different cultural context.

This is a significant opportunity, because the communication dynamics observed on websites are likely to not be exactly replicated on Facebook. Most intriguingly, Facebook's environment may encourage organizations to communicate differently in response to the youth-driven norms of digital culture already established there. Facebook is an online locale that organizations must *enter*. Users must make a choice to communicate in a space that already exists, and already has established norms and practices—most of all, the participatory, networked sharing norms of digital culture. The crucial possibility—and fascinating question—is that organizations responding to the norms of the space, and feeling pressure to adapt to it, may broaden the variety of communications they offer and adopt more actualizing styles. Thus, in contrast to websites, Facebook offers an arena in which organizations not already well-versed in practices and patterns of digital culture—above all what we have termed offline organizations—must at least contend with them.

In addition to the general culture or ethos that has built up around Facebook, Facebook's very functionalities impose structural constraints and guidelines on organizations' communications. Especially if they do not invest in developing their own applications or features, organizations can only do certain things, in certain ways: they must operate within the confines Facebook has established for organizations. As a site specializing in helping entities to develop productive and interactive relationships with supporters, the structural guidance set by Facebook may also lead organizations to adopt more participatory, actualizing communication styles.

As a result, we might reconsider the factors described in Chapter 3 with these dynamics in mind. What they suggest is that, first, general social changes are likely to be more pronounced in organizations' Facebook communications compared to those on their websites. This derives from the fact that organizations operating within Facebook must do so from a shared and relatively constrained set of choices, functionalities, and so on. As such, a relatively new culture, one that we have hypothesized is imbued with norms of digital culture, is likely to have a widespread influence on organizations' communications.

How the impact of organizational leadership and habit on organizational communication will change in Facebook is somewhat less clear. One possibility is that online only organizations' actualizing styles will increase, because the leaders of those organizations are most attuned and responsive to the norms of the environment in which they are operating. According to this *magnifying effect*, leaders of offline organizations may be less responsive—having entered the Facebook space simply because of a perception that it is where the youth are, but with little inclination to engage with its communicative norms. A contrasting possibility is a sort of *ceiling effect*, in which online only organizations continue to offer a reasonable rate of actualizing communications, but other organizations catch up as they for the first time encounter and internalize the new norms.

The problem of media politics suggests a different set of dynamics. This factor should continue to constrain formally political organizations from introducing a great deal of actualizing communications—they still operate in an environment of media politics. As a result, we should still expect to see differences between those groups operating in the formal political sphere and those in a more civic one. The interesting question will be to what extent this constraint will be overcome by the cultural/normative factors pushing in the opposite direction.

All of this paints the move to Facebook as a prime opportunity for organizations to adapt to participatory communication patterns and begin offering opportunities for supporters to share and produce information: if they are not able to adapt to a more actualizing style in this youth-driven, participatory context, we should question whether they ever will be.

Identifying Facebook Pages

I was able to maximize continuity and points of comparison with the analysis of the communication of organizations via websites by building the analysis of Facebook communications largely on the same set of 90 websites analyzed in

Chapter 4. The main sampling challenge was therefore to determine whether an organization had created a presence on Facebook, and what form it took.

Here I was assisted by the fact that Facebook makes available specific features to organizations wishing to create a presence within the site.[11] Two primary organizing modes are dominant. The more informal of these are *Groups*. Groups are collections of individuals who have chosen to identify themselves with a given collection of others. Groups come in several forms, and Facebook's functionalities offer several choices as to how they are set up, who they admit, and who is able to view the group's members and activities. A more formal form of representation on Facebook, created especially for organizations, politicians, companies, and other public figures, is the *Page*, a special kind of profile with which to communicate with supporters. The biggest difference between a Page and a Group or a typical user's *profile* is that a Page is necessarily public: all content on the Page is visible to anyone who might visit. However, the way a Page works, and its basic functionalities, are not substantially different from Groups or profiles, though unlike Groups they are necessarily public, with no control over who views the Page or joins it (by "liking" it), and unlike profiles are enabled with a variety of additional tools such as discussion boards and video and photo sharing tools to which supporters can post. But like Groups and profiles, organizations with a Page on Facebook are able to create *status updates* that are communicated to all of those who have identified themselves as supporters of the organization and constitute the fundamental unit of communication within Facebook—a point that will be crucial in analyses below. (In this chapter, I capitalize Page and Group when referring specifically to the use of Facebook's features by those names to distinguish them from more general uses of the words.)

The construction of the sample for this chapter's study, therefore, was a matter of applying a systematic search process to each of the original 90 engagement websites to determine whether each site had built a Facebook Page. (This process is described in Appendix D.) My research assistants and I also noted the presence of Facebook Groups associated with a given organization's name, to account for other forms that organizations' presences might take. Table 5.1 breaks the numbers down by site category and the kinds of Facebook presences found.

Of the 90 original websites, we found 67 unique Facebook Pages: for 22 of the 90 projects, no Facebook Page was found; another pair of organizations shared the same Page.[12] In half of the cases (11) where an organization did not have a Page, a Group had been created instead; in the remaining cases, an organization either had gone defunct altogether (7) or had no discernible traces on Facebook (4).

Thus, of the 83 websites that were still operational, a good majority—68, or 81.9%—were associated with some Facebook Page, confirming the

Table 5.1 **Facebook Presences of the 90 Websites**

Site category	With FB Pages	Missing FB Pages	Websites missing FB Pages		
			Site down	No FB Presence	Group, no Page
Online only	24* (75%)	11	3	0 (0%)	8 (25%)
Government	9 (75%)	6	3	2 (17%)	1 (8%)
Interest	16 (84%)	4	1	1 (5%)	2 (11%)
Community	19 (95%)	1	0	1 (5%)	0 (0%)
Total	68 (82%)	22	7	4	11

Percentages are out of the number of organizations with still-active websites.

*Includes Servenet, which directed to the Youth Service America (Community) Facebook page.

attractiveness of the medium for organizers of youth engagement projects. Second, the tendency to be represented by a Group, but not a Page, was not evenly distributed across the site categories. The pattern was pronounced among online only projects, where 8 of the 32 active sites (25%) were represented on Facebook by a Group but no Page. This was less common among other types of organizations—a pattern that may be reflective of the overall patterns we have so far been observing, with online only projects more comfortable and open to youth taking the reins of the project, in this case by allowing, and perhaps encouraging, youth to define the project's identity on Facebook through Group formation. Facebook Groups, then, are clearly important sites for some organizations' communications with supporters; the difference between Pages and Groups may even represent two forms of online organizing that roughly align with dutiful and actualizing communication styles.[13]

At the same time, when it came to creating Facebook Pages, there is little evidence that systematic self-selection taking place among organizations: types of organizations that were most dutiful in the website study were no less likely to create a Facebook Page than online only organizations. In fact, interest groups and community organizations were slightly more likely. This should reassure us that self-selection into Facebook is not playing a large role in aggregate results, and that Facebook is indeed a medium attractive to a wide range of civic groups.

To round out the sample, two Pages were added to the 67 identified based on the sample of Chapter 4. These were Sarah Palin's Page, added because she had replaced John McCain (whose Page remained in the dataset) as a figurehead in the Republican party, and was far and away the most popular conservative on Facebook (with 1,536,430 fans at the time of analysis in March 2010); and the Page of the website Puget Sound Off, an innovative online only project of special interest because its design was influenced by the author's previous work.[14] Of these 69 Pages, nine produced no status updates during the three months we followed them. Those nine are excluded from this chapter's analyses, resulting in a final sample of 60 Pages. (These are listed in Appendix E.)

Structure of the Study

STATUS UPDATE COMMUNICATION

What sort of communications would a young citizen interacting with the Pages in our sample have encountered? To investigate the question, we can make productive use of the Facebook functionality of status updates. Status updates are miniposts any Facebook user or organization can create to describe what they are thinking about, doing, reading, watching, and listening to. They appear in reverse chronological order on each user's profile (or on the Page of an organization) in a string of microblogs similar to Twitter tweets. (Some users syndicate their posts to automatically appear in both, and other, social media services.) Any visitor to a profile or Page can then see all the status updates that the user has posted.

But a person need not go to a friend's or organization's profile or Page to see the status updates: one of Facebook's unique contributions to social networking was the news feed, a collection of information presented to every Facebook user that displays information being produced by the individuals, Groups, and Pages in that person's network—subject to user customization and Facebook's algorithms.[15] The dominant type of content present in an individual's news feed is status updates, along with accompanying links and comments, of friends, acquaintances, and Pages of which the user is a supporter. The news feed is thus a customized stream of information from people, organizations, and public figures a user has a relationship with or is interested in. As Rory O'Connor has noted, this is the essence of a personally networked information environment, and represents a new model for receiving information about the world around us: rather than visiting a hub of information produced by a particular organization and visited periodically by news consumers, the news feed lets us know about the information the Pages we have chosen to identify ourselves with, are choosing to share.[16] And though the details of Facebook's interface, functionalities, and, surely, algorithm have changed over the years, the role and makeup of the news feed have stayed remarkably constant.

The status update is thus an essential medium of communication within Facebook, and one that both individuals and organizations use extensively. Here we conceptualize it as the major component of the communicative relationship between an entity (in this case, a civic organization) and its publics in a networked public sphere. Analyzing status updates is thus an obvious place to consider the degree to which organizations offer dutiful or actualizing styles of civic information.

COLLECTION OF STATUS UPDATES

My team gathered organizations' status updates from the three-month period February 1 through April 30, 2010. The period was selected to offer a range of time short enough to make the research feasible, but also long enough that short-term variations in organizations' strategies or styles, such as advocacy on specific policy issues, would not overshadow more typical day-to-day communications.[17]

In all, 1,844 status updates were collected, for an average of just under 31 status updates per organization. Organizations' productivity varied widely, ranging from only a few status updates posted in three months, to the Sierra Club, which posted 326 status updates during the sample frame, of which 109 were collected and analyzed. (In this chapter, reports of raw numbers of various types of communication are reports of exactly the number of posts recorded and analyzed; charts and percentages, and comparisons between organizational types, have been adjusted to correct for the sampling scheme.)

The communications that constitute this study were thus gathered exactly two years after the website communications described in the previous chapter. Both took place during the spring of election years, though election years of quite different sorts. While 2008 was a presidential election year in which the spring presented both a continuing battle for the Democratic nomination and unprecedented anticipation for the coming November election, the political dynamics of 2010 were more subdued, if at least as contentious. In addition to being a midterm election, the national mood was predominantly one of volatile malaise and dissatisfaction, characterized by a struggling economy, the rising influence of the far-right conservative Tea Party faction of the Republican Party, and an electorate poised to turn against the party—the Democrats—whom it had voted into power just two years earlier. Ultimately the election would be one of significantly reduced turnout on the political left—the youth vote, so heavily weighted toward Obama two years earlier, would fall 60% from 2008—and a marked conservative shift in Congress and statehouses across the country with political implications for years to come.[18]

However, in the period that is our focus here—February, March, and April—considerations of the midterm elections were not yet prominent in the news media or organizations' Facebook messages. Still, there was no shortage of political issues and events for the organizations to work through and communicate about: major questions of public policy were being decided, chief among them the health care reform being promoted by President Obama and the Democrats, and resisted with increasing ferocity by Republicans. Within government/party organizations, that issue was a frequent topic of posting, both by Obama and the Democrats and, in opposition, the Republicans. Republicans were also clearly eager to use their Facebook presence to remind voters about problems with the economy and employment. And John McCain posted about immigration and border security, reflecting the concerns of an important segment of his party during this time.

Other kinds of organizations display their own responses to current events. Ten days before the end of the sample period, BP's Deepwater Horizon oil drilling rig exploded and collapsed in the Gulf of Mexico, initiating one of the greatest environmental disasters in American history. Although the full magnitude of the crisis would not be known for months, that event impacted the organizations in the sample with environmental concerns, such as the Sierra Club. Several gay and lesbian rights organizations, such as the Human Rights Campaign, were similarly using current events to agitate for opposition to the controversial "Don't ask, don't tell" policy of the US military. And a host of smaller events affecting one or two of the organizations in the sample were also commented on. The Yushu earthquake on April 14 in southern Tibet, for example, was mentioned in several posts of the organization Students for a Free Tibet. Thus, although there was not the same mood of electoral excitement in 2010 as in 2008, the presence of the many high-profile issues that have become characteristic of our politically and culturally divided polity were clearly in play.

Dutiful and Actualizing Communications in Facebook

As for what we should look for in those status updates, we can again maximize continuity and comparability by applying, with some modifications, the general approach of the website study within Facebook. The approach is summarized in Table 5.2. First, as in Chapter 4, we can identify relatively more dutiful and actualizing ways of offering the two essential varieties of civic information, knowledge and action. Similarly, the repertoire of activities promoted by organizations can be documented. A further opportunity for analysis not feasible on websites is suggested by the networked nature of Facebook, and specifically the common practice of including links provided with status updates.

Table 5.2 **Analytic Elements of Facebook Study**

Measure	Dimension of Information Style	Dutiful Pattern	Actualizing Pattern
Presentation of knowledge and action	Modes of interaction with information	Prescription of knowledge and action to supporters	Appeals to supporters to contribute knowledge and action ideas
Action repertoires	Action preferences	Membership/ management activities	Network-expressive activities
Link destinations	Modes of gathering and interpreting information	Links consistently point to organization's own website, Facebook presence, or other branded destination	Links point to destinations within and outside the organization's sphere of influence

Mode of Interaction

The key distinction between dutiful and actualizing modes of interaction concerns whether organizations prescribe the information supporters should be learning or acting with (dutiful), or whether supporters are invited to share (actualizing) in the presentation of knowledge and action. We developed codes along these lines, with separate definitions for dutiful knowledge, dutiful action, actualizing knowledge, and actualizing action. Each status update could then be assessed for the presence and absence of each form of communication. (Appendix F presents the details and reliabilities of this coding process.) Several brief examples will suffice to illustrate.

As in Chapter 4, dutiful knowledge included all sorts of information that the organization was delivering to supporters. These included facts, opinions, and links presented with messages to "learn more." For example, Students for a Free Tibet posted this example (see Figure 5.1) of dutiful knowledge in the form of a simple fact about the meeting of two leaders (the link is to a CBS story about the meeting of the Dalai Lama and President Obama):[19]

Students for a Free Tibet The Tibetan Head of State with President of the United States of America. http://bit.ly/asZuVl
February 18 at 11:32am · Comment · Like

    and 36 others like this.

Figure 5.1 Status Update from Students for a Free Tibet.

Dutiful action included cases in which organizations urged fans to take part in a particular activity, whether by directly asking them to (e.g., "Please help us raise $1000 by donating today!") or more general forms of encouragement ("Lots of member are donating money today!"). For example, in one status update John McCain's Page appealed to supporters to turn out for a phone bank in support of the Senator's proposals (Figure 5.2).

Actualizing knowledge was the mirror of dutiful knowledge: it represented cases in which an organization used its status update to encourage fans to be the source of information through, for example, asking them to contribute their views or knowledge about a specific topic. In one very explicit example of actualizing knowledge (see Figure 5.3), Youth Service America asked fans to.

Actualizing action, finally, was the mirror of dutiful action and the parallel of actualizing knowledge. These were cases in which an organization's post asked supporters to describe what they were *doing*, or suggest to others what they might do as an engaged young person. For example, early in April the US Environmental Protection Agency Facebook Page presented this status update and link text (Figure 5.4).

This status update contained actualizing action because it asked supporters to post what they were *doing* on Earth Day. (It also included dutiful action because it invited fans to the EPA's own event.)

John McCain Arizona Facebook Fans... John McCain Phone Banks start Saturday and continue for the next eight Saturdays. Join us!! http://www.johnmccain.com /phonebank/

April 8 at 11:57am · Comment · Like

👍 ▉▉▉▉▉▉ and 289 others like this.

💬 View all 195 comments

Figure 5.2 Status Update from John McCain.

Youth Service America Tell us what Service Says to you! Post a comment on our wall beginning with, "Service Says..." For example, "Service Says that I have an opportunity to share my voice and be heard, even though I'm 12."

"Service Says" invites creative responses from around the world | YSA

ysa.org

YOUTH SERVICE AMERICA (YSA) improves communities by increasing the number and the diversity of young people, ages 5-25, serving in substantive roles. Founded in 1986, YSA supports a global culture of engaged youth committed to a lifetime of service, learning leadership, and achievement.

📎 March 3 at 6:55am · Comment · Like

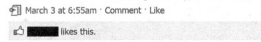
👍 ▉▉▉▉ likes this.

Figure 5.3 Status Update from Youth Service America.

U.S. Environmental Protection Agency Made your Earth Day plans? What are you up to? We're having a big shindig on the National Mall and other events around the country.

Find an Event or Volunteer Opportunity Near You | Earth Day | US EPA

www.epa.gov

To commemorate the 40th anniversary of Earth Day and EPA, we are hosting a celebration event Saturday, April 24 (10am – 6pm) and Sunday (10am – 5pm), on the National Mall. The event will feature a ...

April 5 at 6:28pm · Comment · Like

and 15 others like this.

Figure 5.4 Status Update from the US Environmental Protection Agency.

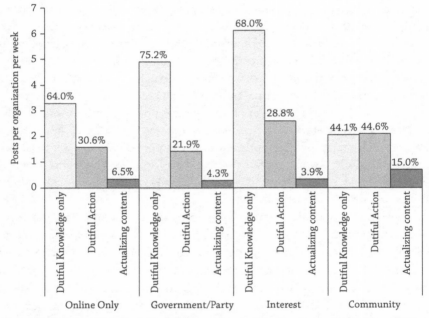

Figure 5.5 Posts With Each Type of Communication Per Organization Per Week.

What modes of interaction were present in organizations' status updates? Figure 5.5 answers the question with broad brush strokes by breaking down the weekly output of the average organization within each site category in terms of the type of information—knowledge or action—and style of communication—dutiful or actualizing—offered. In the figure, bars' total heights indicate the number of posts of each variety produced by each category of organizations, in terms of average number of posts, per organization, per week. Percentages at the top of each bar indicate the percentage of status updates within each organizational category that included each type of communication. (As in the last chapter, dutiful knowledge was so common that it is here isolated into only those posts that included dutiful knowledge *and no other type of communication.* By contrast, actualizing knowledge and action were both so uncommon that they are here combined into a single measure of "actualizing content." Dutiful action and actualizing content could co-occur in the same status update, resulting in percentages within a category summing to slightly more than 100%.)

A couple of patterns are evident. First are somewhat unequal rates of posting status updates between organizations of different categories, as reflected in different total heights of the bars between organizational types. Interest organizations posted more often than other organizational types, with just over 9 posts per organization per week, on average. They were followed by government/party organizations, which posted 6.5 times per week; online only organizations, which posted just over 5 times per week; and community organizations, which posted 4.7 times a week. This difference—a factor of nearly 2 between the most-frequently posting category and the least—indicates a particularly concerted effort to communicate with supporters on the part of interest, and to some extent government/party organizations.

Second, organizations as a whole were clearly using their status updates to inform publics about the organizations' positions and work. This is reflected in the dominantly dutiful nature of most organizations' communications. A solid majority of the status updates posted by organizations were simply conveying information—providing dutiful knowledge *and no other form of communication*: 63.8% of all status updates were of this form. Another third of status updates (31%) were calls to supporters to engage in action along lines defined by the organization: dutiful action.

These heavily dutiful proportions leave only small bars to actualizing forms of information provision: examples of organizations calling upon supporters to share information or opinion (actualizing knowledge) were uncommon across the board, occurring in just more than one status update in twenty (5.6% of all status updates). And calls for action suggestions (actualizing action) were very rare (a tiny 1.1% of status updates). Clearly, Facebook communications were dominated by attempts to simply pass information, and action requests, to supporters. Such small numbers of invitations to supporters to contribute information and action ideas are striking, particularly in the Facebook context, where we expected a powerful participatory ethos to be present.

But these general patterns disguise important differences between types of organizations. Recall Chapter 4's finding that online only organizations offered substantially more actualizing communications than offline organizations. Earlier in this chapter we cited reasons that these differences could become either exacerbated or more muted within Facebook. In fact, we are seeing a mixture of the two: for government/party organizations, it is hard to argue that there has been a move toward actualizing patterns: 75.6% of posts by government groups were dutiful knowledge and nothing else, and a further

21.6% contained dutiful action. By contrast, government/party organizations offered actualizing knowledge *or* action in only 4.3% of posts. Interest groups similarly promoted their own information in 68.0% of cases, and prescribed action in 28.8%. This stands in contrast to a tiny 3.8% of status updates that invited supporter contributions of knowledge or action.

At the same time, even among online only organizations, 64.0% of status updates were only dutiful knowledge and 30.6% dutiful action. Actualizing communications were correspondingly sparse, present in only 6.5% of status updates. What we might draw from these rates is first, that the patterns of the website study held quite constant in Facebook: online only organizations offered more actualizing posts than government/party or interest groups. The caveat at is that all of the rates of actualizing content were so low that they almost appear to be regressions from websites: certainly it was surprising to see online only organizations, half of which had offered actualizing knowledge on their websites, offering it so infrequently in Facebook. (Of course, without benchmarks for comparison, it is difficult to make evaluations of what would be sufficient offerings of actualizing content to constitute communicative autonomy for supporters—an important limitation of exploratory research.) And in terms of our major theoretical concerns then, entering the Facebook context has appeared to make little impression upon the communications of government/party, and interest organizations.

The same cannot be said for community organizations. Those groups both stood out markedly from the others, and made a leap from the website context, offering purely dutiful knowledge in only 44.1% of status updates. They offered a further 44.6% with dutiful action, and most impressive of all, it was community organizations that stood out in their offerings of actualizing content, presenting actualizing knowledge in 11.8% of cases and actualizing action in 3.3%, for a total of some 15.0% of status updates that contained one of the two or both.

What we see here, therefore, is not a straightforward adaptation to the Facebook context. Whereas online only, government/party, and interest organizations entered the social networking space offering highly constrained, dutiful modes of interaction, community organizations have stood out for doing the opposite. For this reason it may be useful to take a closer look at some of the communications there.

What is evident looking in the communications of community organizations is their comfort with—in some cases *passion for*—encouraging supporters to interact with ideas and suggestions. The most prolific organization in terms of actualizing knowledge was the youth news organization Channel One, which invited some kind of response from supporters in a remarkable 36.4% of status updates. Channel One repeatedly offered topics and asked supporters to respond. For instance, one post offered information about one of President Obama's announcements about the space program, and asked for supporters' opinions (Figure 5.6).

Figure 5.6 Status Update from Channel One News.

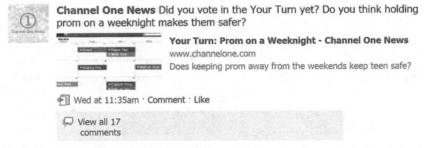

Figure 5.7 Status Update from Channel One News.

Another referred supporters to a feedback feature called "Your Turn" on the Channel One site and asked supporters to offer their thoughts about how to make prom safer for students (Figure 5.7).

The rest of the organizations' status updates are similarly scattered with references to current events, holidays ("Looking forward to a chocolate bunny this weekend?"), and issues of concern to students, many accompanied by some variety of invitation for input.

The Girl Scouts similarly offered plentiful encouragements for supporters to share stories of their participation in the organization, doing so with roughly every fifth status update (21.2%). Famous in the United States for their fundraising Girl Scout cookies, a number of the Scouts' posts involved questions asking supporters to describe their work and what it meant to them (see Figures 5.8 and 5.9).

These are notable uses of actualizing knowledge. First, these are not completely open-ended invitations to share any thoughts on any topic. After all, these are organizations with particular missions and activities. Rather, they are consistently related to the organizations' work—in the case of Channel One, providing information that may inspire young people or help them in their lives; in the case of the Girl Scouts, connecting Scouts to the activities they likely are involved in and care about. As part of this pattern, the prompts typically do include some information provided by the organization—a link

Girl Scouts of the USA Check out some great advice on "How To Sell Like a Girl Scout", straight from girls themselves! Also, share with everyone what works for you...

Girl Scouts of the USA: How To Sell Like a Girl Scout

blog.girlscouts.org

Of the Cookie Program as a whole, Richard Kennedy, president and CEO of the Worcester Regional Chamber of Commerce goes on to say:

March 4 at 7:06am · Comment · Like

and 20 others like this.

View all 33 comments

Figure 5.8 Status Update from the Girl Scouts.

Girl Scouts of the USA Fantastic story involving Girl Scouts, care packages and the Marines! What are your favorite personal stories about sending care packages overseas?

Girl Scouts of the USA: Marine Surprises Girl Scouts With a Visit

blog.girlscouts.org

After giving LaFleur the honor of holding the flag for the scouts' opening ceremony, the girls were welcome to ask the Marine any questions they wanted about his service. They inquired about what it was like to be a Marine and be in a war, among other things. ...

March 17 at 6:18am · Comment · Like

and 34 others like this.

View all 21 comments

Figure 5.9 Status Update from the Girl Scouts.

to information about the president's speech, or an inspiring story about care packages. The organization is playing a key informational role here, bringing stories and information to the attention of young members rather than opening their feeds into a free-for-all of jumbled ideas. (These posts often included dutiful knowledge or action alongside the actualizing forms.) Nonetheless, the organizations are also inviting supporters to add additional meaning to the stories, or to share similar, complementary, or potentially competing stories of their own.

This pattern was much less prevalent among other organizational types. As noted already, it was perhaps most surprising that online only organizations did not offer more of these types of communications. But it is among interest and government/party organizations that actualizing communications were so infrequent that what we really must investigate is what else these organizations were using their status updates for. Taking a look at the posts of the

Sierra Club, a classic interest organization, and the most prolific organization in all of our sample, may be illustrative. The club presented actualizing knowledge in a modest, but roughly typical, for interest groups, 6.4% of the 109 cases we analyzed. The information the club shares in its news feed is a diverse mélange of personal testimonials, descriptions of the club's work and calls for action, and news items—a rich example of the Sierra Club as a news curation source in the new media environment. For instance, in one post the club shared a mainstream news article covering some of the its work (Figure 5.10); in another, it shared information about the passing of a longtime club member (see Figure 5.11).

It is clear that a young member of the Sierra Club who has connected with the organization on Facebook could learn a great deal about the club, its work, and the broader political environment from this stream of posts. However, what the club rarely invited was actual input on the part of fans in response to its posts. In the few cases where that did occur, however, it was in a form quite similar to the examples from the community category just noted: the

Figure 5.10 Status Update from the Sierra Club.

Figure 5.11 Status Update from the Sierra Club.

Figure 5.12 Status Update from the Sierra Club.

club posed a topic of obvious relevance to the organization's work, and invited suggestions and meaning-making from fellow communicators. For instance, as shown in the status update in Figure 5.12.

The indication here is that a meaningful style of actualizing interaction indeed does exist. Among community groups this mode of communicating with online supporters was a regular offering, indicating a willingness to embrace the modes of interactivity and exchange written into Facebook. Such a style is equally available to organizations of other types—there is no reason that more groups like the Sierra Club could not regularly invite input on John Muir's birthday, or hundreds of other topics about which it posts. But the fact that it did not—and that interest, government/party, and even, to a certain extent, online only organizations did not—indicates a systematic difference in those groups' assessments of the risks and benefits to actualizing communication on Facebook.

Repertoires of Action

We shall return to the significance of this finding. Still, let us once again recall that the nature of interaction promoted by organizations in their status updates is but one element of the overall communicative relationships they offer to supporters. As we saw in Chapter 4, even when prescribing activities, different types of activities may be conceptualized as relatively more or less actualizing in style. There we explored the sorts of activities promoted on the webpages in which organizations offered dutiful action; here we can make a comparable contribution. (For reference, see Table 4.3 and Appendix F for full coding details and reliabilities.)

The essential insight of Chapter 4's activities analysis was that different organizations offer different *repertoires* of action—different mixes of activity suggestions—that also constitute an essential element of the communicative relationships they foster. And we conceptualized three primary varieties of

action that make up a repertoire: membership activities, efforts to get supporters to attend meetings and join groups; management activities, the encouragement of specific and prescribed messages to elected officials, or donations; and
network-expressive activities, the encouragement to use communicative connections to convey messages or actions to a personally networked public.

What we saw in Chapter 4 was a decided tendency toward membership and
management activities in organizations' website communications. Except
for online only organizations, in each of the organizational types more organizations offered membership activities than any other kind of activity.
Management activity mentions were correspondingly high, with networked
activities relatively unusual—no community organization suggested a single
network-expressive activity—with online only groups standing out by offering relatively more networked activities. What we concluded from these patterns was, first, that most organizations continue to understand their online
supporters as potentially mobilized to the tasks of twentieth-century activism: to be prodded to attend offline meetings, or donate money or contact an
official about an issue; and second, that online only organizations did differ
from others in beginning to present a set of actions that could position supporters as active curators of their own information networks, and that those
networks could potentially be activated in the service of the organization's
missions.

This set of patterns raises intriguing questions for what we should find in
the social networking space. Once again, Facebook suggests itself as a place in
which organizations might be especially inclined to offer network-expressive
activities: by engaging that space, organizations may position themselves to
reach supporters in precisely the sort of networked environment suited to
managing and leveraging networked communication relationships. If organizations are willing to adjust their understanding of their communicative
relationships with supporters, we should correspondingly expect a rise in networked activity here.

So what do we see in organizations' activity repertoires on Facebook?
Figure 5.13 displays the kinds of activities offered, in terms of the total number of activities offered, by each type of organization during the thirteen-week
sample period. Thus we see that interest sites dominated in offering the most
activities—a product mainly of their overwhelming lead in total numbers of
posts—with 37.2 activities per organization being recorded during our sample
period. Community sites followed, with 32.0 activities. And government/party
and online only sites trailed, with 23.3 and 22.8 activities per organization
respectively.

What is more interesting, of course, is the mix of activities being promoted.
Membership activities, though still the plurality of activity offerings, now
make up fewer than half (46.8%) of all activities. More strikingly, in every
organizational category, network-expressive activities are now more prevalent

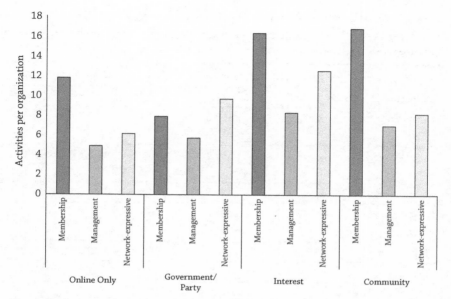

Figure 5.13 Activities Offered By Civic Organizations During 13-Week Sample Period, By Type of Activity and Category of Organization.

than management activities: overall, whereas management activities make up 22.2% of offerings, network-expressive activities make up 30.9%.

This is a marked across-the-board increase in networked activity offerings from the website study. Equally notable is the fact that differences between online only organization and offline ones have disappeared. In fact, it is offline organizations that more avidly present network-expressive actions in Facebook: government/party organizations lead the field, with a plurality of activity offerings (41.6%) being network-expressive. Interest organizations follow, with 33.8%, and online only and community organizations offered network-expressive activities 27.0% and 25.6% of the time, respectively. This is a decided shift in the constitution of the action repertoire being offered by civic organizations attempting to communicate with youth.

NETWORK-EXPRESSIVE ACTIVITIES

The rise in network-expressive activities documented in organizations' Facebook communications deserves closer attention. To get a clearer look at exactly what organizations were promoting on Facebook that resulted in the finding, recall that the set of activities defined as network-expressive included sharing multimedia materials, creating web content, joining an online group, general appeals to spread the word, posting something to a social networking space, and sharing information with friends. Table 5.3 breaks down total actualizing activity offerings into those components.

Table 5.3 **Breakdown of Network-Expressive Activities. Entries are percentages of all network-expressive activities that took each form, by organizational category.**

	Online Only	*Government*	*Interest*	*Community*	*All*
Share multimedia	23.9	21.6	9.0	9.8	14.7
Create and share content	35.9	10.3	13.4	20.3	19.3
Participate in an online group	11.1	12.4	36.8	35.8	26.6
"Spread the word"	12.8	30.9	13.9	14.6	16.9
Post to a social networking site	13.8	21.6	26.9	16.3	20.6
"Tell a friend"	2.6	3.1	0.0	3.3	1.9
Total	100	100	100	100	100

No single activity dominates here, lending some credence to our notion of a category of activities. But overall, the most common type of network-expressive activity recommended was to join some sort of online collective or group. This was especially common among interest and community organizations, making up more than a third of the network-expressive activities of each. A typical example comes from the interest group GLSEN, which urged supporters to show support by becoming a fan of their Page dedicated to the gay-rights-awareness event Day of Silence (Figure 5.14).

These sorts of encouragements are notable. Though we typically think of joining a group as a sort of social act or a contribution to the building of collective power, in these online spaces they take on a meaning that is at least as much about personal expression. Here, GLSEN exploits the fact that a person's decision to "like" an organization has at least three network-expressive qualities. First, as we have seen, liking an organization signs up a user to stay in touch with the group by receiving its status updates in the user's news feed. In this sense, liking is the opening of a communicative relationship that will keep the organization and supporter connected via status updates. Second, the expressive quality of the action is manifested in the support that an individual demonstrates by liking—support that will be visible to networked peers in the form of a status update alert that a friend has liked a particular Page, or in the list of Pages liked on a user's profile. Finally, support is communicated to others through both the total number of "fans" the organization has attracted—an indicator of its popularity and thereby influence. In this sense, the liking is a sort of online vote of confidence in the organization's mission that the Page displays to all Facebook

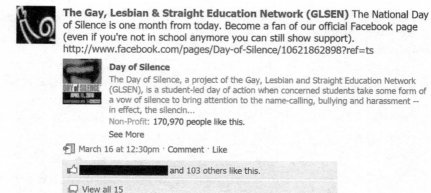

Figure 5.14 Status Update from GLSEN.

users. This case illustrates the transformation of what would be a joining variety of action in the predigital era to one that also has a decidedly communicative element in a networked public space such as Facebook.

The next most common form of network-expressive activity we identified was closely related. By posting to a social networking site or liking a particular Page, supporters were similarly called upon to use the networked communication environment to demonstrate their support and accord the organization additional power. This type of activity was particularly strongly promoted by government/party and interest organizations, which posted messages they thought could gain a broader audience through their supporters. For example, one post from the National Youth Rights Association asked supporters to use their Twitter accounts to send a message about lowering the voting age to their networks (Figure 5.15).

In another example, Greenpeace combined a direct appeal to a corporation with the public qualities of calling out that corporation on its Facebook Page (Figure 5.16).

The latter case makes explicit the contested public nature of communications within the Facebook space. In it, Greenpeace calls upon supporters to disrupt the public relations presence of Koch Industries on Facebook—a virtual defacing of the company's brand. Such activities are at the heart of the network-expressive category: they give supporters both an active role in disseminating a message of concern, while simultaneously offering them the opportunity to publicly associate themselves with the cause.

A further variety of activity that falls along these same lines are instances in which organizations asked supporters more generally to spread the word, a sometimes generic admonition that was interpreted here as implying that they should do so over digital networks. Once again, government/party organizations led in this activity, led by Barack Obama and the Democratic Party, each of which created posts encouraging it multiple times. A characteristic example from Obama is shown in Figure 5.17.

In this case, the activity called upon is the transmission of information favorable to a particular cause—in this case, advocating what would become the Affordable Care Act of 2010. It is an attempt at creating an alternative pathway for information to reach potentially supportive publics that is not dependent upon the particular necessities of the broadcast media. Of course, Obama's team was doing its best also to compete in the mainstream media space: but

National Youth Rights Association Today is the 16th! If you have a Twitter account, be sure to send out tweets today about lowering the voting age using the #16tovote hastag!

April 16 at 3:03pm · Comment · Like

🖒 ▇▇▇▇▇▇ and 3 others like this.

Figure 5.15 Status Update from the National Youth Rights Association.

Greenpeace USA Tell the climate criminals at Koch Industries, Inc. that you're NOT their fan on Facebook.

Go over to their Facebook page and leave a comment saying something like "I'm not a fan of Koch Industries' funding of climate change denying front groups and think tanks." Or ask them why they erased all the comments concerned c...

See More

The search for David Koch continues, and we need your help! - Greenpeace USA Blog
members.greenpeace.org
content

🕐 Wed at 3:44pm · Comment · Like

🖒 ▇▇▇▇▇▇ and 64 others like this.

💬 View all 17 comments

Figure 5.16 Status Update from Greenpeace.

 Barack Obama 41% of adults under the age of 65 have accumulated medical debt, had difficulty paying medical bills, or struggled with both during a recent one year period.

 Health Reform by the Numbers: 41
origin.barackobama.com
The White House is highlighting a new fact or figure each day to make the case for why we need to pass health reform now. Spread the word—share this post with your family, friends and online networks.

🕐 March 12 at 11:53am · Comment · Like · View Feedback (11,677)

Figure 5.17 Status Update from Barack Obama.

through individuals already supportive of the health care bill *and those supporters' own personal networks* the team hoped to reach a large and supportive constituency. This is essentially an update of the "one-step flow" that some scholars see emerging in the digital media environment.[20] Yes, here Obama is reaching supporters directly, without the mediation of journalistic media—but he is doing so less by targeting atomized and algorithmically selected individuals than by calling upon information exchange among personal networks.

Two further activities within the network-expressive category asked individuals to contribute multimedia or other content to an organization's Page or website. Exploring the high percentage of government/party posts dedicated to this kind of activity, it is notable that the US EPA was responsible for 6 of the instances recorded for that site category. And exploring that organization's status updates reveals a series of three video contests called "Faces of Grassroots Environmental Justice," "Burn Wise," and "It's My Environment," each of which was promoted by two of the status updates collected. A typical promotional status update, accompanied by a link to the contest's webpage, looked like Figure 5.18.[21]

A similar instance of an invitation to produce media from the government/party category was a one-off invitation from John McCain's Page (Figure 5.19) to create a video in support of the candidate.

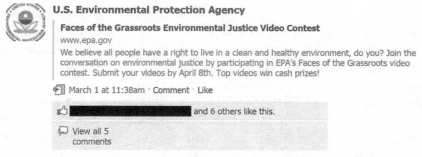

Figure 5.18 Status Update from the US Environmental Protection Agency.

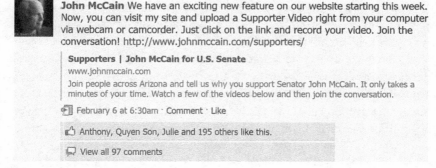

Figure 5.19 Status Update from John McCain.

Such cases highlight the "expressive" component of network-expressive activity. Not unlike the actualizing mode of interaction, in these cases organizations encourage supporters to present their own meanings of issues, positions, or organizations. Those expressions, in turn, are to be presented—subject, undoubtedly, to moderation or editing—in networked public spaces maintained by the organizations themselves. They are thus further means by which organizations can inspire and collect supporters' identifications with the cause.

Organizations across the sample were embracing the possibilities of network-expressive action. Organizations of all four types found ways—often creative ways—to encourage supporters to enact their membership or support through posting, joining, sharing, and media creation—the essence of network-expressive action. In the terms of the actualizing civic information style described since Chapter 2, these features of online action complement well the practices of digital culture, as inscribed in web platforms like Facebook. And as we will discuss further, these kinds of opportunities suggest themselves as possible entry points into civic engagement for many young actualizing citizens.

Links Embedded in Status Updates

Our first two measures of actualizing patterns of communication in organizations' Facebook presences have thus yielded results that are not entirely complementary: on the one hand, most organizations did not substantially embrace interactive patterns in their day-to-day status messages. Most continued to be primarily unidirectional and lacked invitations to supporters to comment, respond, or add their own meanings. On the other, we have seen the expansion of a form of action—network-expressive activities—that we have conceptualized as aligned with the actualizing style. We will do our best to reconcile this inconsistency in future pages.

But for the moment, it is worth noting that the Facebook context invites a further form of analysis of civic information style. Its networked nature, and in particular its many connections to the wider Internet, suggest that we might expand upon the notion of information bricolage discussed in Chapter 2 to investigate how organizations position their communications in the broader media environment. Facebook status updates can—and as we shall see, usually do—carry links to any web destination, either within the status update text or with Facebook's link function, that presents the link below the status update with an icon and preview of the link's destination. Organizations can thus use status update links to highlight something happening somewhere within its own Page, its webpage outside of Facebook, or to note an occurrence reported by a news organization, or a video posted to YouTube, or any other form of online content. And the combination of status update and link means that the organization can use the status update to comment on the link, point to it as a site for information or action, post something unrelated, or post the link with no commentary.

As has been discussed throughout this book, these possibilities position organizations as a new variety of communicative actor. No longer are organizations necessarily peripheral to mainstream news processes, dependent on mainstream news processes to carry their messages to mass publics, and relegated to providing context and meaning of news to narrow constituencies. In the networked media environment, organizations can provide to supporters a full range of information about a particular topic or concern—potentially commenting on it, contextualizing it, and generally serving as information mediators in the way they did early in the twentieth century.[22] The interesting question is how organizations use this newfound capacity.

Our earlier theoretical discussions suggest that many organizations may have a tendency to use links to point to their own content: after all, they want users to continually visit their Facebook Page and website to participate. For example, many organizations link to locations on their site in which they are posting news about the organization or issues of interest. Or they link to videos produced by members, or ask supporters to make contributions. Such behavior is understandable, but it also does not help supporters to develop a rich network of action locations and opportunities; it treats supporters like members whose primary orientation is toward being a member of the organization—the antithesis of the actualizing civic orientation as we have characterized it. Most importantly, because it runs counter to our discussion of actualizing citizens' preference for networked information sharing, we shall view it here as a dutiful style of providing information aligned with an earlier period of jealously guarding members' attention.

In contrast, some organizations may use status update links to point to webpages or Facebook resources that are not their own, to highlight an online action being taken by another group, or to point to news from another source that may be of interest to supporters. This is much more in line with an actualizing, networked style of providing civic information, in which supporters are not treated as members to be addressed with only organization-specific information, but as autonomous agents actively constructing their own networks of action and interested in information and action opportunities wherever they occur—not just through one organization. To the extent that organizations are embracing these possibilities, they might be seen as developing their potential as information portals—making themselves useful to members because of their ability to creatively and helpfully curate the world's information on a given topic of concern.

LINK ANALYSIS

The key measure called upon by the preceding discussion is a fairly simple one: do organizations' links direct to a destination clearly a part of or sponsored by that organization, or do they point to information not affiliated with it? To examine this question, we collected the links contained in the status updates discussed throughout this chapter.[23] We then investigated each link and made two determinations. The first was whether the link was an *internal* one, meaning that it directed to the organization's website, Facebook page, affiliate organization, or news article specifically about the organization; or an *external* one, meaning that it directed to some other web location that was not in any way visibly affiliated with the organization. Then, to further develop our understanding of the information resources called upon by the use of external links, we also categorized the sites to which such links directed—distinguishing links to other Pages within Facebook, the website of a government agency, of another civic organization, or of a news organization.[24]

INTERNAL AND EXTERNAL LINKS

Links were present on a striking 90% of the 1,844 total status updates, meaning that 1,622 links were available for coding. This demonstrated that organizations were consistently using links to direct fans to content beyond the status update itself—to connect their Facebook communications with the broader web. Across the site categories, community organizations used links slightly less often, doing so in 74% of posts, as opposed to over 90% for each of the other organizational categories.

As Figure 5.20 demonstrates, across the sample, internal links were the dominant variety. Eighty-four percent of links were internal, meaning only 16% directed supporters to content beyond the organization itself. This meant that the vast majority of the time, when an organization used a link, it was using it to direct to information about itself.

The figure also makes clear modest but noteworthy differences between organizational types. Online only organizations were relatively more prone to posting external links, doing so with 20.3% of links. This is set next to somewhat comparable rates of 18.2% and 15.9% among interest and community organizations, respectively, and a tiny 6.7% among government/party organizations. In terms of the dutiful-actualizing nature of the communicative relationships being fostered by these organizations' communications, the story here runs very much parallel to the patterns we observed when considering mode of interaction: online only organizations are demonstrating their (relatively greater) willingness to break open their particular communication sphere, and expose their supporters to a wider range of informational resources. Most of the offline organizations, by contrast, and most of all the government/party

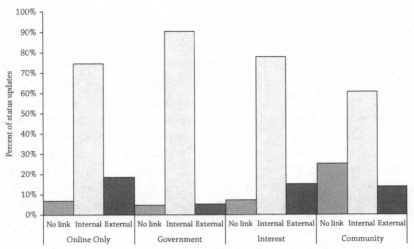

Figure 5.20 Status Updates Containing No Link, an Internal Link, or an External Link, By Category of Organization.

groups, kept their communications directed largely to information that they themselves had created and controlled.

There are three prominent explanations we should consider in understanding this finding. First, the high rate of internal linking demonstrates a high degree of what we could call *networking narcissism*, a tendency to privilege one's own content, and the message that one wants to promote, over others—and especially, in this context, to infuse supporters' news feeds with as much organizational content as possible. In these terms, organizations communicating through Facebook are simply using all the bandwidth available to them to communicate their own, honed messages: if an audience's attention is already attenuated by hundreds of posts and general communicative clutter, why spend one's brief time in front of a supporter sharing another's message? Second, it suggests a further reflection of the emphasis on message control that we have discussed in some detail in the context of the dutiful mode of interaction. An external link is a door into another set of information experiences: it means the possible loss of a supporter's attention, as well as an abdication of responsibility over what a young supporter might do once released into the wilds of the web. In this connection, the fact that it was government/party Facebook Pages that were most reticent to point supporters to other web locations is a resounding echo of Stephen Coleman's observations that government web projects tend to be intensely concerned about not only the experiences, but also the *safety*, of youth who visit them.[25]

Third is the problem of information quality and reliability. To the extent that an organization's reputation rests on its communication of information that is not reliable, we can expect groups to be less willing to share other groups' content that they have not had the chance to verify. From this perspective, we might interpret the finding as suggesting that organizations understand links to other groups' content to be endorsements of that content's validity.

These explanations bolster our understanding of the linking patterns as essentially representations of dutiful modes of communication on the part of organizations. And we must not lose sight of the potential cost of this insistence of self-referential information networking. This, we might contend, is the possibility of a rich, varied, *curated* information experience provided by some of the web's most successful services. As we argued in Chapter 2, understanding an organization in communicative terms means recognizing it as a networked actor that can share not only its own information, but also point supporters to other sorts of information of interest—and in the process, help supporters to make sense of the civic-political world and their place in it. To illustrate this possibility, let consider some of the cases in which external links *were* used, and what they were used for.

Figure 5.21 offers a breakdown of this form of link use aggregated across all organizations in the sample. Though there was some minor variation between what sorts of external resources different organizations pointed to, by and large the patterns of Figure 5.21 replicated across the site categories.

Clearly, news outlets played a prominent role in the information resources organizations pointed to—links to news sites constituted nearly half of all external links organizations posted. This fact confirms once again the great importance that news organizations continue to play in the information ecology, and points to the potential role of organizations as information curators piecing together (bricolage) an informational narrative of interest to a particular public out of a variety of news sources. A representative illustration comes from the College Republicans,

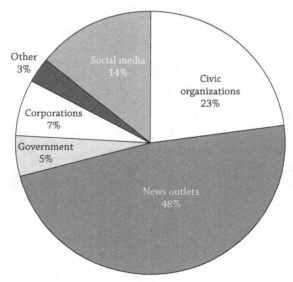

Figure 5.21 Destinations of External Links.

who posted a link to a story in the *Pittsburgh Tribune-Review* describing possible growth in conservatism among young citizens (Figure 5.22).

Such use of news sources both allows an organization to make the case of its importance or success to supporters while also exposing them to a wider set of ideas about the world than they would have from purely internal organizational communications. In the same vein, Girls Inc., an online only organization focused on the empowerment of young women, posted a series of updates concerning the place of women in business, sports and society (see Figures 5.23 and 5.24).

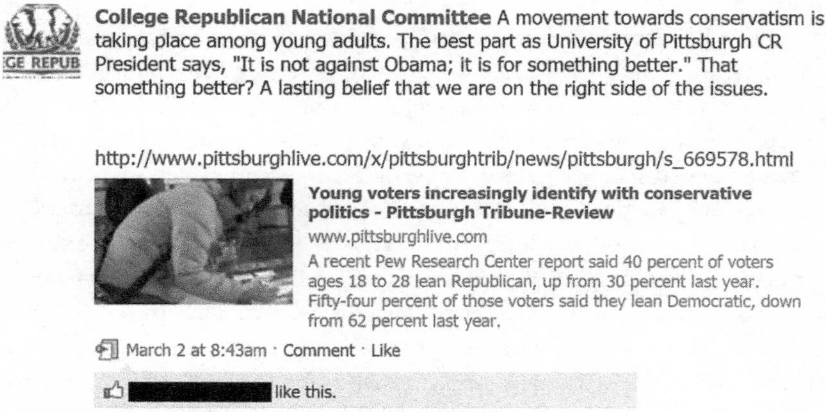

College Republican National Committee A movement towards conservatism is taking place among young adults. The best part as University of Pittsburgh CR President says, "It is not against Obama; it is for something better." That something better? A lasting belief that we are on the right side of the issues.

http://www.pittsburghlive.com/x/pittsburghtrib/news/pittsburgh/s_669578.html

Young voters increasingly identify with conservative politics - Pittsburgh Tribune-Review
www.pittsburghlive.com
A recent Pew Research Center report said 40 percent of voters ages 18 to 28 lean Republican, up from 30 percent last year. Fifty-four percent of those voters said they lean Democratic, down from 62 percent last year.

March 2 at 8:43am · Comment · Like

▉▉▉▉▉▉▉▉▉ like this.

Figure 5.22 Status Update from the College Republicans.

Girls Inc. Time magazine explores why women are not allowed to ski jump in the Winter Olympics: http://bit.ly/bqeMZY

Why Can't Women Ski Jump in the Olympics? - Winter Olympic Games - TIME
bit.ly
Lindsey Van holds the record among both men and women for the longest jump off of Whistler, B.C.'s normal ski jump, built for the 2010 Vancouver Olympics. The 25-year-old skier trains...

February 16 at 11:55am · Share

2 people like this.

Figure 5.23 Status Update from Girls Inc.

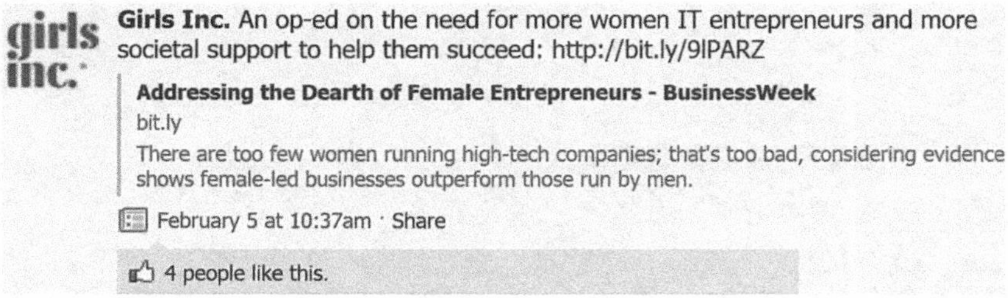

Girls Inc. An op-ed on the need for more women IT entrepreneurs and more societal support to help them succeed: http://bit.ly/9lPARZ

Addressing the Dearth of Female Entrepreneurs - BusinessWeek
bit.ly
There are too few women running high-tech companies; that's too bad, considering evidence shows female-led businesses outperform those run by men.

February 5 at 10:37am · Share

4 people like this.

Figure 5.24 Status Update from Girls Inc.

In addition to news organizations, posts of external links also pointed to other civic organizations doing important work, as well as a variety of sorts of multimedia and other content hosted on social media sites Facebook, Twitter, YouTube, and Flickr. Such links are notable for the fact that they represent a willingness on the part of organizations to share the attention of their supporters with other organizations. As competitive entities locked in what may be perceived as zero-sum game contests for supporters' attention, it is notable from a strategic standpoint that organizations would do this—and reflects a willingness to engage in practices not uncommon in the evolving networked information environment.

Another handful of links, not surprisingly, pointed to government-sponsored content, which took place in order to draw supporters' attention to government activities, such as livestreamed hearings on topics of interest. Such cases, not surprisingly, were dominated by interest organizations encouraging their supporters to learn about or observe governmental workings on issues under the organization's purview. And 7% of external links pointed to corporate content, a pattern that at first blush is somewhat puzzling. This type of linking was dominated by community organizations, which linked to corporations in 17% of external links. Looking into the pattern further, what we uncover is a series of partnerships in which community organizations stood to fundraise or otherwise benefit from attracting supporter attention to a corporate online space. 4H was particularly intent on urging supporters to visit Tractor Supply as part of a promotion (see Figure 5.25).

Similar status updates revealed a concerted pattern of corporate-civic partnerships in which promotions or competitions spurred organizations to point their supporters to companies offering some incentive. In another instance, the community organization LIFT apparently took part in Pepsi's Refresh Everything Project, in which supporters could vote for various charities on Pepsi's website, with the winning charities receiving grants (see Figure 5.26).

The major point here in this interesting mix of civic life, brand promotion, and consumer culture is the success with which companies appear to be

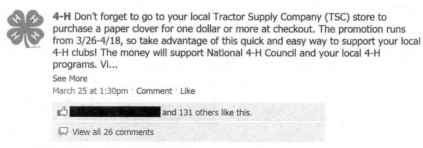

4-H Don't forget to go to your local Tractor Supply Company (TSC) store to purchase a paper clover for one dollar or more at checkout. The promotion runs from 3/26-4/18, so take advantage of this quick and easy way to support your local 4-H clubs! The money will support National 4-H Council and your local 4-H programs. Vi...
See More
March 25 at 1:30pm · Comment · Like

and 131 others like this.

View all 26 comments

Figure 5.25 Status Update from 4-H.

LIFT Final day for voting! You have a little over 7 hours left to vote for LIFT at http://www.refresheverything.com/LIFT. Please support LIFT and help us win $250,000 to pull families out of poverty!

Pull thousands of families out of poverty by training LIFT volunteers | Pepsi Refresh Everything
www.refresheverything.com
Vote for the most refreshing ideas to win Pepsi Refresh Project grants for Neighborhoods

📑 February 28 at 1:26pm · Comment · Like

Figure 5.26 Status Update from LIFT.

inserting themselves into civic organizations' networks. Pepsi's primary reason for setting up the grant-giving program in this way, in addition to generating good will, is to drive target markets to their website.

These examples of the use of external links point to the *possibility* of a rich and varied information experience provided by organizations to their supporters. Drawing on various external resources, organizations occasionally drew in the ideas, experiences, and media of many different types of content. Of course, what we saw more often was protectiveness of supporters' attention, and repeatedly drawing that attention back to various aspects of the organization's own work. Once again, therefore, the story here is of predominantly dutiful communication style across the civic web, with notable qualifications in some sectors. Most of the time, organizations are not using their links to expand the networked information gathering processes of supporters; nor are they demonstrating themselves to be omnivorous information consumers. In short, they are not by and large adopting a posture as an informational resource within the new information environment. Rather, in violation of what we have characterized as a norm of digital culture, most of the time organizations are resolutely linking to themselves—trying to drive their supporters, time and again, to resources elsewhere on their Facebook Page, to their website, or, occasionally, to news coverage of themselves.

From Websites to Social Media

We asked in Chapter 3 what difference the shift from communicating on websites to doing so on Facebook would make to the civic information styles presented by organizations. The findings of this chapter and the last offer the opportunity to consider this question. Two measures of actualizing communications were common between the two studies: mode of interaction (dutiful or actualizing knowledge and action) and types of activities (membership, management, or network-expressive).

With respect to the former, a formal, numerical comparison is difficult because the units of analysis between the two studies were so different: on websites, the units were entire webpages—substantial portions of sites that could contain sophisticated interactive features or databases; whereas on Facebook, units were status updates that invited discourse. Correspondingly, each website had only one to three pages with which to deliver participatory invitations, while most organizations in Facebook posted many more than three status updates.

But in the case of participatory invitations, we do not need sophisticated measures to derive the basic story: most organizations, on both their websites and in Facebook, did not often present their content in a way that invited comment and discussion from supporters. That is, most of their communications were dutiful when it came to the mode of interaction promoted. That this pattern would persist as strongly as it did in Facebook was something of a surprise, and may speak to the limits of the communicative context in influencing organizations' choices—or the resolute risks they feel to inviting supporter contribution. It was, after all, community organizations that *did* stand out in offering a steady stream of actualizing invitations for supporters to comment and respond—precisely the set of groups we anticipated would not feel the dampening effect of media politics as strongly as others. Nonetheless, this pattern of findings speaks to the general claim that the move to social networking spaces does not entail a wholesale shift in organizations' communication modes.

If shifts in organizations' offerings of actualizing interaction modes were not notable for most groups, the changes in what kinds of activities they offered were striking. Happily, the comparisons here are more straightforward: since multiple activities were coded on both webpages and Facebook status updates, we can compare percentages of activities that were of each of the three activity types. Table 5.4 offers those percentages by breaking down the activities of each organizational type that were membership, management, and network-expressive.

Table 5.4 **Percentage of Activities Each Type, By Category of Organization and Web Medium**

	Membership		Management		Network-expressive	
Medium →	Web	FB	Web	FB	Web	FB
Online Only	39.3	51.6	39.3	21.4	21.2	27.0
Government	47.2	33.9	30.6	24.5	22.2	41.6
Interest	59.5	43.9	28.6	22.4	11.9	33.8
Community	63.0	52.5	37.0	21.9	0.0	25.6

The story here could hardly be clearer. Except for online only organizations, each of the organizational categories dialed back their offerings of both membership and management activities in favor of network-expressive activities. For government/party organizations, the proportion of activities that were of that latter variety nearly doubled; for interest groups, they tripled; and community organizations, which had offered not a single version of a networked activity on their websites, did so with one out of four activities on Facebook. Thus, whereas in terms of the mode of interaction organizations promote, the move to Facebook yielded little evidence of change in organizational communications. But when it came to what they asked supporters to do, the change was impressive.

Organizational Communications in Social Media

A certain degree of controversy surrounded discourses over the rise of social media in the 2004 to 2008 period.[26] Whereas some saw in the development of new networking platforms such as Friendster, MySpace, and Facebook a paradigm shift in the nature of web communication, others—including some of the web's own creators—felt that possibilities and norms of sharing and interactivity had been written into the deeper structure of the web.[27] The analyses of this chapter located us in the heyday of Web 2.0 excitement, enabling an examination of possible changes in organizations' communications as they entered what by 2010 was becoming the archetypal social networking site, at least in the United States. Entering that space, to what degree would organizations adapt to and embrace the information sharing and participatory norms of the social networking world, and to what degree would they continue to hew to modern conventions of civic communication?

The three varieties of analysis presented above do not all point in the same direction, but may in fact tell a coherent story about the future of the organization–citizen relationship as constituted through networked digital communication. When it came to the mode of interaction invited by organizations in their status updates, most organizations stuck to very dutiful patterns of providing information and knowledge as though to citizens just waiting to be informed and mobilized. Overall rates of actualizing knowledge were quite low and actualizing action very low. Although it is difficult to define exactly what constitutes a high rate of actualizing content, at least in the case of government/party and interest organizations, which offered it in tiny portions of status updates, we can safely say they did so very little. For their part, online only organizations replicated their relatively greater offerings, at least in comparison to interest and government/party organizations, but if anything underperformed their website rates. But the most prolific site category was the community set of organizations, surprising us with their nearly regular offerings of actualizing knowledge and action.

Our analysis of the informational resources organizations drew on in their posts—via our link analysis—tells a similarly dutiful story. Across the site categories, the posting of links to content beyond an organization's own sphere of influence was limited. Thus an attentive fan of an average interest organization's Facebook page—one of the stronger posters of external links—sees about nine posts per week from that organization. Nearly all of those posts are accompanied by links, offering a potentially rich source of information about whatever topic the organization concerns itself with. But only one, or on a good week two, of those links directs the user to information about anything besides the organization itself. In the terms of networked information sharing that we characterized as a hallmark of the actualizing civic information style, this suggests a squandering of communicative potential: the opportunity to share with interested fans further information about an issue, to add context, or learn about what is happening with the issue on a broader scale—such as how current legislation affects the issue.[28] Instead, in the vast majority of cases, what we saw was the incredible potential of information sharing on Facebook reduced to links to other Facebook content by the same organization, or—even more often—links to the organization's website, which a given Facebook user would have been perfectly capable of doing on their own. Thus, rather than the beneficiary of being connected a node rich with a diverse menu of content about the issue of concern, the fan just described effectively receives a newsletter from the organization about its activities—*every day*. If we compare such organizations to people in a given person's network, they fail miserably: most would consider a friend who post only content about themselves 90% of the time quite dull.

On these two measures, then, we detected a deep reticence on the part of organizations to allow their supporters to be even the least bit distracted by information beyond the organization, its work, and what the supporter might do in support. The effort to control message, to maintain the attention of supporters as much as possible, and to avoid the dangers lurking amid media politics clearly continue to be very strong influences. Organizations seem to see themselves as addressing committed members and partisans—hardly the kinds of networked citizens and semimembers who might be intrigued by interesting information and connections posted by daring and enterprising organizational types. They continue to present themselves as organizations to which members should be absolutely devoted—not as nodes in the networks of complex, multifaceted citizens now accustomed to managing and sifting diverse information networks.

THE TRANSFORMATION OF ACTION

The story is different, and potentially much more interesting, when we look to our measure of activity recommendations. The array of activities organizations recommended to supporters expanded greatly beyond what was present in their websites, and moved decidedly toward encouraging supporters to employ personal networks and self-expression to both enhance individuals' engaged with the organization and promote the organization's message.

This is a notable shift in the structure of action opportunities being presented to supporters. While the dominant message of organizations' websites was that the best way to get involved with the organization was to join offline groups and activities—or give money—within Facebook a new array of web-based ways to take action through communication and self-expression took hold. As noted in Chapter 2, there is reason to believe that these types of activities fit relatively better with young citizens' actualizing information preferences than either membership activities, rooted as they are in an earlier social era of strong geographically based social commitments and identities, or management ones, which presuppose a highly dutiful role for supporters. And as we shall discuss further in Chapter 6, there are ways of imagining how these kinds of activities could become entry points into other kinds of political engagement.

The story that emerges from this set of findings is that a shift is taking place in many organizations' understandings of who their supporters are and what they are capable of. Many are indeed calling upon supporters to engage in a set of information sharing and self-identification practices that implies a changing understanding of what communicatively connected supporters are and what role they play in an organization's work. At the same time, most groups do appear deeply hesitant to engage in what may be a higher bar for actualizing communication: genuinely engaging with a public and asking it to actively participate in constructing the meaning—perhaps even direction?—of an organization's work. In the Facebook context, we found this pressure to be especially prohibitive for organization's working in the formal political sphere, where untoward supporter contributions might be especially feared. Such a combination implies a sort of "thin digital citizenship," in which digital citizens' inclinations are indeed appealed to—particularly through encouragements to take on the task of spreading the word—but in which the real nature of the organization's communications are hardly postinstitutional.

6

Conclusion

Communicating Civic Life to Digital Citizens

Young citizens of the early twenty-first century have a great deal going for them. In the industrialized world at least, most young citizens simply have not known material deprivation; on the contrary, they have enjoyed standards of living unprecedented on the planet. Unlike their grandparents and great-grandparents, personal involvement in catastrophic war is a remote possibility, not a nearby certainty. Similarly, medical advances in treating and eradicating diseases mean that young people are nearly free from a host of scourges that in living memory crippled millions of youth. We don't often pause to recognize these wages of living in late modern society, especially in times of ongoing economic crisis—but in the scope of civic and democratic history, they are quite recent occurrences with great consequences for how young people relate to public life.[1]

Contemporary young people also enjoy some of the highest levels of education in all of history. They are the most tolerant of difference, especially in terms of race, religious identity, and sexual identity.[2] And despite continuing problems of crime and violence, many Western societies have recently enjoyed a decline in violent crime—a trend almost unimaginable only two decades ago, in the throes of the so-called crack epidemic that decimated (especially American) urban life. Instead, cities from New York to San Francisco to London to Berlin have revitalized themselves, inspiring a generation of young adults to forgo the once-attractive security of suburbs for the interest and diversity of urban environments.[3] Given these very genuine advantages, it should be heartening and inspiring that many young people are demanding active, participatory opportunities for engagement in many aspects of life, including the civic.[4]

This is not to say that the lives of contemporary young people will be untroubled. As a generation, they face a host of challenges that are in some ways the byproducts of a prolific twentieth century that has run out of steam. One the economic front, the globalizing postindustrial economy and postmodern financial system have dissolved the employment base and social safety net of many working people. One result is a social order in which differences of economic class are hardening: the political scientist Robert Putnam has described recent visits to his own hometown of Port Clinton, Ohio, and the social chasm that now separates the descendants of his own high school class. The children of students who, like him, followed (often local civic organizations') scholarships to college and the middle and upper-middle classes now reliably send their own children to elite schools. But the children of other peers who followed what at the time was a reasonable alternative—well-paid blue collar work in local factories—now find themselves trapped in a decaying rust belt city with an eviscerated civic infrastructure, scarce employment prospects and crippling social problems.[5] Infamously—for believers in the classic American dream—it is becoming widely known that the United States is no longer the land of opportunity, at least in terms of one's ability to transcend social class by hard work and education.[6] A deep inequality, with its accompanying ills, is setting in, an unwinding of the progress of twentieth century. Alongside inequalities of economic power are racial injustices and antagonisms that remain unresolved fifty years after the Civil Rights movement's greatest victories. And few prospects for amelioration are in sight.[7]

Another byproduct of the industrial age, climate change, is only beginning to make itself felt, but will bedevil global politics as the young generation comes of age. Increasingly erratic weather patterns will disrupt food supplies, markets, and landscapes around the world. Global instability driven by resource competition will exacerbate existing conflicts and create news ones. While a few industrialized countries innovate with technology and policy, the biggest contributors to the problem remain intransigent due to so-far insurmountable internal political dynamics. Future efforts to address the problem will be expensive, highly contentious, and possibly too late.

Perhaps worst of all, the very processes needed to right course on these and a host of other pressing problems are in states of severe disrepair: political systems across the Western world are showing signs of strain, with some reduced to positive dysfunction. In the United States, a period of seemingly endless polarization and partisan gridlock has set in, and now lends its hue to nearly every issue the government tries to address.[8] Public opinion research is revealing irreconcilable differences not simply in normative beliefs about how to apply values to public policy, but increasingly in the basic facts of the world.[9] In Europe, questions about the viability of a common economy and monetary system are being raised as the German economic engine chugs ahead, but other countries are trying to dig out from externally enforced austerity without the flexibility—or political will—to make necessary changes. The turmoil caused by the collapse of the Iraqi state in 2014 has also made clear the failure of many European states to provide satisfying opportunities to large populations of children of immigrants from the Middle East and North Africa, as hundreds of disaffected young citizens have traveled to Iraq and Syria to oppose the very form of society in which they were raised.[10]

It is clear that the generation of people who are now young will need great collective will to address problems of this magnitude. But as of now it is unclear whence that collective will will come. Many young people show, in creative, passionate, and committed ways, their willingness to engage with issues beyond themselves. But for many, improving the world around them does not intuitively have much to do with the practice of politics: a shift from political styles of engagement to more civic ones, involving personalized, highly flexible activities such as volunteering and the practice of lifestyle concerns, signals a lack of inclination to understand social problems in political, maybe even collective, terms.[11]

Another set of young people clearly have conceptualized the world's problems in those terms. We saw in this book's opening chapter how much youth civic energy is being devoted to demonstrations, protests, and other resistance that demand change. But these movements have offered few concrete demands, and generated little political pressure for making them reality.[12] Resistance to engaging issues through conventionally political channels has stymied most of their efforts, and many of those emergent in 2011 are fading from the scene or have been lost in larger political struggles over which they have little influence. Even more troubling, in some cases bursts of protest activity have actually served to undermine slower-moving but meaningful democratic reform. A case in point was the short tenure of Paul Schell as mayor of Seattle. An ardent champion of devolving city authority and funding to neighborhood councils—now seen by many as a triumph of participatory governance—his missteps in directing the police response to the public unrest of the 1999 WTO protests cost him his office after only one term. His successor, Greg Nickels, was much less supportive of local governance and undid much of the work.[13]

Meanwhile, the social form that has historically channeled movement energy into coherent political leverage, the civic organization, has lost much of its credibility and appeal among young people. In addition to larger social-structural transformations that make group-based associations less relevant to the lives of young people, many young activists have explicitly rejected opportunities to join or form more bounded, official groups—to trade any degree of autonomy for the efficiencies and increased potency of bureaucratized associations. Thus, though traditional civic organizations continue to function, much of their young supporter base has deserted them.

But something new is afoot. As digitally networked media have developed, and norms of interaction in online spaces evolved, we have seen the possibility for a reformulation of associational relationships. These have included the emergence of novel forms of organizing (and nonorganizing), but also potential new dynamics with established groups. Civic organizations now find themselves inhabiting a communication environment in which they may reach out to young individuals directly—and those young people can reach back—in a multidirectional communication experience. This relationship is potentially fraught: as we have seen, it exists within a political culture that both demands institutional openness to user contributions, but also punishes ruthlessly for communicative missteps. This is new, and something that associations of all kinds are grappling to comprehend and master.

It is precisely this complex, tendentious, but above all important relationship between civic organizations and young citizens that we have interrogated in this book. In this concluding chapter, we shall place the book's perspective, findings, and contributions into the larger context of the conversations to which it speaks. First, we consider the consequences of thinking about the relationship between organizations and citizens in communicative terms, and what that has helped us to see about dynamics of civic information and engagement in the current time. Especially, it has helped us to specify the terms of a *disconnect in civic information styles*, as many organizations continue to communicate in a mode built on the habits and concerns of the last century, despite young citizens' demands for other forms.

But pervasive though it is, that disconnect is not evenly distributed: it is concentrated, perhaps distressingly, among those organizations with the most formal, direct connections to the politics of policymaking. In contrast, civic organizations without formal political ties sometimes appeared more willing to open their communication to user contributions—as we demonstrated in the enhanced offerings of actualizing communications by community organizations in Facebook. A further contrast was revealed between organizations with their feet firmly planted in the offline world and those created more recently, and primarily online: those online only organizations also stood out for relatively more actualizing communication style on both websites and in Facebook. This finding adds a further dimension to previous claims that we are witnessing the *emergence of new kinds of organizations*,[14] and we were able to detail more specifically the nature of the communicative relationships on which membership is based.

There is also an important qualification to the largely dutiful information experiences designed by organizations. With *the rise of network-expressive activity*, we saw a shift underway in how organizations view their young members: from individual satellites connected to the central node of the organization to active nodes in themselves managing significant information networks within a much broader communicative sphere. Notably, the emergence of network-expressive activity was not nearly as restricted to nonpolitical, or online only groups, raising questions as to how the organization–citizen relationship is evolving. In particular, it draws us to more closely consider how contemporary organizations can manage the divide between audiences' demands for autonomy in action and bureaucratic needs for sustained commitment to political process, how dynamics of supporter commitment to organizations may play out when relationships are largely mediated by digital media, and the "participation paradigm" currently at full strength in our society and scholarship.[15]

An Organizational Perspective on Civic Communication Through Digital Media

Existing treatments of late modern civic disengagement can be roughly sorted into two major bodies of insight. One has emphasized the place of the individual citizen in later modern social and civic life and his or her inclinations to become involved with civic and political causes. This work has often found its way to a focus on young people because they have stood out as among the less engaged, and has made great progress in theorizing why young people behave as they do and how changing civic identities and notions of citizenship affect decisions about engaging with politics.[16] The other has examined organizational dynamics and the implications of changing media opportunities and risks for them. Again, we have an array of exciting insights being created there, as research documents the transformations in collective action taking place as new media has diminished the cost of many-to-many networked communications.[17]

Up to this point, however, these two important and voluminous literatures have rarely met in conversation, leaving unanswered crucial questions concerning the possibilities of youth civic engagement in the digital age. What do the cultural shifts described by scholars of changing youth engagement patterns have to do with emergent organizing forms? What do "typical" citizen activists make of the new forms of engagement? What sorts of relationships do they engender with their supporters, how do those relationships compare to those of the past, and what are the participatory consequences of those relationships?[18] Joining the insights of these two bodies of work has the potential to yield great insights: the aim of this book, by placing its focus on how organizations communicate engagement to young people with late modern, digital culture-informed sensibilities, has been to do just that.

The conceptual work necessary to do so was accomplished by recalling the foundational place of organizations in American civic life, as well as the historic—and potentially future—capacity of organizations to provide informational resources to supporters. This led to focusing our analysis on the question of *civic information*, and how its meaning, and the roles it assigns to key players in a sociopolitical context, have changed, with great implications for networked citizens and organizations. Specifically, what we saw in Chapter 1 was that the high modern paradigm of civic information—as a discrete, authoritatively produced set of messages called "news" to be used on a regular basis by citizens preparing themselves for future engagement opportunities—is breaking apart. Citizens have lost a great deal of faith in previously unassailable news figures, most have lost the habitual consumption of key news formats, and many have turned a great deal of their media consumption in directions that now keep them removed from news. For their part, news organizations are struggling to find funding bases in a world without classified advertising, questionable advertising revenue models, and unlimited choice on the part of their consumers. Some have softened, attempting to steal back audience members who might accept a more palatable take on daily affairs, though this has hardly cured the malady, and for many serious consumers of news has probably exacerbated it.[19]

The breakdown of high modern civic information, in combination with the digital transformations that are a part of its downfall, opens the doors to new actors, and new roles, in how society informs itself. We have been particularly interested in exploring the possibilities that civic organizations might begin to play an increasingly important role in providing civic information to young citizens. What the networked digital media environment provides is the possibility for any actor—no matter how small or resource-constrained—to reach supporters at any time and place without mediation by news-making logics outside their control. Intriguingly, what we saw in Chapter 3 is that such a role of civic organizations is in some ways a return to a time in which organization played a dominant role in providing civic information and knowledge to the citizenry.

The combination of an enhanced role for civic organizations in providing civic information, the possibilities of multidirectional communication enabled by digitally networked technology, and norms of information exchange emergent in digital culture led us to conceptualize the *communicative relationship* between young people and civic organizations as a productive location for exploring the new dynamics. In doing so, we learned in Chapter 2 that many young citizens of the digital era are disattaching from the civic information norms held by their parents and grandparents—and the major institutions of civic life. In place of those norms are a set of practices and inclinations informed by both shifting civic identities and the culture written into digital media. These emerging preferences, which we termed an *actualizing* style, include exchange and peer learning in the information experience, networked sharing of content, and view of communication as inherently powerful. Where might young people find the kinds of civic information experiences in these terms?

For their part, political organizations and their communications are also profoundly changing in adaptation to digital media, which has been treated in some detail from the perspectives of organizational structure and strategy. But reconsidering organization–citizen interactions in communicative terms offered a window on how organizations have managed and encouraged their memberships over time, and how constraints originating in institutional history and habit, as well as the political communication environment, complicate those efforts. Many civic organizations have quite clear reasons for resisting precisely the actualizing relationships young people may desire—and instead continuing to communicate in a *dutiful* form that places citizens in a restricted, circumscribed role within the organization's work and communications.

There is reason to believe, therefore, that the recent legacy of the organization-young citizen relationship is troubled, leading us to some skepticism about the likelihood that young citizens and civic groups would meet productively over digital media—at least in the near term.

The Disconnect

Examining directly the communications of a large sample of organizations enabled us to document this disconnect. As Chapters 4 and 5 showed, most civic organizations, most of the time, frame their communications as though targeting dutiful citizens eager to be informed about the organization's work and execute a specific action—most often, writing a check. Organizations did not often use their spaces of online communication to foster interaction or collaborative knowledge building:[20] rather than inviting information and action suggestions from supporters, they dictated official and strategic organizational statements. Uses of links (in Chapter 5's analysis) directed predominantly to organizational content, a pattern that suggests the siloing of young supporters' attention within the organization's sphere of influence, rather than using online presences to expose youth to a wealth of online content. And, at least when it came to website communications, organizations' action requests were by and large encouragements to meet the organization in offline spaces or donate money. (We discuss the notable rise in networked-expressive activity documented in Chapter 5 below.) The possibility that a young supporter might engage in interactive, expressive, and constructive acts through public online communications was not often on offer.

At the same time, organizations were not equally duty-driven in their communications. As anticipated, recently created groups whose work takes place predominantly online (online only organizations) stood out considerably from their counterparts in offering more opportunities to share information on their sites. And, at least when it came to their Facebook communications, brick-and-mortar civic organizations without formal ties to politics (community organizations) produced a relatively large number of participatory invitations—even more than online only groups in that medium. These patterns supported our proposition that less overtly political organizations might more willingly offer actualizing communications than more political ones, and presented the greatest evidence in the direction of our hypothesis that the move from websites to Facebook would result in generally more actualizing communication.

Let us consider the implications of these findings for our understanding of the future of digitally enabled engagement. We begin with the relative performances of formally political organizations and their nonformally political counterparts, before turning to the rise of a new, online only category of organization.

THE PROBLEM OF POLITICS

The great surprise in the shift from websites to Facebook was the performance of community organizations, and specifically their embrace of participatory opportunities on the social networking site. That finding was in line with our expectations of the effect of Facebook, and will be discussed below. But first, let us take note of what we did not see: unlike community organizations, the more overtly political organizations—government/party and interest ones—showed little adaptation to actualizing communication, even in the social media context where we most expected it.

These findings comport in broad brushstrokes with other research on the communicative offerings of political figures online. As far back as the 1998 American midterm elections, scholars have described the often limited experience offered to citizens via online communications. Kirsten Foot and Steven Schneider early on termed this variety of communications "brochure-ware," indicating the most strategic, directed, and reductionist use of the web.[21]

Clearly, web campaigning has come a long way since 2000.[22] Yet as we saw in our analysis of Barack Obama's 2008 website in Chapter 4, increasing web sophistication and the incorporation of new tools has not overturned the underlying dynamic, which is that strategic campaigns create content and online experiences and consumers consume them. Indeed, the case that we made was that as much as anything else, Obama created a successful brand of exchange and interactivity, but that the structure of his communications carefully sequestered them in a safe, internally networked portion of the site.[23] Other recent studies have come to similar conclusions. For example, in a study of the British General Election of 2010, Todd Graham and colleagues explored the practices of politicians on Twitter. They found that candidates' consultations with voters were quite rare, and instead that candidates typically employed a "broadcasting" strategy, using Twitter to send messages about what the campaign was doing, and responding to events in the campaign, rather than soliciting comments from supporters.[24]

What underlies campaigns' deep resistance to actualizing communication? One factor is that when it comes to the large institutions of politics, we seem to still be looking at a politics of management.[25] As we described it (in Chapter 3), in communicative terms the politics of management is about simultaneous concern with maintaining strict message discipline and strategy, and the danger associated with allowing an institution's name to be associated with potentially volatile supporter contributions, which we termed *communicative risk aversion.* Message discipline is a logical and necessary response to the opportunities presented by the political-media structure: organizations seem willing to minimize the role of participants in exchange for a focus on developing power within the capitol, and that focus seems to have been expressed in a dearth of participatory invitations through both websites and Facebook. As for communicative risk aversion, in the world of media politics, organizations and campaigns became very adept at insulating themselves from potentially damaging messages. They learned to highly prize their brands and protect them at all costs—above all, from scandals and prying journalists.[26] These instincts directly contradict the participatory impulse: they urge organizations to maintain strict control of message and carefully craft it to the appropriate audiences.

What potential is there for progress in this area? There is considerable debate occurring about whether the public's tolerance for embarrassing information might increase as information about the lives of individuals, public figures and organizations is increasingly available;[27] it is conceivable that the fear of losing control of organizational and corporate brands may also weaken under those conditions, but such shifts are still beyond the horizon. Instead, any change that comes in this area is likely to come as organizations recalculate the relative costs and benefits of opening themselves to increased participation. We also should be aware that organizations—along with corporations—are likely to become increasingly adept at aping participatory opportunities while remaining resolutely in control of message.

Another observation on this trend is the fact that government institutions themselves are deeply rooted in an institutional framework. That institutional-ness naturally means that organizations that work with the formal structures of government must tie themselves more to specific modes of operating than organizations not trying to accomplish formal political goals. That limited flexibility of governmental institutions is a challenge to fundamental change in how civic organizations operate.[28] Will it change, and can it be changed? A considerable line of research is now investigating how governmental processes might be made more amenable to citizen input;[29] it would be interesting to explore how such changes in governmental process will give way to new forms of organizing aimed at influencing politics through those processes.

A third factor we must bear in mind is the simple force of institutional habit. The large campaign organizations may be the most rooted in a dutiful model of citizenship as a product of institutional history and the instincts of older officials. This element of the trend is likely to weaken as younger individuals more comfortable with the norms of digital media rise within even the most dutiful organizations.

Whatever the underlying cause of the result, the implications for youth engagement in politics are concerning. From this book's opening chapter, we have made the case for the historic and continuing importance of civic organizations in shaping, developing, and promoting citizen involvement in politics and their interactions with civic information. To the extent that existing organizations are unable or unwilling to forge communicative relationships that young citizens find appealing, their potential to energize youth participation—through digital or any other media—may be limited.

The Rise of Online Organizing Forms

Alongside differences between more and less formally political organizations, organizations created recently, and operating entirely online, stood out from those that exist primarily in brick-and-mortar form. That online only organizations tended to be more willing to offer supporters more actualizing forms of information fit with the theory discussed in Chapter 3: and by and large, it was indeed online only organizations that led the field in inviting supporters to contribute information and action ideas, in sharing information from a diverse array of sources (in the Facebook study), and promoting networked-expressive activities. What does our confirmation of that hypothesis tell us about the nature and future of political organizations online?

For one thing, it supports and adds weight to claims that we are witnessing an era of "organizational fecundity," the creation of a host of new kinds of organizations, by showing that one reason that such organizations are likely to attract increasing support is that they can offer communication experiences relatively more in line with many young people's preferences.[30] Through them, young people will have increasing opportunity to engage as more online only organizations develop and further experiment with actualizing citizen-organization relationships. We can thus anticipate many more experiments with different ways of organizing citizens emerging online, and different ways of delivering entrepreneurial engagement opportunities.

All of this is fine, but it does not answer a further question. The very position of online only organizations—as organizations recently created, with little heritage on the political scene—means that their influence in political matters is already limited. And the most serious challenge facing these new experiments may be how to both offer actualizing information experiences that appeal to young supporters, and convert many autonomous contributions into a politically significant force. Although organizations seem to be moving toward postbureaucratic forms, the institutions of government remain—and are sure to remain—resolutely bureaucratic. The question for new organizations is clearly finding a balance, or innovative approach, to both preserving individuals' autonomous opportunities and combining those contributions into a meaningful and politically significant whole. David Karpf, in his explication of the success and enduring influence of MoveOn's style of mobilizing millions of supporters, is acutely aware of just this problem:

> MoveOn will never sit down across the table from management to negotiate a new collective bargaining agreement. Democracy for America has no policy experts or research scientists on staff. DailyKos isn't going to employ a field staffer or lobbyist in every state capital . . . Some valuable functions require substantial overhead cost, regardless of the changing information landscape. A few of these tasks have migrated, covered by "phantom staff" or netroots infrastructure organizations. Others, however, represent a troubling net loss for American political associations and the interests they represent.[31]

In this way, the communicative dynamics of online only organizations position them as a variant of precisely the networked social movements that opened this book. That is, their raison d'etre is as much about creating spaces in which young citizens can self-actualize and express as about creating a forum for significant political change. As Daniel Kreiss and Zeynep Tufekci observe about late modern social movements including Occupy, the personalization of politics and the increasingly dominant role of personal identity expression (as opposed to facilitation of instrumental action) have seriously complicated the process of organizing, because "the legitimacy of movement organizational forms is entwined with their realization of personal expression."[32] Rather than active participants willing to have their participation subsumed, to some degree, into the necessities of the action—which arguably is the truer story of the success of Obama in 2008[33]—such associations are instead hampered by supporters unwilling or unable to detach the internal functioning of the association from the realities of the political world that they seek to affect.

This is "the tension between self-expression and strategic institutional action" perhaps more acute than at previous moments in history;[34] in some ways, it is a defining problem of our civic era, which our focus on the intersection of changing civic information preferences and organizational communication has brought into sharp relief. Is communicative autonomy compatible with bureaucratic civic participation—that is, with modern democracy as we know it?

The answer of the anarchism-tinged ideologies of Occupy would hold that it is not—this is precisely their radical critique.[35] But developing scholarship is uncovering other, sometimes surprising, possibilities.

Bridging the Gap Between Autonomous Contribution and Bureaucratic Effectiveness

One approach to contemplating the possible combination of autonomous action and organizational effectiveness has come from the logical intuition to look to the past: the fact that earlier eras successfully blended the two has led scholars to ask what organizational resources were available that might be recreated. In this book's discussion (mainly in Chapter 3), two organizational features stand out: the interpersonal nature of interaction in earlier organizations, and associations' federated structure.

For Robert Putnam, what is essential to citizen investment, trust, and political engagement is interpersonal interaction in the context of group processes. From that starting point, he has expressed skepticism that digitally mediated communication can be a substitute for interpersonally produced social capital. As a result, he argues passionately for a return to the sort of face-to-face associations that was the center of social capital development up to the mid-twentieth century. These he sees as essential to the development of the aspects of social capital that are most important—the skills of communicating oneself to others and organizing a (small-scale) collective action, norms of pluralism, tolerance and deliberation, trust, and reciprocity.[36]

And we should not discount the likelihood that regular interpersonal interactions engendered a high degree of mutual obligation among supporters, such that they became relatively resistant to urges to leave if organizational actions didn't go their way: in Albert Hirschman's terms, interpersonal interaction created levels of "loyalty" that tipped the balance for many participants from "exit" in favor of "voice."[37]

Of course, considerable subsequent work has explored conditions under which these desirable traits may be fostered in online contexts lacking face-to-face interaction, with some convincing evidence that they can.[38] This raises the question of to what degree the beneficial outcomes that Putnam ascribes to face-to-face interaction might be, to a greater extent, a product of an individual's role in deciding what is to be done in his/her name, and having a say in how it is executed—in short, their communicative autonomy? Though Putnam focuses on the fact that the "tertiary" organizations that have replaced the associations of the mid-twentieth century are much less face-to-face, he elides the fact that they also have largely removed such autonomy from the individual's membership experience.

And in fact, some of the evidence Putnam cites suggests this conclusion. First, he notes that participation in voluntary associations was most significant in the development of civic skills for people of working classes, because they apparently did not have those opportunities in the workplace. They were less critical for professionals, who apparently benefited more from workplace experiences. What is the key difference between these groups' workplace interactions? It is not the degree of face-to-face interaction, which we might imagine to be roughly equivalent; rather it is the fact that professionals have a much greater degree of control and autonomy over what they do and how they do it. Second, citing Sidney Verba and colleagues, Putnam notes a similar pattern between members of Catholic and Protestant churches, with Protestants reporting much more opportunity to participate in many forms of civic work.[39] The difference there again is not the mode of interaction, but the opportunity to make decisions about the self and the group.

But the bigger point should be that the interpersonal conditions Putnam described are simply not returning. The context that allowed productive interpersonal interaction to take place was about much more than the specific structures of any particular organization: it was a society-wide pattern of deep group-based social and identity attachments. As a result, creating a new group with features thought to be in imitation of those of earlier periods is unlikely to create an experience appealing to contemporary citizens. By contrast, the notion that communicative autonomy might be a key factor in the development of some of the desirable traits often ascribed to social capital is an important one if we seek to rethink how to bridge young citizens' information preferences with major institutions' established routines.

The second historical feature cited by scholars interested in this problem is the federated nature of civic organizations. Autonomy could exist in such organizations because local chapters made possible a great deal of decision-making on a citizen's scale: it is when a local chapter has only 20 to 100 members that individual members have real opportunities to take charge (e.g., of a committee), make decisions, and express themselves. Federated structure of civic communications lent participation at the time the simultaneous quality of rich interactive and expressive experiences for involved persons and structures that could direct, implement, and structure those actions into all levels of political power.

Once again, we can question the degree to which organizations are likely to refederate: in contrast to organizations of the classic civic era of the early twentieth century, many of which were umbrella groups made up of many local associations that found common cause, those founded more recently have started at the top and subsequently developed local chapters with mixed success.[40] But intriguingly, some scholars of new media information flows appear to implicitly expect them to follow a federated logic. In the new media environment, we have the capacity for member input on a host of issues. Members are not inherently excluded as they were during the check-writing era: direct mail went one way (and the checks went the other). How to deal with the potential cacophony of so many voices speaking together? Yochai Benkler and Clay Shirky have proposed variations on the notion of filters at various levels that can judge the usefulness of information at a local level and pass it to the next. Benkler's primary purpose in his discussion of filters is to illustrate the public sphere potential of networked filtering of information; but we could equally conceptualize a networked organization as one federated into many levels of increasingly small filter groups in which participants have highly autonomous experiences—while also raising issues and concerns brought to wider attention.[41]

There is intriguing potential here. But one problem standing in its way is that most organizations are not federated in their communication style, and consequently will have difficulty in productively scaling up members' inputs into meaningful directives for organizational aims and strategy. Filters necessitate that there be coherent levels in place for filtering within an association, and from whatever an organization's series of filters produce to policymakers. Further, citizens must be willing to devote significant attention to a level of discussion and operation that may not first appear to have great relevance or impact: one consequence of news media, politicians, organizations, and all other members of the new media ecology being able to communicate directly with citizens is that most people's primary information exposure now comes from the top, managed and produced by communication professionals, not local or intermediary levels. Citizens will be correspondingly skeptical about investing in lower levels of participation that they may not perceive as influential enough to be worth the effort. So once again we run into the problem that organizations are operating in a society that no longer is organized on a space-based logic: organizations of the classic period were surely help by the fact that the center of gravity of political power was still much more local and state-based than it became in the latter half of the twentieth century.

Nonetheless, to a greater extent than developing richly configured interpersonal interactions, contemporary organizations may have the opportunity to create what we might call networked-federated structures. Indeed, there is an argument to be made that blogging communities such as DailyKos have done exactly this: they are not federated in a strictly Skocpolian sense—into chapters based on location, for instance. But they are somewhat federated by interest, with various members focusing to a greater or lesser degree on particular issues more than others. And indeed, some are especially interested in particular states or cities, giving some areas of the community a quasi-geographical organization.

But most importantly, what is available in such communities are opportunities to express oneself and *have oneself heard*—even if only by a relatively small audience of peer average citizens. What is more, the possibility of having one's contributions, or even personal reputation, elevated to a greater level of exposure and influence within the community gives is a character of potential importance always a good blog post or comment away. It would be interesting to see more attempts by established civic organizations to develop communities of these types; considerable work would be needed, once again, to negotiate the transition from member passion to policy platform, but the potential is intriguing.

Hybrid Organizations

A further possibility for forms that can offer both autonomy and real political connectedness comes from more recent analyses of hybrid organizations.[42] The key question then becomes, how are they connected and—equally important for a risk-averse political campaign—distinctly separate? The organization of the artistic festival Burning Man may be an illustrative example. As Katharine Chen has shown, the Burning Man organization successfully mediates between very discrete realms: the creation of the city on the one hand, and administrative tasks on the other. As long as the administration does not place too many burdens on autonomous participants, participants seem happy to let them rule unimpeded.[43] Clear delineation between structures of autonomy and bureaucracy appears to allow both to function in parallel.

But those structures may in fact be so clearly delineated that Burning Man cannot be taken as a model for participatory engagement in more formally political contexts. Pursuing this observation reveals that Burning Man has particular characteristics making it conducive to a structure such as this one. And, in fact, it shares those features with other of the exciting examples often cited on behalf of arguments for the capacity of large networked groups to produce value, including open source software development and online knowledge repository Wikipedia. It is one thing to build something new: that is what horizontal networks have exceled at. At Burning Man, participants mostly autonomously build a city in the middle of the Nevada desert; open source communities identify problems or interesting challenges and build new code to address them; Wikipedia has built an extraordinary a storehouse of knowledge. In these places, contributors exercise a great sense of agency and often have a great deal of autonomy. But one notable feature of these instances is that they stand largely alone: they do not have to contend with the many external forces that make political action so fraught.[44] Yes, Burning Man has to deal occasionally with local governments—and such circumstances are precisely where it has bureaucratized.[45] But Wikipedia has no external enemies; there is no defeat in Wikipedia. Similarly, the open source movement operates largely independently, with Microsoft a whipping boy but no genuine existential threat.

Politics is different: it is a process involving enemies, interminable discussions, endless meetings, long waits—and, after all that, frequent failure. This is the essence of the democratic process.[46] These features have significant implications for the tolerances of participants. First, the possibility—even likelihood—of failure means that participants in political movements are likely to be much more discerning as to the ends to which their contributions are put. An individual artist creating an installation for Burning Man may derive great satisfaction from the creation of her masterwork; that satisfaction is largely unaffected by either the degree of successful coordination with peers or Burning Man LLC's ability to leverage that contribution on an external target. By contrast, political movement participants make contributions in the hope that together, the collective successfully achieves an uncertain outcome: with failure, there is nothing. This fact serves to closely tie together individuals' contributions and the structures that unite them in a way foreign to autonomous collectives.

This is not to say that autonomous individual contributions and formal political activity can never be bridged. The presidential campaigns of Howard Dean and Barack Obama have often been cited as examples, including in this book. Clearly, this is a rich area for research: what kinds of organizational components go into an effective hybrid campaign? What we tend to see in such cases is a division of the campaign along somewhat discrete lines: in the case of Barack Obama's 2008 and 2012 campaigns, for example, we can identify at least three: the war room-style central campaign; the campaign's new media operation, tasked with connecting with supporters online and facilitating online community; and considerable unofficial support from the wider websphere.

We also cannot write off—or let off the hook—traditional, highly bureaucratic institutions' ability to connect with interested public when they are appropriately designed to do so. Perhaps foremost, this includes institutions of government: Carmen Sirianni's accounts of participatory governance in such cases as the City of Seattle and the US Environmental Protection Agency make clear that participation can be built into even the most bureaucratic of systems. The EPA's devotion of resources and staff to building local communities' concern and civic capacity around watershed protection beginning in the early 1970s stands as an example of how a massive institution fostered both the development of existing associations' expertise and the formation of new movements in response to opportunities the EPA helped create. This is in fact an overlooked emphasis of Tocqueville's account of American civic activism. Usually understood primarily as depicting spontaneous, organic civic behavior in response to community concerns, Tocqueville was well aware of the importance of institutions that could provide context and outlet for that energy.[47]

Today, we cannot allow our interest in emergent ahierarchical organizing forms to overshadow careful study of the successful innovations in older forms, complex and unglamorous though they may be.[48] Especially, it suggests a word of caution to proposals that lean too heavily on technology to create economies of scale and efficiencies in governing.[49]

However, there again we raised questions about to what extent member participation was genuinely incorporated into organizational functioning, and to what extent participatory opportunities may be offered that mimic genuine consultation but that are in fact kept at an arm's length—from policymaking within the organization, and from the organization's closely guarded public image. How will we recognize the difference? How will citizens? The clear danger is that "spectacles of participation may be made to stand in for mechanisms of democratic accountability," with no great gain for campaigns, citizens or civic involvement.[50]

One further possibility for the accommodating of supporter communicative autonomy with bureaucratic effectiveness—one that suggests a shifting of the terms of organization–citizen interaction more so that the structures of association—deserves our attention. It is one that emerges from our documentation of a sharp rise of networked-expressive activity as organizations communicated through Facebook.

The Rise of Network-Expressive Activity

If the more politically oriented organizations in our sample failed to offer frequent opportunities for contribution of ideas, we saw more potential in their communications to young supporters in the activities they recommended. We proposed in Chapter 2 the attractiveness of online actions that allow young supporters to create a novel message in an expressive form—on a social networking site, or via a homemade video. Terming these activities *network-expressive*, we documented in Chapter 5 that they also are becoming vital to the action repertoires organizations are communicating in Facebook. Indeed, this was the clearest shift observed in organizational behavior as we moved from their websites to their Facebook communications: whereas organizations only occasionally suggested network-expressive action on their websites, they did so fully a third of the time they offered action on Facebook.

This shift in what citizens are asked to do is a potentially striking one, with implications for the place of citizens in their relations with organized groups. Network-expressive activities occur at the intersection of an increasing need among younger people for identity construction and expression, a technology that enables self-expression on an unprecedented scale, and an organization recognizing the potential for supporters to spread a message widely. They allow a young person to incorporate civic or political concerns into a tapestry of identity that is being created through constant online self-presentation. This is a significant development that should point scholars in the direction of thinking about an expressive style of citizenship online that may parallel other forms of citizenship—a sort of digitally expressive citizenship—and what that means for the future of civic engagement.[51]

Given this, the key question is what these kinds of activities really mean: what they accomplish, either for the actor him or herself, or for any broader political issue on which he or she hopes to have an impact. Because research in this area is still in an embryonic stage, what can be presented here is nothing like a definitive answer to this question, but rather a sketch of potential directions for future research.

The meaning of these activities that have received the most attention are what we might call their symbolic value.[52] While not directly affecting the outside political environment, this type of role may nonetheless be highly consequential for the individual citizen, as it allows him or her a space in which to experiment with and try to understand a new political identity—which might allow them then to make decisions about who they want to be politically and what kinds of political action they want to invest in more.[53] And we can imagine how networked-expressive activities may be taking the place of the identity-building roles that organizations played in the modern society. Where their parents or grandparents developed civic identities out of group membership and regular interpersonal interactions, young people could develop their version of identity from interacting with information and learning to express themselves to a networked public.

This is Zizi Papacharissi's vision of a "private sphere," a space of personal exploration and occasionally public (or networked) expression. Papacharissi contrasts the private sphere to the (idealized) public sphere in which participants meet in public, agree to publicly held norms, and debate about matters of the public good. The private sphere, by contrast, is considerably more self-defined: participation does not depend on the acquiescence of others to a particular mode of discourse of topics of concern. These are concerns only of the networked individual. All of this is plenty narcissistic. But the private sphere is not completely disconnected from public life. Its quality of being networked into a web of others means that participation that happens within the private sphere is *potentially* public: action in the private sphere is always riding the blurred boundary between private and public. It is this is "civic narcissism," the actions within personal networks with potentially civic consequences that may have conventional engaging effects such identity development might have.[54]

The development of identity through networked-expressive activities might then contribute to further investment in other, potentially more consequential forms of civic activity, such as organizing meetings or engaging in a larger movement—in "loyalty."[55] Future research should consider the role that online expressions play in the development of young people's conceptions of themselves as political actors. To return to the example of the Obama campaign in 2008, it is possible to picture a young person for whom dutiful information and conventional politics are a foreign language becoming interested in the media being posted by friends in a network and the persona of the candidate being developed by peer posts. Their first action might be commenting on a friend's video about Obama; then posting the first link in their network to the next cool video. From there we could imagine a person's sense of location in the political-media world developing, and ultimately doing something more traditionally political to help Obama get elected.

But the account of network-expressive activity that ascribes them only symbolic value may underestimate the degree of change occurring in the political-communicative sphere. A stronger case for the significance of networked-expressive activity from a traditional perspective on civic engagement is that they might have some kind of *instrumental* impact: that they might affect in some way the outcomes of politics, whether through influence on public opinion, larger media processes, or on officials themselves. Eric Bucy and Kimberly Gregson, in their prescient elaboration of the concept of "media participation," anticipated the rise of just this sort of political activity.[56] In this reading, young citizens are not—at least not only—acting out needs of evolving civic identities but also are accurately reading the communication environment and rationally acting in it. As colleagues and I put it:

> Some are finding it hard to distinguish communication acts and participatory behaviors. In previous eras, communication could be conceptually distinguished from participation. The digital information environment disrupts this neat separation. Citizens are using communication online not only for consumption of information, or even for deliberation or expression of views. They also are using digital media to directly influence others' ideas—as direct participants in the competition of ideas and public opinion.[57]

There is a direct parallel here between citizens focusing their participation on the communication sphere and processes of "mediatization" identified in political communication scholarship since the 1990s.[58] Mediatization refers to the complex interplay between political actors and communication processes, and their intertwining to the point that it becomes unclear where actual power lies. Under such circumstances, we see communication processes rise from a role of mediation of political relationships to having political significance in themselves. Under mediatization the practice of politics takes on strange forms, as communicative possibilities and limitations become foremost in the formation of policy and other political considerations: how a policy, action, or candidate will play in the press becomes at least as consequential to the policy, action, or candidate's success as any other, more "real" considerations such as economic feasibility or objective qualifications.

For its part, journalism is by no means immune to raw communicative influence as a measure of political legitimacy. Illustrating the seductive power of mediatization perfectly, Todd Gitlin has recently described his conversation with Tim Russert over the latter's choice to invite Rush Limbaugh onto "Meet the Press" to discuss Iraq. According to Gitlin, Russert's rationale for the choice was "'He speaks to twenty million people,' not 'He knows about Iraq.'"[59] To Russert, Limbaugh's legitimacy, even authority, comes from his communication power—not expertise—which apparently is perfectly suitable justification for awarding him further communication power.

These facts have been well recognized—at least in the realm of elite political actors.[60] But we have been less inclined to perceive their likely implications for citizens, perhaps a product of the fact that prior to the most recent decade citizens had few opportunities to engage meaningfully with the larger communication environment in which mediatization operates: under a broadcast media regime, one can observe the often surreal orchestrations of media politics, but do very little about it. The shift of the media system to one of networked digital media changes this, though it is not yet at all clear how or to what degree.[61] What is evident is that citizens are finding it meaningful to interject their opinions and perspectives into semipublic networks via social media (as we saw in Chapter 2), and that increasingly organizations are giving them specific prompts and encouragements to do so (detailed in Chapter 5).

Could such activity make a difference, in the crude terms of political potency? The possibility deserves considerably more investigation. Several possibilities of how this might work present themselves. For example, at the end of the 2008 Presidential campaign, the Obama campaign produced digital images of Barack Obama and Joe Biden that reminded people to vote. They made the images available online, and encouraged young supporters to substitute those images as their own Facebook photos for the week of the election. It is imaginable that a young person otherwise not likely to vote might be persuaded to when presented by a Facebook friends list overwhelmed by these blue and white images encouraging them to turn out on Tuesday, and in fact emerging research suggests that it very well might.[62] Future research could ascertain whether this kind of communication, from one young person to their network, in fact has any substantial effect on the vote—if it did, even the most skeptical civic engagement scholars would have to acknowledge the significance of at least some networked-expressive activity.

Network-expressive information sharing may also contribute through the spread of politically significant media such as viral videos. In a few cases, such videos have been produced by typical young people, but more often young people have contributed to a video's power by embedding, commenting on, or linking to a particular video through their own blog or social networking site. The will.i.am "Yes We Can" video, for example, though certainly aided by its star power and a good amount of traditional media coverage, was clearly shared across a wide range of blogging and social networking platforms. Contributing to the success of that video, which became an important element in the development of Obama's youth-friendly identity, should also be considered an instrumental accomplishment of networked-expressive activity. Similarly, young citizens' groups have been reported collecting Super PAC money specifically for the professional creation and (hopefully viral) dissemination of videos advocating particular positions.[63]

A counterargument holds that any individual's contribution to such political media accomplishments is hardly consequential: that their post or link is only one of millions, and one that only a handful of like-minded people are likely to see. But the same criticism could—and has—been made about the vote, as one person's opinion measure in a sea of others', so inconsequential in itself as to be hardly worth casting.[64] From this perspective, network-expressive actions might be viewed as the information-age equivalent of the vote: a kind of voting for a generation that recognizes that is greater power may be in influencing the mediated world around them, making a small but noticeable difference in the communications that are flowing through the networks of the people connected to them—and possibly, in cases of viral flow, beyond. Such networked-expressive activities are hardly "narcissistic":[65] they could very well have fully instrumental effects, and young people employing them might have fully instrumental intentions when deployed.

But the most provocative interpretation of the finding of rising network-expressive activity is what it potentially heralds for the organization–citizen relationship. Could the development of network-expressive activity be the federated form of our age? Here, citizens are not assigned to specific chapters of much larger federated organizations, with all of their activities taking place under the organization's rubric. Instead, networked-expressive activity potentially portends a civic era in which large organizations again federate themselves—this time by connecting not with associations on the ground, but with networked individuals managing complex identities that include civic or public concerns. The prevalence of the networked-expressive form of activity strongly suggested that organizations see their supporters as potential actors in those terms. What we saw in networked-expressive activity is a potential bridge between actualizing networked individuals and highly strategic organizations.

The Question of Commitment

A question lingering behind the problem of bridging autonomous individual action with effective collective efforts is whether individuals' levels of commitment to organizations with whom they interact on a sporadic, communicative, and mediated basis is likely to be sufficient to maintain the momentum necessary for political change. This dynamic has been the subject of a great deal of recent debate. What keeps an organization going in the face of those defeats, interminable discussions, and long waits?

One critique of emerging paradigms of online civic behavior is the "clicktivism" or "slacktivism" objection, made perhaps most famously (and concisely) by Malcolm Gladwell in a *New Yorker* essay.[66] Gladwell's case is that online activism and political expression may feel good to participants, and give them the sense of contributing to an issue they are concerned about (all part of constructing a positive sense of identity, in the terms of the private sphere), but that in fact such activities are substantially less good at fostering groups of individuals ready to undertake challenging and even possibly risky engagement actions than are interpersonal groups, in which trust and reputation are more readily fostered. He particularly contrasts the dense network of interpersonal connections that made participants in the civil rights movement willing to shoulder very great risks in support of the movement. Surveying the history of Internet-based civic movements, he finds few cases comparable to 1960s activism—and several, such as the use of new media tools during the Iranian riots of 2009, that were substantially overhyped. Gladwell's conclusion is that online activism seems to be restricted to a quite thin level of commitment.

Comparing street protest with online activism, Ulises Mejias voiced similar concerns (several years before Gladwell):

> Protests represent actions against the established order, which means the act of protesting involves a certain risk. Many forms of onsite and online protests . . . have removed that risk almost entirely, which results in the anomie of feeling like our actions have no consequences. I believe new media can help translate online engagement into more meaningful participation, but only if the individual is willing to assume some risk.[67]

Without cost or risk, participants demonstrate minimal commitment to an action, and are likely to receive minimal response from the broader civic community. But we might note that not only is commitment required for personal risk taking, as is the case in street protest, but also for enduring the inevitably dull, frustrating, and often fruitless conduct of formal politics. Just as a participant is more likely to desert a fraught action if he does not feel social support (and pressure) from peers with whom he has relationships, so is he more likely to stop coming to meetings that are contentious, or stop following an issue that is cognitively taxing.

This is in fact a classic problem in organizations and collective action. Albert Hirschman's "exit, voice and loyalty" framework can go some way toward explaining the problem of sustaining engagement over flexible networks. Put simplistically, his model is one of interaction and balance between participants' choices between exercising exit (leaving) or voice (self-expression, sometimes complaint). This choice is moderated by loyalty.[68]

This book has shown that we have some sense of how exit and voice operate in late modern civic life. A principle concern is that exit from organizational relationships based on check-writing or weekly emails is too easy: citizens unsatisfied by an organization's positions, or success rate, or a condescending email may have few ties encouraging them to stay with the organization. As for voice, our measures of actualizing communications are in some ways comparable to the idea of voice as the possibility of offering communications that can challenge an institutions ways of operating.[69] Interpreted this way, most Hirschman makes clear that the combined circumstances of ease of exit and minimized opportunities for the expression of voice is a recipe for mass desertion, which is arguably exactly what we have seen.

The question raised, and not sufficiently answered by scholarship, is what are the conditions under which online activism may foster levels of commitment or loyalty that keep participants engaged even with ease of exit. In particular, at least two problems underlying challenges to commitment under digital connections.

First, the very circumstances of identity-driven movement participation likely reduce individuals' inclinations and abilities to form loyal attachments. Action has been disentangled from political ends.[70] And when civic action is motivated more by personal identity achievements than by instrumental goals, participants become unwilling to accept any constraints on their expressive participation. The nature of their participation becomes disconnected from concerns over whether an action is going to make a difference.

Following these observations is a further question that has been something of a third rail in studies of youth civic engagement. Is it possible that the civic and identity circumstances to which young people have been exposed has inhibited their inclination to form sustainable attachments? Most studies of youth engagement have avoided this problem, or elided it by emphasizing the many ways in which young people are engaging "by other means."[71] But there is evidence that such an aversion may in fact exist, with potentially large civic consequences generally obscured in contemporary conversations. In describing his own preferences for low-commitment activity in the occupational sphere, one young man told Tapscott: "A commitment of three years or more [to a job] would make me hesitate. I don't want to get locked in to something I may not enjoy 10 years down the road. I want the freedom to try new and different things ... I view my twenties as a period of self-discovery and self-realization."[72]

What the previous chapter's theory and findings point to is the question of how loyalty can work for citizens under these conditions. In particular, drawing on a notion of changing civic identities and information styles, it leads us to ask whether loyalty might be created out of experiences that satisfy those preferences. Is it possible that having voice itself could yield loyalty? This would place even greater weight on our calls for organizations to increase their offerings of invitations to young supporters to contribute information and action ideas. Likewise, we have represented networked-expressive action as a digital citizen version of what once would have been group-based interpersonal activity. Might the sense of responsibility that youth feel for managing a personal communication environment and network give way to greater commitment to a given cause? Further research may be able to demonstrate in more specific terms the role that networked-expressive activities play, both instrumentally and as precursors to other kinds of civic action.

Another area that has not been explored enough are the civic outcomes of the interplay between online communication and physical spaces, such as neighborhoods. A growing literature on community problem-solving has pointed up the impressive capacities of citizens when they are confronted with problems and opportunities in their vicinity.[73] At the same time, a host of formats and applications, from neighborhood blogs to localized parent listserves to Meetups and Foursquare offer connections between the cyberworld and physical space. We have anecdotal evidence of complementarity, such as the "Mass mobs" attending churches, especially in the American rust belt.[74] But we have little systematic evidence for the longer term consequences of such phenomena: whether attendees ever return, whether there are enough of them to substantially shift a church's or a neighborhood's trajectory, how they influence voice and loyalty. The interaction of local space and digital media is a rich area for future research.

The Audience Comes Alive: Participation as the Ideal of Late Modern Engagement

Before concluding, a final comment on one of the largest, ubiquitous, and therefore nearly unseen frames of the present work and others in the area. A defining feature of scholarly interest in new media technologies, and especially in the specific implications of new media for democracy and polities, is a preoccupation with the possibility that new media may enable new varieties and quantities of *participation*. This preoccupation surely has a variety of sources: from traditions of audience research that long grappled with the question of how active, exactly, the audiences of mass communication channels could be, digital media in which any person is potentially a producer and distributor to a networked public enables a possible transcendence of even the category of active audience to a participatory one.[75] From scholarship on civic engagement, declining rates of involvement over the latter half of the twentieth century similarly primed scholars to consider the participatory possibilities afforded by new media. And, as we saw in Chapter 2, the ethos of digital culture has long been a participatory one holding that contributions from a wide array of actors is a good thing, and thanks to the filtering capabilities of digital networks can be productively sorted to yield tangible public goods.[76]

The obsession is not limited to communication, or even academic scholarship: our society at large has become obsessed with participation. As Francesca Polleta puts it, "participatory democracy has gone mainstream. It is championed by businesspeople and political strategists, municipal bureaucrats and social workers."[77] Why? One reason is doubtless the cultural trend, traced throughout this book, against authoritative certification of value, of information, of experience. The resulting widespread skepticism of absolute values, of elites, of experts, opens a legitimacy gap in all of our politics and institutions. To fill that gap, we are trying to replace the practice of politics by elites with the legitimacy of mass participation.

Building on these perspectives, we developed a conceptualization of young citizens as demanding participation in nearly every aspect of life. We have good reasons to suppose so: and though the studies presented in this book did not directly gauge the effects of the different styles of communication on young citizens, a growing body of research supports the general proposition that younger citizens respond positively to the opportunity to contribute information to a political communication experience. In one experiment, young respondents who had the chance to visit an interactive online experience gained a significantly greater degree of personal political efficacy than those who were exposed only to a unidirectional one.[78] And in a separate study involving the same sample as that of Chapter 4, with colleagues I found that more actualizing communications were indeed associated with a great level of supporter participation on organizations' websites.[79]

Still, what we are talking about when we talk about participation has tended to go badly undertheorized, or at the least be applied highly idiosyncratically. As a result, the notion that participation is good has taken on often-unquestioned reverence, when there is little clear idea of what sort of participation is good or under what conditions. The major story of the contrast between the dearth of actualizing invitations to propose information or action ideas on organization's websites or Facebook profiles and the significant rise in invitations to networked-expressive action is that organizations appear to be reaching out to citizens to participate *in their own networks*—but not in the organization's own spaces.

Another truth that scholarship has not always been willing to recognize is that the participatory impulse is stronger, and one might even say primarily a concern of, the political left. Looking at the Occupy movement, Michael Kazin sees a contemporary anarchistic ethos involving deep skepticism of institutions, and an unwillingness to turn any element of personal autonomy over to authority: "[The Occupiers] are the cyberclever progeny of Henry David Thoreau and Emma Goldman, streaming video and organizing flash mobs instead of writing essays about the wilderness or traveling around the country touting feminism and free love."[80] Once again, we can trace the roots of this style to both the New Communalist counterculture and Silicon Valley: whereas the main emphases of the 1960s and 1970s new left were radical equality and consensus, the emerging digital culture has adopted more a Silicon Valley libertarianism that prizes autonomy and self-determination.[81] By contrast, the notions of radical participation do not figure in recent movements on the right, with the Tea Party being the most obvious example. Though in some ways they are highly participatory, the Tea Party has primarily been cast as a reactionary movement intently focused on policy. And indeed, for a movement with a far-right platform, steady (if by no means universally accepted) undertones of racism, and candidates who need to distance themselves from the dark arts, it has been wildly successful in American politics.

The leftist bias of the participatory impulse should caution us against placing too much weight on what may be a culturally specific trend. The greatest danger may be that we will be led astray by a fad, or worse, unconsciously narrow our understanding of participatory preferences by focusing too much on the activities of one side of the political spectrum. It is true that young people, at least in the United States, have shown a strong leftward shift in recent years; this may be no coincidence given the combination of relatively participatory campaigns offered them—combined, of course, with policies to which they are more favorable. But as researchers, we must remain aware of the potential blindspot here, and keep our eyes open to forms of involvement attracting young people from across the political spectrum, and from a variety of cultures of engaging with problems of public life.

Conclusion: Political Communication for Engagement in a Time of Social and Media Change

In 2011 the Oxford Internet Institute held a symposium titled "A Decade in Internet Time," but was careful not to specify which decade. Are we witnessing the beginning of the end of the Internet's social ramifications? The end of the beginning? Are we still observing the Internet's infancy? Or, indeed, are we entering a prolonged period of increasingly rapid change such that future researchers will look back on our era as one of relative stasis?

Whatever the answer, in current times, and in studies of social processes mediated by digital tools in particular, the pace of change is outstripping our ability to sufficiently contemplate the scale of what we are seeing: it is impossible to take accurate measurements on a quickly moving target. The change surrounds us, and is occurring not only in the technologies of communication: since the birth of modernity our social structures and relations have had their own Moore's law of evolution, as the very foundations of economics, power, race, sex, identity, and much else shift.

At the same time, the core observation of this book is that *everything is not changing equally*. In particular, processes of democratic governance are remarkably inflexible—or stable, depending on your perspective. In many ways, their inertia in longstanding democratic societies have proved to be keys to social stasis: but the depiction offered here is that they also create dislocations in citizens' abilities and inclinations to participate in the process. Between the rapid social change and government processes, we have argued, are forms of organization. When mediating these fundamental relationships in times of change, these associational forms find themselves in impossible positions. For the relationships to right themselves, these associations need to find new forms of mediation in the new environment. We have depicted several possibilities for how this to happen. However it is accomplished, it is necessary to the successful functioning of a society based on making decisions out of the will of the people.

Appendices

Appendix A: Website Selection Process

In line with previous research on the constituents of the youth civic web, organizations of interest were identified by drawing on a number of resources. The catalog was begun with sites appearing in earlier research on youth civic engagement.[1] Next, to ensure inclusion of major nonprofit organizations that have not appeared in studies of youth-only sites, Google searches were conducted using the names of the United States' 100 biggest nonprofit organizations paired with the search terms "youth," "student," "college," and "social networking."[2] Finally, a more open-ended search was conducted to identify organizations working on contemporary issues and political or religious ideologies that had not been uncovered. Those searches combined 54 key civic and political terms with the youth-related search terms above.[3]

The catalog of civic organizations with live websites identified through these methods was then screened for sites or sections of sites having a primary focus on engaging young people, yielding a total population of 264 living websites dedicated to promoting youth civic engagement.[4] These were categorized by research assistants and checked by the author according to the type of organization that created them. If a site was entirely online, without identifiable reference to an offline organization, it was placed in the *online only* category. Fifty-six sites fell in that category. A focus on a government agency or program, a candidate for office, or a political party placed a site in the *government/party* category (28 sites). Sites promoting advocacy for a cause or particular political interest group were placed in the *interest* category (98 sites). And organizations providing community or service involvement without explicit advocacy were placed in the *community* category (84 sites).

To obtain rough estimates of traffic, www.compete.com was used, and a preliminary list of the most-trafficked sites in each category was selected. These clusters were then adjusted to include organizations representing local levels of large multibranch national organizations, and those that might have eluded the mechanical search terms as primarily youth oriented, but that offered explicit invitations youth engagement.

Specifically, to include the kinds of local, community sites that most youth would be likely to interact with, the sites of several national-level organizations in the community/service category were replaced with those of local branches, selected based on searches using randomly generated zip codes. For the Girl Scouts the site of a Madison, Wisconsin chapter was used; for the Boys and Girls Clubs the site of Metropolitan Denver's Clubs; for the Boy Scouts a Council in Texas; and for 4H the site of 4H in North Carolina.

Second, even though they are not focused primarily on youth, the 2008 political campaign sites of John McCain, Barack Obama, and Hillary Clinton were added to gauge any differences in the way they communicated engagement to young voters; several major interest organizations that eluded our search for organizations that had an explicit focus on youth, but that offered sections targeted at youth on their websites, were included in the sample. These included the ACLU, NRA, and Sierra Club. In these cases, we focused on website sections targeted at youth.

Based on the size of the coding challenge, the sample was cut off at 90, with an oversample of 35 in the online only category (to accommodate the great diversity of sites in that category), 15 in the government/party category (reflecting the smaller numbers and more limited youth focus in this category), and 20 each in the interest and community categories. The final sample of sites is presented in Appendix B.

Appendix B: List of Organizations in Website Study (Chapter 4)

The websites of ninety youth civic organizations were included in the website study. The sites, and their organizational sponsors, can be found in Table A.1.

Appendix C: Coding Details for Website Study (Chapter 4)

Coding for the website study of Chapter 4 had three elements: a page selection process, dutiful and actualizing coding, and activities coding. These processes, and corresponding reliabilities, are described on the two following pages; specific codebooks for the three are presented in Appendices C.1, C.2, and C.3, which follow.

Page selection. In the page selection process, three analysts independently evaluated each website for the presence of knowledge and action. Navigating from the home page, the coders looked at each page linked to from the main menu bars. The analysts' selections were limited to pages one link from the homepage, a choice that reduced the potential for error resulting from different search patterns through idiosyncratically designed websites, while capturing websites' most prominent communication spaces and making the process manageable.

The coders assessed each page to determine whether it was primarily presenting information that supporters should know (knowledge), actions a supporter should take (action), both information and actions, or neither. The task was somewhat simplified by some degree of consistency in labeling across websites. Many of the websites in the sample, for example, clearly labeled pages with names such as "Learn more about [this issue/candidate/organization]" (a clear indication of knowledge being communicated) or, very frequently, "Take Action" or "Action Center" (clear indications of action).

Analysts were instructed to select up to three pages per site for knowledge, and up to three for action (see codebook in Appendix C.1). The percent agreement across three coders for the presence of knowledge on a given site was 83.9%, and of action 89.7%. Agreement on whether specific pages contained those goals was also very high.[5] Cases in which analysts differed were resolved by consensus discussion to produce a set of up to 3 pages per website for knowledge and up to 3 for action.[6]

Coding dutiful and actualizing knowledge and action. A different team of four trained coders coded the pages selected in the page selection process to determine whether the knowledge or action was presented in a dutiful or actualizing

Table A.1 **List of Organizations in Website Study (Chapter 4), By Category of Organization**

Site Name	Site URL	Sponsoring organization
Online Only		
Battle Cry	www.battlecry.com/	Teen Mania Ministries
Black College View	www.blackcollegeview.com/	Howard University Department of Journalism
bullying.org	www.bullying.org/	bullying.org
Campus Activism	http://campusactivism.org/	Campus Activism
CampusProgress.org	www.campusprogress.org/	Center for American Progress
Conservative Punk	www.conservativepunk.com/	Conservative Punk
Declare Yourself	www.declareyourself.com/	Declaration of Independence, Inc
Do Something	www.dosomething.org/	Do Something
FreeCulture.org	http://freeculture.org/	Students for Free Culture
Future Majority	http://futuremajority.com/	Future Majority
Girls Inc Online	www.girlsinc-online.org/	Girls Inc.
Global Kid's Digital Media Initiative	www.holymeatballs.org/	Global Kids, Inc
Idealist.org	www.idealist.org/	Action Without Borders
It's Getting Hot In Here	http://itsgettinghotinhere.org/	It's Getting Hot In Here
Libertarian Rock	www.libertarianrock.com/	Libertarian Rock
MySistahs	www.mysistahs.org/	Advocates for Youth
Newz Crew	http://newzcrew.org/	Global Kids, Inc, Newshour

PEACEFIRE	www.peacefire.org/	Peacefire
PEARL World Youth News	www.pearl.iearn.org/pearlnews/	iEARN, Daniel Pearl Foundation
peta2.com	www.peta2.com/	PETA
Progressive U	www.progressiveu.org/	College of San Mateo
Razoo	http://community.razoo.com/	Razoo
Reznet News	www.reznetnews.org/	University of Montana School of Journalism
Rock the Vote	www.rockthevote.org/	Rock the Vote
servenet.org	http://servenet.org/	State Farm Companies Foundation
Spank!	www.spankmag.com/	Lopedia
TakingITGlobal	www.takingitglobal.org/	TakingITGlobal
Think MTV	http://think.mtv.com/	Viacom
Think Youth	www.thinkyouth.org	Think Youth
Tolerance.org: Mix It Up	www.tolerance.org/teens/	Southern Poverty Law Center
TrueU.org	www.trueu.org/	Focus on the Family
U4Prez	www.u4prez.com/	U4Prez
WireTap Magazine	www.wiretapmag.org/	AlterNet.org, Tides Center
YouthNoise	www.youthnoise.com/	YouthNoise
Youthresource	www.youthresource.com/	Advocates for Youth

Government/Party

2020 Democrats	www.2020democrats.org/	2020 Democrats

(continued)

Table A.1 **(Continued)**

Site Name	Site URL	Sponsoring organization
Barack Obama	www.barackobama.com/	Obama for America
Boston Youth Zone	www.bostonyouthzone.com/	Boston Youth Zone
College Democrats of America	www.collegedems.com/	College Democrats of America
College Republican National Committee	www.collegerepublicans.org/	College Republican National Committee
College Republicans	http://storm.collegerepublicans.org	WeTheCitizens
EPA Student Center	www.epa.gov/student/	US EPA
HillaryClinton.com	www.hillaryclinton.com/	Friends of Hillary
John McCain 2008	www.johnmccain.com/	John McCain 2008
Peace Corps {teens}	www.peacecorps.gov/teens/	Peace Corps
Republican National Committee	http://youth.gop.com/GroupPage.aspx?	Republican National Committee
Storm	<no longer available>	College Republicans
The Democratic Party	www.democrats.org/a/ communities/ young_people_and_students/	The Democratic Party
USA Freedom Corps for Kids	www.usafreedomcorpskids.gov/ youth/	USA Freedom Corps
YDA	www.yda.org/	Young Democrats of America
Interest		
Arctic Youth Network	www.taiga.net/ayn/home.html	Walter and Duncan Gordon Foundation

Organization	Website	Abbreviation
Gay, Lesbian and Straight Education Network	www.glsen.org/cgi-bin/iowa/all/home/index.html	GLSEN, Inc
Gay-Straight Alliance Network	www.gsanetwork.org/	GSA Network
Greenpeace Students	http://members.greenpeace.org/students/	Greenpeace
HRC	www.hrc.org/issues/youth_and_campus_activism.asp	HRC
Kids for Saving Earth	www.kidsforsavingearth.org/	KSE Worldwide
NAACP	www.naacp.org/youth/	NAACP
National Youth Rights Association	www.youthrights.org/	National Youth Rights Association
NRA Youth Programs	www.nrahq.org/youth/	The National Rifle Association of America
OutProud	www.outproud.org/	OutProud
SADD	www.sadd.org/	SADD National
Sierra Club	www.sierraclub.org/youth/	Sierra Club
Student Conservation Association	www.thesca.org/	The Student Conservation Association
Students for a Free Tibet	www.studentsforafreetibet.org/	Students for a Free Tibet
Survivors of the Abortion Holocaust	www.survivors.la/	Survivors of the Abortion Holocaust
The Foundation for Jewish Campus Life	www.hillel.org/index	Hillel
UNICEF	www.unicef.org/voy/	UNICEF
Young America's Foundation	www.yaf.org/	Young America's Foundation

(continued)

Table A.1 (Continued)

Site Name	Site URL	Sponsoring organization
Youth & Civil Liberties Council	www.aclu-wi.org/youth/	Youth & Civil Liberties Council of WI Foundation
Youth for Socialist Action	www.socialistaction.org/ysa.htm	Youth for Socialist Action
Community		
Boys & Girls Club of Metro Denver	www.bgcmd.org/	Boys& Girls Club of Metro Denver
BSA Circle Ten Council	www.circle10.org/	Boy Scouts of America
Center for Teen Empowerment	www.teenempowerment.org/	Teen Empowerment
ChannelOne.com	www.channelone.com/	Channel One
Constitutional Rights Foundation	www.crf-usa.org/	Constitutional Rights Foundation
Girl Scouts of Blackhawk Council	www.girlscoutsofblackhawk.org/	Girl Scouts of Blackhawk Council
HarlemLIVE	www.harlemlive.org/	HarlemLIVE, Inc
HighSchoolJournalism.org	www.highschooljournalism.org/	ASNE
iEARN	www.iearn.org/	iEARN

Key Club	www.keyclub.org/	Key Club International
National Student Partnerships	http://nspnet.org/	National Student Partnerships
NC 4-H Youth Development	www.nc4h.org/	NC State University
Seattle YMCA	www.seattleymca.org/	YMCA of Greater Seattle
Teen Ink	http://teenink.com/	Teen Ink, The 21st Century, The Young Author's Foundation
The CityKids Foundation	www.citykids.com/	CityKids Foundation
The National Beta Club	www.betaclub.org/	National Beta Club
Volunteer Work for Teens	www.volunteers.com/	Landmark Volunteers
Youth Venture	www.genv.net/	Ashoka
Youth With A Mission	www.ywam.org/	Youth With A Mission International Communications
YSA.org	www.ysa.org/	Youth Service America

way. For knowledge, page features that presented users with information from the site or other authoritative sources, such as site sponsors, news stories, public officials, or other external sources, were coded as dutiful; appeals for, or clear opportunities for user knowledge-sharing, were coded as actualizing. For action, actions organized or recommended by site sponsors or affiliated organizations and authorities were considered dutiful; peer generated actions suggested or reported upon by site users were actualizing.

Reliability. After the four coders were trained, a random 16-site subsample was selected for a reliability test. The reliabilities (pairwise percent agreement for four coders) were: 100% for organization-driven knowledge (every site presenting knowledge offered it in at least an organization-driven form); 78% for supporter-driven knowledge; 98% for organization-driven action; and 91% for supporter-driven action.[7]

Activities coding. Informed by the three categories of civic activity developed in Chapter 2 and a survey of the dataset, the catalog of action opportunities described in Table 4.2 were developed. Archived copies of all pages coded as containing dutiful action from the first stage of coding were collected and coded by the author and an undergraduate assistant. In all, 120 pages had been identified in that first stage, and were subject to activities coding. (In six cases—5%—data errors made recoding of the pages impossible, leaving 114.)

Reliability. The coders independently coded a randomly selected subset of sixteen (14%) of the 114 pages coded as having dutiful action. On each page, they determined whether each of the activities noted above was present or absent. Their overall intercoder reliability, combining all coder decisions on all pages and all 17 types of activities, yields a test of 272 decisions (16 pages x 17 activities). The coders agreed on 266 of the 272 decisions (97.8%).[8]

APPENDIX C.1: CODEBOOK FOR PAGE SELECTION PROCESS

Repeat the following process for each learning goal (knowledge and action), on each website:

1. Using the site's main navigation bars (which may be displayed across the top and/or down the left side of the page), look at the pages to which each of the menu items direct.
   a. If the main menu bars are drop-down menus, choose the header link (the one visible without the cursor on it). For drop-down menus in which the header item is not a link, explore each item on the drop down menu as though they were separate menu bar items.
2. For each webpage, assess it for the following question:

a. *Does the page represent the site's main effort (or one of the site's main efforts) to deliver the given type of learning goals?* A site's main effort is that page (or pages) on which the site has made offering a particular learning goal a priority. Almost all sites are divided into different sections based on the type of material and experience they contain. Here we are interested in which pages offer predominantly knowledge, expression, publics, or action skills.

b. Broken down by learning goal:

   i. *Does the information on this page represent the kind of knowledge the site hopes to deliver to its users?* Knowledge is the set of static information that the site suggests an engaged citizen should know. It may take several forms, and come from either site administrators or users, but it is a set of "facts" that the site offers as important. It is a static information source, and so does not include forms of information that change, such as news, blogs, or forums. Classifieds material and material about the projects themselves (typically on "About" pages) are also not knowledge, as they do not represent information that the site believes users need to be engaged.

   ii. *Does this page represent how the site hopes its users take action?* "Take Action" pages are dedicated to offering users opportunities to *do something*. Such pages offer one or more suggestions about things users can do—online or offline—that fulfill the mission of the site. Explicit encouragements (such as "buy Fair Trade") and examples (such as "I became a vegetarian") both constitute taking action. Events pages and calendar pages, however, are not "Take Action" pages. Also, pages that simply describe the actions of the group, or of group members, without suggestion or enabling actions to the audience, also do not count.

3. If the page does represent a main effort to deliver that learning goal, code it "yes" (1). If it does not, code it "no" (0).

4. If none of the learning goals are present on any of the pages linked to from the top and left bars, or if there are no top or left menu bars, use the links from the right menu bar. If none of the learning goals are linked to from any of the pages linked to from the right menu bar, or there is no right menu bar, look on the front page for each learning goal.

5. For some websites, no page will be coded "yes" for one or more learning goals.

6. Likewise, some websites will have more than one page coded "yes" for one or more learning goals.

7. And in some cases, the same page with be coded as a main location for more than one learning goal.

For example, on www.gaia.com/community/, for the knowledge learning goal, the page linked to from the "Wisdom" button on the top menu bar is an obvious choice because it seems to be the site's primary place for conveying knowledge to users. For the expression learning goal, "Explore" is a good choice, because that page shows users engaged in a number of types of expression, including videos, blogs, and discussions. For the joining a public learning goal, both "Friends" and "Groups" are good choices. Those pages suggest ways that users can connect with others and become a part of groups. This website's page for "Take Action" is less obvious, but the "Exchange" page is a good choice for that learning goal. There, the site names a number of actions that it hopes its users might take.

Here are several words often used by sites to designate the uses for particular pages. They do not constitute an exhaustive list, and they are clues to—not determinants of—a page's purpose.

For *knowledge*: Causes; Information; Issues; Get Informed; Wisdom

For *action*: Take Action; Get Involved; Volunteer; Do something; Take charge; Campaigns; Get Started; Project databases; Donate

Other notes

- Do not select pages that are clearly labeled as for adults in the menu bar, for example, links that say "For parents/teachers/corporate/educators."
- Blogs are NOT pages for knowledge.
- About pages are NOT pages for knowledge.
- Classifieds pages are NOT pages for knowledge.
- News pages are NOT pages for knowledge.

APPENDIX C.2: CODEBOOK FOR DUTIFUL AND ACTUALIZING CODING

Setup

There are two categories of civic learning (knowledge and action). Those are lettered a and b in the codesheet.

For each learning category, there are two different learning modes that we want you to look for. These are numbered 1 and 2 for each learning goal. The data file thus has columns for codes 1 and 2. NOTE: the different modes will not occur on every website you check, so do not assume that they will be present on every page. Just note them when they are clearly present.

Directions

For each learning category you will see a list of *sites*. Beside each site will be a list of the exact *pages* where we would like you to look for the presence or absence of the two learning modes in each category. (For most sites one page will be listed, but some will have two or three.)

For each learning category, go to each site and look through the set of pages to see if you find any examples of the first learning mode. When you find something that qualifies, mark it as "present" (value=1) and move on to look for the second learning mode in the same page(s). If you look through all of a site's pages and don't find any examples that support the code, mark it "absent" (value=0) and move on. If the only support for a code is questionable, mark it "not sure" (value=2) and move on.

When you have coded all the pages for all the sites in the first learning category, move on to the next category and repeat this procedure.

The Codes

1. Knowledge (issues, get informed, causes, information, projects)
   a. Some sites want users to be able to find out more about issues or related matters when they are on the website. Some sites have pages that are specifically for this purpose. Looking at the pages selected from this site:
      i. Do any of the pages contain a listing of facts or background reports (on issues, problems, or how some political process works) *produced by experts or by the operators of the site*?
         1. For example, some sites might have sections such as "what they never told you," or "inform yourself on important issues," or "what you should know about X (e.g., global warming)."
      ii. Do any of the pages *encourage users to share what they know* about community or public issues or related matters with other users?
         1. For example, some sites enable users to post their own reports and projects in order to share they have learned about a particular problem with other users.
2. Action
   a. Many sites want users to take action in response to public problems. Looking at the pages selected from this site:
      i. Does *the site name one or more actions* for users to undertake?
         1. For example, sites might suggest that users "Volunteer for Senator Obama here," 'Sign our petition asking Congress to fight Global Warming!," or they might talk about the importance of buying fair trade products or not driving too much.
         2. Some sites may offer tools for accomplishing particular actions. If in the process they name an action that could be taken with the tools, that action counts.
      ii. Do any of the pages contain *users suggesting actions* to undertake, or talk about their own actions, or *are users encouraged to suggest actions*?
         1. For example, some sites encourage users to post their own actions or projects. Others show groups started by users to work on particular actions. Still others show users talking about their own actions that they are undertaking or want to undertake. To qualify, user statements about actions must be associated with a username or avatar.

APPENDIX C.3: CODEBOOK FOR WEBPAGE ACTIVITIES CODING

For each page in the spreadsheet, click or copy/paste the link to open the archived page in a web browser. Look over the webpage to get a sense of what is being offered. Look only on that page, and do not click any of its links. In this coding, we are looking for the kinds of actions that the organization is asking supporters to take.

There may be only one or two actions being encouraged on the page, or there may be several. Use the action column to record the activities being encouraged by this page. These are the activities that the page is being dedicated to, and they probably occur more prominently than other activities, as indicated by:

- their placement in the page itself (not in menu bars);
- their placement nearer the top of the page (thus *earlier* if a viewer was reading down the page);
- the text's frequent mention or emphasis of them, or use of the text to describe how to do them.

On many pages, there will be only one action listed; on most there will be only one or two. Multiple actions should only be recorded when those actions really are equally emphasized, such as when they all occur in the same list within the text of the page.

Finally, occasionally no actions will be visible on a page, or action mentions will be visible, but not clear enough to lead to an actual code. (For example, if a page writes something like "Read here to learn more about what you can do.") In these cases, the code recorded should be "NV."

Appendix D: Process for Identification of Facebook Pages (Chapter 5)

Two researchers independently searched for each project's presence on Facebook to ensure comprehensiveness. As a first step, they visited the website of the project and determined whether a link to a Facebook Page was present there. If there was, the job for that project was done: clearly the project had a Facebook Page, and the presence of a link on the website to that Page was taken as an official endorsement. If the project's website offered no link to a Facebook Page, the researcher proceeded to Facebook and conducted three sets of searches to reveal a project's presence. These involved: the organization's official name, with spaces, just as it would look on the header of a webpage (e.g., "Do Something"); the organization's official name, without spaces, as it might look in a URL without the first-level domain (e.g., "dosomething"); and the project's official web address, with first- and second-level domain (e.g., "dosomething.org"). The separate forms of search were employed based on tests in which it was found that some organizations in the sample appeared in some of the searches but not others.

CODEBOOK

The goal of this process is to accurately locate and identify (a) whether an organization has an official Facebook Page; (b) exactly which Facebook Page is the official one for that organization; and (c) whether the organization also has Facebook Groups associated with it.

1. Visit the organization's website and look for links to Facebook Pages. If there is a link to a Facebook Page, that will be considered the official Facebook Page. Continue to Step 2 to search for Groups, skip Step 3 and do Step 4.
2. If the organization's website does not include a link to a Facebook Page, go to Facebook and search for the organization there, using the following search terms:
   a. The organization's official name, with spaces, just as it would look on the header of a webpage (e.g., "Do Something").
   b. The organization's official name, without spaces, as it would look in a url without the extension (e.g., "dosomething").
   c. The organization's official web address, with domain and extension (e.g., "dosomething.org").
3. For each set of search results, assess the Pages returned as results. Determine the organization's official Page of those delivered from all three searches. Record the official Page, the method used to locate it; in cases where it is unclear which is the official Page, record multiple Pages. The following criteria should be used to determine the official Page:
   a. Number of fans: more fans suggests greater likelihood that a Page is official.
   b. Use of organization logo: use of the official logo suggests a Page is official.
4. While executing Step 3, also look at Groups returned as results for each organization. If any Groups apparently related to the organization (i.e., using their logo or otherwise likely to be affiliated) are returned, record the largest one.
5. Record the number of fans (for each Page) and members (for each Group) listed in your worksheet.

Appendix E: List of Organizations in Facebook Study (Chapter 5)

Sixty nine Facebook Pages were analyzed, as shown in Table A.2.

Table A.2 **List of Organizations in Facebook Study (Chapter 5), By Category of Organization**

Facebook Page	Organization URL
Online Only	
Battle Cry	www.battlecry.com/
CampusProgress.org	www.campusprogress.org/
Declare Yourself	www.declareyourself.com/
Do Something	www.dosomething.org/
Future Majority	http://futuremajority.com/
Girls Inc Online	www.girlsinc-online.org/
Global Kid's Digital Media Initiative	www.holymeatballs.org/
Idealist.org	www.idealist.org/
It's Getting Hot In Here	http://itsgettinghotinhere.org/
Libertarian Rock	www.libertarianrock.com/
peta2.com	www.peta2.com/
Progressive U	www.progressiveu.org/
Puget Sound Off!	http://pugetsoundoff.org
Razoo	http://community.razoo.com/
Reznet News	www.reznetnews.org/
Rock the Vote	www.rockthevote.org/
Think MTV	http://think.mtv.com/
Tolerance.org: Mix It Up	www.tolerance.org/teens/
YouthNoise	www.youthnoise.com/
Government/Party	
Barack Obama	www.barackobama.com/
College Democrats of America	www.collegedems.com/
College Republicans	www.collegerepublicans.org/
Democratic Party	www.democrats.org/a/ communities/ young_people_and_students/
John McCain	www.johnmccain.com/

(continued)

Facebook Page	Organization URL
Peace Corps	www.peacecorps.gov/teens/
Republican Party	http://youth.gop.com/
Sarah Palin	http://sarapac.com
US EPA	www.epa.gov/students/
Young Democrats	www.yda.org/
Interest	
American Civil Liberties Union	http://aclu.org
Gay, Lesbian and Straight Education Network (GLSEN)	www.glsen.org/ cgi-bin/iowa/all/home/index.html
Gay-Straight Alliance Network	www.gsanetwork.org/
Greenpeace	http://greenpeace.org/
Human Rights Campaign	www.hrc.org/
NAACP	www.naacp.org/youth/
National Youth Rights Association	www.youthrights.org/
National Rifle Association (NRA)	www.nrahq.org/
Oasis Magazine	www.oasisjournals.org/
Students Against Destructive Decisions	www.sadd.org/
Sierra Club	www.sierraclub.org/youth/
Student Conservation Association	www.thesca.org/
Students for a Free Tibet	www.studentsforafreetibet.org/
Survivors of the Abortion Holocaust	www.survivors.la/
UNICEF	www.unicef.org/voy/
Young America's Foundation	www.yaf.org/
Community	
4-H	www.4h.org/
Boys & Girls Club	www.bgca.org/
Boy Scouts	www.boyscouts.org/
Center for Teen Empowerment	www.teenempowerment.org/

(continued)

Table A.2 **(Continued)**

Facebook Page	Organization URL
Channel One News	www.channelone.com/
Constitutional Rights Foundation	www.crf-usa.org/
Girl Scouts	www.girlscouts.org/
Key Club	www.keyclub.org/
LIFT	· http://liftcommunities.org
Seattle YMCA	www.seattleymca.org/
Teen Ink	http://teenink.com/
The National Beta Club	www.betaclub.org/
Youth Venture	www.genv.net/
Youth Service America	www.ysa.org/
Youth With A Mission	www.ywam.org/

Appendix F: Process for Collecting Facebook Status Updates (Chapter 5)

To gather the status updates, the author and four undergraduate assistants went to each Page's wall and applied Facebook's built-in filter to make only the organization's status updates visible. Wall posts by users other than the official organization Page were thus excluded. They then unfurled each wall until all the status updates for the sample period were visible, and copied and pasted the text of each status update into an Excel file. Six pieces of information were gathered from each status update: the date; the text of the status update itself; any text associated with a link attached to the status update; the destination of the link, if there was one, including the final destination of shortened links; the number of comments the status update had received; and the number of likes the status update had earned. (In compliance with Facebook's Statement of Rights and Responsibilities, the content of the comments, and other information containing the identities of those who had liked a given post, were not gathered; see Appendix H.)

Each organization's status updates were checked at two independent times to ensure reliability and completeness: once as a signed-in user of Facebook, and once not signed in. While we anticipated, from preliminary testing, a certain degree of unreliability in the status updates Facebook retrieved—both over time and between logged-in and nonlogged-in users—in fact we found minimal variation: in only three cases was a status update visible to the logged-in user when originally gathered and not visible when not logged in, which was tested between one and three weeks later. Two of these involved instances in which supporters from the researchers' location were being specifically appealed to—and thus apparently had drawn on the user's personal information. These cases were replaced with status updates visible when not logged in; thus, all status updates in the analysis were visible to a user not logged in to Facebook.

Appendix G: Facebook Coding Process (Chapter 5)

Coding for the Facebook study of Chapter 5 had three elements: dutiful and actualizing coding, activities coding, and links coding. These processes, and corresponding reliabilities, are described on the two following pages; specific codebooks for the three are presented in Appendices G.1, G.2, and G.3, which follow.

Reliability for Coding of Dutiful and Actualizing Knowledge and Action in Status Updates

Two coders were trained to identify each type of communication, and a reliability test was conducted on a random 10% of each organization's posts during March (181 status updates). This test revealed highly reliable measures of the communication types: for dutiful knowledge, the average pairwise percent agreement was 92.63%; for dutiful action, 87.85%; for actualizing knowledge, 95.95%; and for actualizing action, 99.26%.[9] The complete dataset of status updates was then coded by the author and two assistants. One-third of each organization's posts were coded by each of the three coders to ensure than any remaining unreliability was randomly distributed.

Reliability for Coding of Activities

As noted in Chapter 4, the cataloging of activities to be identified and coded was done in parallel for the two studies. This meant that essentially the same set of activities presented in Chapter 4 was assessed in the Facebook study.[10] (Appendix H presents the details of how it was applied to Facebook.) A reliability check was conducted on those status updates that were coded as having dutiful action. Overall percent agreement for identification of presence/absence of each activity on each status update was 97.7%, between two coders.[11]

Reliability for Link Analysis Coding

The author and a graduate student assistant coded a subset of 184 (10%) of the 1,844 total status updates in the sample. In determining whether a link was internal or external, the reliability was 98.7% (Krippendorff's alpha of .940).

The remaining sample was then coded by the author. In five cases (0.3% of sample) the link had expired and it was no longer possible to analyze it.

APPENDIX G.1: CODEBOOK FOR DUTIFUL AND ACTUALIZING CODING

Codebook

This codebook guides the analysis of Facebook status updates, including the text of notes and links visible with status updates on a Page's wall.

WHAT TO ANALYZE

This codesheet will be applied to elements on an organization's Facebook wall that meet certain criteria:

1. The text of status updates.
2. The text of notes and links visible on the wall, usually accompanying a status update.

Each piece of posted material should be analyzed as a package. Thus, if a status update contains a link, the whole package should be analyzed for the presence or absence of the four communication types.

Those four types are described in detail on the next page. They are:

- Organization-driven knowledge
- Organization-driven action
- Fan-driven knowledge
- Fan-driven action

For each post on a wall, each type of communication is either present or absent. The types are thus independent, and might occur in any combination (e.g., organization-driven knowledge and fan-driven action). It is possible but unlikely that all four will be present in a single post, and very unlikely that none of the four will be present in any post. Most posts probably will present one or two of the types.

For each post, record either a 1 or 0 for each type of communication (1=that form is present in this post; 0=that form is absent from this post).

SPECIFIC CODING INSTRUCTIONS AND GUIDING NOTES

With *organization-driven knowledge*, the organization presents information that it wants fans to know. This may be general news relevant to the organization, or it may describe events or happenings within the context of the organization. The information does not need to be substantial or even true; it simply needs to include *information* that the organization wants users to *know*.

- Because this is a very typical use of status updates and notes, most posts will include some organization-driven knowledge.
- NO: A message that describes an action that users are being asked to take, either implicitly or explicitly, should *not* be considered organization-driven knowledge, but organization-driven action (unless it is also accompanied by a separate element of the message that is itself knowledge). The key question is: Is there information here beyond the information that suggests action?
- NO: Similarly, information that explains *how* to do an action should not be considered knowledge unless there is information present *beyond the context one would need to participate in the action.*

With *organization-driven action*, the organization presents opportunities for action that it wants fans to take. These are any activities that fans are being asked to *do*.

- NO: Cases in which an organization asks fans to contribution information to their Page or website (e.g., "share your opinion with us!") should *not* be considered organization-driven action—*unless* it involves structured processes, as below.
- NO: Cases in which an organization asks fans to learn more/read more/watch.
- YES: Cases in which an organization asks fans to contribute information to a web location that is not explicitly affiliated with the organization should be considered organization-driven action.
- YES: questions that ask fans if they have done or will do something should usually be coded as organization-driven action. (They're asking you because they want you to do it.)
- YES: appeals to fans to participate in a structured organizational process, even if that process includes contributing information or opinion (for example, voting for something, nominating someone for a specific award, creating a video).

With *fan-driven knowledge*, the organization invites fans to contribute information or opinion, or invites them to participate in information exchange somewhere on its Page or website.

- YES: Cases in which an organization asks fans to contribute an opinion, or participate in a discussion that takes place on a Page or website affiliated with the organization should be considered fan-driven knowledge.
- NO: Rhetorical questions, such as when an organization opens with a question that clearly leads only to presentation of information, should *not* be considered fan-driven knowledge. (For example, from PugetSoundOff. org: "Do you take AP classes? Are they worth the pressure? This video features stories of students and teachers of AP classes and the pressures they face in our achievement-obsessed culture.")

- NO: appeals to fans to contribute information or opinion through a structured/institutionalized process (for example, voting for something, nominating someone for a specific award) are NOT fan-driven knowledge; rather, fan-driven knowledge occurs where an organization appeals to fans to share information/opinion in an open forum, such as the organization's Page, or it's website's discussion board. It includes most appeals to share information/opinion in general (without a specific location or process).

With *fan-driven action*, the organization invites fans to suggest actions that others could take, or describe action that they themselves are taking.

CLARIFICATION OF DIFFICULT CASES

1. Rhetorical questions pose a challenge because sources sometimes present their information with a question that is not meant to be answered, but rather to stimulate interest in the topic. In coding status updates, it can be particularly unclear whether a question is meant to be answered when the question is accompanied by a link providing some kind of information related to the question.
2. In posts that have questions that are ambiguously rhetorical, err on the side of fan-driven knowledge. Sometimes, posts will include questions that are clearly rhetorical, with the organization clearly not looking for a response. But if it is ambiguous enough that you aren't sure whether the organization is looking for an answer, assume that it is.
3. In posts that are ambiguous about the kind of information being solicited from fans—where it is hard to tell whether the organization is asking fans to submit knowledge or action—err on the side of fan-driven action. In such cases where it is unclear whether the thing to be contributed is knowledge or action, err on the side of coding it as action.
4. Some posts recommend an action to be taken in the form of a statement about the possibility of that action by supporters. These posts should be considered organization-driven action, and not organization-driven knowledge, unless there is also a separate piece of knowledge delivered with the action statement.
5. If an action could only be taken by a subset of group members (e.g., those over 18, women, Sam's Club Members), it still counts as action.

APPENDIX G.2: CODEBOOK FOR ACTIVITIES CODING

Instructions for Assessing the Kind(s) of Activity Present in Status Updates
Read the text of the status update, and the text of any corresponding link *that is visible with the status update.* (Thus, in the Excel sheets, read the text in the "text" and "link/note text" columns.)

Assess the kinds of activities the organizations is encouraging supporters to do. Use the checklist of activities to decide what kinds of activities those are, and enter the letter of those activities in the "Letter code" column on the right. Most status updates will only present one kind of activity; but where more than one kind of activity is presented, enter each letter, separated by commas.

Notes for clarification:

- *If it is not clear whether the organization is asking supporters to take an action*: When it is not clear that an action is present, or it is not clear that the organization is asking supporters to take an action that is described, assume that the action *is* being encouraged. Assume that when organizations are telling supporters *about* an action, they probably are asking/inviting them to take part in it.
- *When NOT to follow a link*: When the kind of action the organization wants supporters to take (that is, the action that is the purpose of the status update) is clear from the text of the update itself, it is NOT necessary to click on the link.
  - *Likewise,* Links should also NOT be investigated where there is at least one clear action named in the status update—even if there are other, unspecified actions alluded to in the post. In that case, the specific action named in the post should be coded.
- *When TO follow a link*: Links should be investigated only where there is an action encouraged in a status update, but its nature is unclear, for example, when an organization suggests you urge an official to do an unspecified thing, or to help seals, but in an unspecified way.
  - *Example*: For example, in one status update, Peta2 states, "Top five ways to help animals while poopin'!" In this example, there are clearly actions being encouraged by Peta2, but it is not clear what they are from the status update itself—supporters must click a link to find out what those five ways actually are. In this case, the link SHOULD be followed.
  - *However,* if the post had read, "Don't eat meat! And four other ways to help animals," ONLY the "don't eat meat" part of the action should be coded—and the link should NOT be followed. (Because there clearly are other ways to help animals, but it is the not eating meat that Peta2 is choosing to highlight.)

APPENDIX G.3: CODEBOOK FOR LINK ANALYSIS CODING

For each status update, coders will examine up to one URL, which can be found in the link_dest field of the datasheet. If the organization has not used Facebook's link feature (in which case the link_dest field will be N/A or blank), no link will be analyzed for that status update.

For each URL, two variables will be measured: first, the extent to which organizations link to themselves, or to information clearly about themselves, which will be referred to as *internal* versus *external* links; and second, the types of sites that are linked to (such as different kinds of websites, and social media applications).

INSTRUCTIONS: INTERNAL/EXTERNAL LINK CODING

This coding explores the extent to which organizations use links in Facebook to direct supporters to more information about themselves (using internal links) or to a broad range of information from diverse sources and about diverse topics (using external links). In essence, the question is whether the page is being linked to because it is affiliated with the organization—its own page, or a page that talks about the organization, or, for example, an op-ed written by a director of the organization (internal)—or because it is new information the organization wants to notify supporters about (external).

1. Be aware of which organization posted each link. The organization's name is available in column A, "Page_name." Of course, it is necessary to know which organization posted the link to assess the relationship between the organization and the content of the link destination.

2. Look at URL itself. If the URL is clearly affiliated with the organization (for instance, by containing the organization's domain, or including the organization's name in its extension), it is an internal link. No further internal/external examination needs to take place.

3. If the URL is NOT clearly affiliated with the organization, it may still be a link associated with the organization; click the link to see the page. Look over the whole page to which the link directs, but do not click further into the website. (The one exception are Facebook links to external content, in which Facebook warns the user that they are leaving Facebook. Coders should click through that page to arrive at the true destination of the link.)

   a. Scan the page for the organization's name. If it appears, it is an internal link. If there is NO mention of the organization anywhere on the page, it is an external link.

   b. Look particularly at the top and bottom of the page, where organizations sponsoring a page are often presented. If the organization's name is present, it is an internal link.

   c. If the page is a news article, scan the article for the organization's name. If the organization's name appears, it is an internal link.

   d. If the page is a Facebook Page, look for the organization's name. For Pages, determine whether the Page is the organization's own Page, or one sponsored by the organization. For photos, determine whether the photos were posted by the organization.

4. Use the "Internal/External" column in the datasheet to record your determination. Use 1 to indicate that the link is an internal one; use 2 to indicate the link is an external one. For status updates that had not link, leave this field blank.

5. If the link directs to a page that is no longer available, or content within a site that has been removed (AND the URL itself does not make evident what sort of link it is), mark "Unavailable" in both coding columns.

INSTRUCTIONS: TYPE OF SITE CODING

This coding records the *kinds* of sites directed to by the links. It asks coders to catalog the social media affordances directed to, and to roughly characterize the kinds of websites directed to.

6. Whether the link destination is internal or external, use the appropriate column to record what kind of page is linked to (e.g., webpage, Facebook page). The other column should be left blank.
   1. Facebook (or other social networking site; if other, indicate—e.g., "MySpace")
   2. YouTube (or other video sharing site; if other, indicate—e.g., "Vimeo")
   3. Flickr (or other photo sharing site; if other, indicate)
   4. Twitter
   5. Websites
      (a) Own website, affiliate website or website sponsored by organization
      (b) Civic organization (use only if NOT own website)
          Nonprofit civic, charity, or political organizations, including other organizations from the sample
      (c) News organization (use only if NOT own website)
          Recognizable news organizations, including well-known online sources (e.g., *Washington Post, New York Times, Huffington Post, Talking Points Memo*)
      (d) Government agency (use only if NOT own website) (e.g., EPA, White House)
      (e) Gorporate entity (use only if NOT own website) (e.g., Coca-Cola, Walmart)
      (f) Other/unclear

Appendix H: Complying with Facebook's Statement of Rights and Responsibilities

One issue that has concerned researchers studying Facebook is the need to comply with Facebook's Statement of Rights and Responsibilities, which governs use of the site. First, it is not clear that the statement applies to this research. The data to be gathered are available to users not logged in to Facebook, a property of all Facebook Pages, which Facebook makes clear are public spaces.[12]

Academic research has generally treated publicly available web information as open to collection and analysis, though the statement also states that: "By using or accessing Facebook, you agree to this Statement." Nonetheless, whether or not the statement is meant to apply to this kind of research, the study presented in Chapter 5 was being designed to comply with its letter and spirit.

The statement contains two items that pertain to how Facebook participants will gather and use others' information within the site. Item 3.2 states: "You will not collect users' content or information, or otherwise access Facebook, using automated means (such as harvesting bots, robots, spiders, or scrapers) without our permission." And item 5.7 states: "If you collect information from users, you will: obtain their consent, make it clear you (and not Facebook) are the one collecting their information, and post a privacy policy explaining what information you collect and how you will use it."

Although this study collects Facebook content, it is unreasonable to interpret 3.2 as pertaining to manual archiving of content one status update at a time. Facebook gives specific examples of the kind of data-gathering it intends to prohibit, indicating that by "automated means" Facebook is trying to prohibit the use of tools that can be set to gather data without human input—that is, at regular intervals or across a large number of pages, presumably to keep its service clear of bandwidth-intensive automated tools. (While a copy-paste command, such as the ones used to gather status update text here, could technically be considered automated means, the fully literal interpretation of that phrase would also include accessing Facebook using web browsers, which is clearly not the intent of the clause.)

Similarly, with respect to item 5.7, Facebook makes it quite clear that by "information" they are referring to "facts and other information about you [that is, users], including actions you take" (item 17.4). This is distinguished from "content" in section 17, and it is made clear that content is meant to cover what people post. Thus, 5.7 does not refer to the content that will be the bulk of the data gathered here, including all the status posts.

Notes

Chapter 1

1. The People's Assembly is Egypt's lower house of parliament. Results for the upper house, the Shura Council, were similar; BBC, 2012.
2. Kirkpatrick, 2013.
3. Blitzer, 2011; Minder & Erlanger, 2012.
4. Moynihan, 2012; Newman & Moynihan, 2012; Skocpol & Williamson, 2012.
5. Kazin, 2011; Buckley & Moynihan, 2011; Gitlin, 2011; Spiegel, 2011; Tremlett, 2011.
6. Karpf, 2012.
7. Tocqueville, 1863/1964; Skocpol, 2003.
8. And their forbears in networked movements concerning globalization, fair trade, and war; see, e.g., Bennett, Breunig, & Givens, 2008; della Porta & Tarrow, 2005.
9. See, e.g., Schudson's citation of Rousseau's lament that "we have physicists, geometers, chemists, astonomers, poets, musicians and painters; we no longer have citizens"—and that was in 1750! Schudson, 1998, p. 365.
10. Hayes, 1983; Skocpol, 2003.
11. Putnam, 2000; Wattenberg, 2008; Zukin et al., 2006.
12. E.g., Bennett, 2008; Bennett & Segerberg, 2011; Bimber, 2003; Bimber, Flanagin, & Stohl, 2012; Karpf, 2012; Kreiss, 2012; Papacharissi, 2010; Thorson, 2010.
13. E.g., Boyd, 2014; Livingstone, 2009; Palfrey & Gasser, 2008.
14. See, e.g., Bennett & Segerberg, 2011; Earl & Kimport, 2011; Flanagin, Stohl, & Bimber, 2006; Papacharissi, 2010.
15. Almond & Verba, 1963; Skocpol, 1999, 2003.
16. Shirky, 2008; important exceptions include Bimber 2003; Bimber et al., 2012; Karpf, 2012; and Kreiss, 2012.
17. Van Laer & van Aelst, 2010; Bimber et al., 2012 make the important point that what we are in fact seeing is not a replacement of one kind of organization with another, but rather a proliferation of different kinds of organizations.
18. Bimber, 2003; see also Kreiss, Finn, & Turner, 2010.
19. This special category is roughly coextensive with the set of new types of organizations Karpf, 2012, analyzes.
20. Hayes, 1983.
21. Van Laer & van Aelst, 2010.
22. Baym, 2010; Hallin, 1992.
23. Williams & Delli Carpini, 2011.
24. Ibid.
25. Boyd, 2014.
26. Bimber, 2003; Schudson, 1998; Starr, 2004; Williams & Delli Carpini, 2011.

27. Dahl, 1989, p. 13.
28. Delli Carpini & Keeter, 1996, p. 25.
29. Arendt, 1958; Habermas, 1962/1989.
30. Lee & Fouts, 2005, p. 133.
31. Dahl, 1989, pp. 19–20; Pasley, 2002; Sheehan, 2009.
32. Carey, 1993; Darnton, 2010; Habermas, 1962/1989.
33. Carey, 1993, pp. 6–7.
34. Bailyn, 1967.
35. Anderson, 1983/1991; Habermas, 1962/1989; Schudson, 1998.
36. For a rich discussion of James Madison's concerns about providing communications to knit together a diverse republic closely—but not too closely—see Sheehan, 2009.
37. Koschnik, 2001.
38. Carey, 1993; Schudson, 1998, p. 19.
39. Carey, 1993; Habermas, 1962/1989; Nerone, 2011, p. 745; Sheehan, 2009.
40. Bimber, 2003; Starr, 2004.
41. Carey, 1993.
42. Nerone, 2011, pp. 745–746.
43. Bimber, 2003, p. 51; John, 1998; Starr, 2004.
44. Bimber, 2003, p. 55.
45. Nerone, 2011, p. 746; Pasley, 2002.
46. Nerone, 2011, p. 747.
47. Pasley, 2002.
48. Ibid., p. 11.
49. Clemens, 1997; Nerone, 2011; Schudson, 1998; Skocpol, Ganz, & Munson, 2000.
50. Pasley, 2002; Nerone, 2011.
51. Sheehan, 2009; see Kielbowicz, 1983, for an analysis of the actual cohesiveness of party newspapers in 1832.
52. Schudson, 1978.
53. Grimsted, 1972; John, 1998.
54. Schudson, 1998.
55. Levine, 2000.
56. Skocpol, 2003.
57. See Skocpol & Fiorina, 1999.
58. See, e.g., Odegard, 1928.
59. Almond & Verba, 1963, p. 245.
60. Schudson, 1998, p. 196.
61. Lippmann, 1922, p. 11.
62. Hallin, 1992.
63. Mindich, 2004; See also Zaller, 2003.
64. Blumler & Kavanagh, 1999; Hallin, 1992, 2006.
65. Castells, 2009; Iyengar & McGrady, 2006; Zaller, 1999.
66. On the "political spectacle," Edelman, 1988; on dysfunctional relationships between politicians and media figures; Blumler & Kavanagh, 1999; Cappella & Jamieson, 1997.
67. On a "democracy without citizens," Entman, 1989; "crisis in public communication" comes from Blumler & Gurevitch, 1995.
68. This is Skocpol's "diminished democracy," 2003; See also Hayes, 1983, for an early perspective on this trend.
69. See, e.g., Hindman, 2008; Prior, 2007.
70. For example, see Rheingold, 1993, and Turner, 2006 on the Whole Earth 'Lectronic Link and digital networking in the 1980s.
71. Purcell, Rainie, Mitchell, Rosenstiel, & Olmstead, 2010.
72. Kreiss, 2012; Plouffe, 2009; Trippi, 2004.
73. Lessig, 2005, p. 43; see also Shirky, 2008; on the macaca moment see Gueorguieva, 2008; on guns and religion, Reid, 2008.
74. Bimber, 2003; Bimber, Flanagin, & Stohl, 2005; Karpf, 2012.

75. E.g., Palfrey & Gasser, 2008.
76. Rheingold, 2003.
77. Bimber, Flanagin, & Stohl, 2005.
78. Kreiss & Tufekci, 2013.
79. Bennett et al., 2008; Karpf, 2012.
80. Bennett & Segerberg, 2011; Papacharissi, 2010.
81. Franzen, 2011; Tufekci & Wilson, 2012; van Laer & van Aelst, 2010; see Bennett & Segerberg, 2011, for an optimistic view.
82. Cf. Bimber et al., 2012.
83. Bennett, 2008; Dalton, 2009; Inglehart, 1997; Zukin et al., 2006; we also might include the oft-used "millenials," though this term is more often used to refer to a generation than a set of behaviors or attitudes.
84. Rheingold, 2003; Shirky, 2008.
85. Morozov, 2011.
86. Kreiss & Tufekci, 2013; Gladwell, 2010; Morozov, 2011; van Laer & van Aelst, 2010.
87. Kreiss et al., 2011.
88. Rainie & Wellman, 2012; Wellman, 2001.
89. Putnam, 2000, and Skocpol, 2003, both describe structures and social contexts that are hard to imagine returning.
90. Bimber, 2003; Rainie & Wellman, 2012.

Chapter 2

1. Franklin, 2009.
2. Linkins, 2009.
3. On the uniqueness of Cronkite, see Brinkley, 2012; on changes in broadcast news style, see Baym, 2009; on soft news, see Patterson, 2000; on profit motives, see Hamilton, 2004; on press-state relations, see Bennett, Lawrence, & Livingston, 2007 and Cook, 1998; on the collapse of political consensus, see Hallin, 1992.
4. Baym, 2009; Hallin, 1992.
5. Prior, 2007.
6. Mindich, 2004; Patterson, 2007; Wattenberg, 2008.
7. Benson, 2000; Hallin, 2000.
8. Baym, 2009, p. 64.
9. Thorson, 2010.
10. Levine, 2007.
11. See, e.g., Beck, 1999; Beck & Beck-Gernsheim, 2002; Blumler & Kavanagh, 1999; Castells, 1996, 2009; Giddens, 1991.
12. Giddens, 1991.
13. Kreiss et al., 2010; Lupia & Sin, 2003.
14. Bimber, 2003.
15. Putnam, 2000; while Putnam's argument has received criticism from nearly every side, there is general consensus on the decline of citizen participation in formal organizations. See, e.g., Bennett, 1998.
16. Castells, 1996.
17. See, e.g., Tarrow, 2005.
18. Bennett, 1998; Giddens, 1991.
19. Papacharissi, 2010, p. 97; Tarrow, 2005.
20. Bennett, 1998.
21. Beck, 1999.
22. Ibid.; Giddens, 1991.
23. Blumler & Kavanagh, 1999.
24. Bennett, 1998, 2008; Hallin, 1992; Zukin et al., 2006.
25. Inglehart 1997, p. 299.

26. Schudson, 1998.
27. Putnam, 2000; Skocpol, 2003.
28. Castells, 1996, p. 23.
29. Ibid., pp. 23–24.
30. Mentioned in Skocpol, 2003, p. 119.
31. Giddens, 1991, p. 243.
32. Ibid., p. 215.
33. Blumler & Kavanagh, 1999, following Ulrich Beck, detect a trend toward "aestheticization" of all aspects of life; on lifestyle politics, see Bennett, 1998; Giddens, 1991.
34. Rainie & Wellman, 2012; Wellman, 2001.
35. Rainie & Wellman, 2012; see also Castells, 1996.
36. Livingstone, 2009; Papacharissi, 2010.
37. Blumler & Kavanagh, 1999.
38. Skocpol, 2003.
39. Bennett, 1998; Zukin et al., 2006.
40. Brokaw, 1998; Putnam, 2000.
41. Whether the mid-twentieth century in fact represented a high point of civic activity is the subject of some debate. Though Putnam traces declines in group membership from the mid-twentieth century, there is some evidence that many civic practices were already falling by then; Schudson, 1998.
42. On knowledge and interest in politics and voting see Wattenberg, 2008; on news consumption, see Mindich, 2004, and Patterson, 2007; on a sense of obligation, see Zukin et al., 2006.
43. E.g., Zogby, 2008; a significant portion of the scholarship on creative youth uses of digital media suggest this perspective as well—e.g., Ito et al., 2009; Jenkins, 2006; Palfrey & Gasser, 2008.
44. Dalton, 2009, p. 68; Dalton also presents a number of methodological critiques of the decline narrative, including the data on which it (e.g., Putnam, 1995; 2000) is based. Dalton thinks the commercial surveys Putnam uses have issues with sampling and inconsistent wording, and that the use of voting age public instead of voting eligible public in describing voter turnout leads to misleading conclusions. This critique is in line with others that also note that given only slightly modified (updated) survey items, several of Putnam's key findings greatly weaken (Sirianni & Friedland, 2001).
45. Following Tilly's repertoires of contention at the level of social movement, engagement repertoire here refers to the set of civic actions available to and selected by individuals; see also Bimber, Flanagin, & Stohl, 2012; van Laer & van Aelst, 2010.
46. Zukin et al., 2006, pp. 8, 61.
47. Levine, 2000; Macedo, 2005.
48. Bennett, 1998; Giddens, 1991.
49. Scammell, 2003; Stolle, Hooghe, & Micheletti, 2005.
50. Carr, Gotlieb, Lee, & Shah, 2012; Zukin et al., 2006, p. 77.
51. Zukin et al., 2006, p. 76; the same patterns are reported by Dalton, 2009.
52. Targeting corporations and business entities, on the other hand, is: Zukin et al., 2006, report that the youngest citizens in their study were more than twice as likely than baby boomers to feel that business and corporations have more impact on their lives than government; p. 117.
53. Ibid., p. 93.
54. Inglehart, 1997; Dalton, 2009; Bennett, 2008; Schudson, 1998.
55. Thorson, 2010.
56. Ibid.
57. E.g., Bennett, Freelon, & Wells, 2010.
58. Bimber et al., 2012.
59. See, e.g., Deuze, 2006; Ito et al., 2009; Palfrey & Gasser, 2008.
60. Palfrey & Gasser, 2008.
61. Livingstone, 2009.

62. Ibid.; Boyd, 2014.
63. Livingstone, 2009, p. 117.
64. Deuze, 2006, n. 1.
65. Ibid., p. 63.
66. Deuze, 2006, identifies the first two of these.
67. Ibid., p. 68.
68. Giddens, 1991, for example, sees the drive for participation as one of hallmarks of the modern era's "emancipatory politics." See also Papacharissi, 2010.
69. This is the "secularization" described by Blumler & Kavanagh, 1999.
70. Deuze, 2006; Thorson, 2010.
71. Deuze, 2006, p. 68.
72. Jenkins, 2006.
73. Palfrey & Gasser, 2008.
74. Jenkins et al., 2008.
75. Lankes, 2008; Rainie & Wellman, 2012, p. 229.
76. Purcell et al., 2010.
77. E.g., by Boyd & Ellison, 2007; Livingstone, 2009; Palfrey & Gasser, 2008.
78. Bennett et al., 2010; Earl & Kimport, 2011; Earl & Schussman, 2008.
79. Reynolds, 2009. As of this writing, "United Breaks Guitars" and several sequels have cumulatively received well over 10 million views on YouTube: www.davecarrollmusic.com/ubg/song1/.
80. McCartney, 2010b.
81. McCartney, 2010a.
82. These topics will be important ones in Chapter 3. See Bennett & Segerberg, 2011; Bimber, Flanagin, & Stohl, 2005.
83. Blumler & Kavanah, 1999.
84. Castells, 2009.
85. E.g., Earl & Schussman, 2008.
86. Rainie & Wellman, 2012, p. 78.
87. Turner, 2006.
88. Ibid., p. 237.
89. Bimber et al., 2012.
90. Bennett, 2008; Dalton, 2009.
91. Bennett et al., 2009.
92. Baym, 2009.
93. Purcell et al., 2010.
94. Corburn, 2005; Sirianni, 2009.
95. Bennett, 1998.
96. Lankes, 2008.
97. O'Connor, 2009.
98. Karpf, 2012; Morozov, 2011.
99. E.g., Verba, Schlozman, & Brady, 1995.
100. Earl & Kimport, 2011.
101. Zukin et al., 2006, p. 76.
102. Smith, Schlozman, Verba, & Brady, 2009, p. 40; Only 16% of young citizens (18–24 years old) took part in at least two of the five key traditional online activities asked about in the survey (contacting a government official, signing a petition, sending a letter to an editor, donating money, or contacting a political group). Meanwhile, 20% or more of each of the older age categories, until age 65, engaged in at least two of the activities. When only Internet users, as opposed to the whole population, are considered, the divide widens further because younger people are more likely to be online.
103. Smith, 2009, p. 45; it should be emphasized that we are comparing across individuals who use social networking sites; thus, the fact that younger citizens were more likely than their elders to use social networking sites in 2008 does not explain the activity difference described here.

104. Ibid., p. 42.
105. Smith, 2013.
106. Bucy & Gregson, 2001.

Chapter 3

1. Boyte & Kari, 1996; Knoke, 1981; Schlozman & Tierney, 1986.
2. E.g., Truman, 1951; Walker, 1991.
3. Barakso, 2004; Eisinger, 1973.
4. Castells, 1996; Chadwick, 2007; Rainie & Wellman, 2012.
5. Scolari, 2012; Truman, 1951.
6. A small sample of relevant citations includes: on interest groups, Barakso, 2004, Berry & Wilcox, 2005, Berry, 1999, Schlozman & Tierney, 1986, Truman, 1951, Walker, 1991, Wilson, 1973; on social movements and social movement organizations, Della Porta & Tarrow, 2004, Earl & Kimport, 2011, Davis, McAdam, Scott, & Zald, 2005; on voluntary associations, Lipset, Trow, & Coleman, 1956; Putnam, 2000; on collective action, Hirschman, 1970, Olson, 1965; Bimber et al., 2012.
7. Clemens, 2005; Davis et al., 2005.
8. Boy Scouts of America, n.d. Of course, in recent years the Boy Scouts have been drawn into politicized issues such as the membership statuses of gay Boy Scouts and leaders; Eckholm, 2012.
9. Karpf, 2012.
10. Putnam, 2000.
11. E.g., Bimber et al., 2012.
12. Almond & Verba, 1963; Clemens, 1997; Walker, 1991.
13. For account of some of the earliest American examples of explicitly political organizations making themselves known to potential supporters through newspapers, see Koschnik, 2001; Nerone, 2011.
14. Walker, 1983, p. 396.
15. Baym, 2010.
16. Tocqueville, 1835/1964; see Koschnik, 2001; Nerone, 2011.
17. Karpf, 2012.
18. Pasley, 2002.
19. Jones, 2009.
20. Barakso, 2004; Bimber, Flanagin, & Stohl, 2012, p. 83.
21. Barakso & Schaffner, 2008.
22. Michels, 1915.
23. Schlozman & Tierney, 1986, p. 134.
24. Knoke, 1981, p. 143.
25. Hirschman, 1970; the importance of communication channels to organizational democracy is emphasized by Lipset et al., 1956, in their study of the internal politics of a labor union.
26. Tocqueville, 1835/1964, p. 181.
27. Clemens, 1997; Crowley & Skocpol, 2001.
28. Skocpol, 1999, pp. 53–54.
29. Clemens, 1999; Lipset et al., 1956.
30. This point is clear in the formation of various of the antialcohol associations at the end of the nineteenth century. Both Willard (1883) and Odegard (1928) show that larger-level (national) organizing structures followed more local organizations. Later organizations, by contrast, often created chapters as after thoughts to the main, federal-level organization: see Barakso, 2004, p. 33, on the founding of the National Organization for Women (NOW) in the late 1960s; and Lipset et al., 1956, p. 395 for a similar comparison.
31. Putnam, 2000; Skocpol, 1999, p. 67.
32. Levine, 2000.

33. Pasley, 2000.
34. Quoted by Odegard, 1928, p. 77.
35. Tapia, 1997.
36. Ibid., p. 15.
37. Ibid., p. 11.
38. Willard, 1883, p. 125.
39. Skocpol, 1999, p. 46; Walker, 1983.
40. Nerone, 2011.
41. Pasley, 2002, p. 9.
42. Odegard, 1928, p. 75; I thank Matthew Hindman for pointing me to this historical evidence.
43. Ibid.
44. Verba, Schlozman, & Brady, 1995; Wilson, 1973.
45. Almond & Verba, 1963.
46. Clemens, 1997, p. 197.
47. Putnam, 2000; Sirianni & Friedland, 2001; Skocpol, 2003; counterexamples can be found in Barakso, 2004, and Bimber et al., 2012.
48. Blumler & Kavanagh, 1999; Walker, 1991.
49. Sirianni & Friedland, 2001.
50. Skocpol, 2003, pp. 201–202.
51. Skocpol, 2003; the same trend is identified by scholars of interest groups, though with more emphasis on the expansion of representation for many citizens. Walker, 1983, notes: "there are many more interest groups operating in Washington today than in the years before World War II, and citizen groups make up a larger proportion of the total than ever before" (p. 395).
52. Edelman, 1988; Entman, 1989.
53. Castells, 2009; Zaller, 1999.
54. Castells, 2009.
55. Blumler & Kavanagh, 1999, p. 214.
56. Gibson & Ward, 2012; Stromer-Galley, 2000.
57. Bimber et al., 2009; Skocpol, 2004.
58. Though see Bimber et al., 2012 for findings indicating that interpersonal interactions happen in wider a variety of civic groups that we might assume.
59. Fisher, 2006.
60. Hirschman, 1970.
61. Putnam, 2000; Wattenberg, 2008; Zukin et al., 2006; also see discussion in Chapter 1.
62. Benkler, 2006; Shirky, 2008.
63. On transnational movements, see Tarrow, 2005; Rheingold, 2003; on multiplayer games, Jenkins, 2006; on alternative modes of cultural production, Benkler, 2006.
64. Benkler, 2006, pp. 3–4.
65. Jenkins, 2006; Wojcieszak, 2010.
66. Olson, 1965.
67. Shirky, 2008.
68. See, e.g., Morozov, 2011.
69. Davis & Zald, 2005.
70. Flanagin et al., 2006, p.32.
71. Bimber, Flanagin, & Stohl, 2005; Olson, 1965.
72. Bimber, 2003.
73. Flanagin et al., 2006, p. 31.
74. Kreiss, 2012.
75. Karpf, 2012.
76. Scolari, 2012.
77. Credit is due Coleman, 2008, for an early elaboration of the notion of autonomy in the context of web communication.
78. Clemens, 1997, p. 36.

79. Gitlin, 2011.
80. The prevalence of such discourses is highlighted best by its ironic counterpart in satirical newspaper *The Onion*: "Internet Users Demand Less Interactivity: 'We Just Want to Visit Websites and Look at Them,' Users Say" (2013).
81. Corburn, 2005.
82. Flanagin et al., 2006.
83. Wilson, 1995, p. 247.
84. Barakso, 2004, p. 3.
85. Bimber et al., 2012, emphatically make this point about the diverse types of organizations, and citizen involvement possibilities, at play in the contemporary civic arena.
86. Bimber, 2003, p. 98.
87. Karpf, 2012.
88. Coleman, 2008; Wells, 2010.
89. Foot & Schneider, 2006.
90. Ibid., 2006.
91. Palfrey & Gasser, 2008.
92. See, e.g., Raynes-Goldie &Walker, 2008, who report 130,000 total profiles for TakingITGlobal as of 2006.
93. McGirt, 2009.
94. Raynes-Goldie & Walker, 2008.
95. Smith, 2009.
96. Lenhart, Purcell, Smith, & Zickuhr, 2010.
97. Bimber et al., 2012.

Chapter 4

1. Lenhart, Purcell, Smith, & Zickuhr, 2010; Toma & Hancock, 2010
2. Berners-Lee, 2010.
3. Foot & Schneider, 2006.
4. In keeping with the book's focus on young people's engagement, organizations were only included if they explicitly focused on youth engagement or otherwise offered specific resources for youth involvement, such as a particular portion of a political party's website; see Appendix A for sampling details.
5. I follow Wells, 2010 in identifying websites that are online only as a discrete category.
6. Bimber, 2003.
7. Sirianni, 2009.
8. Zukin et al., 2006.
9. For sampling details, see Appendix A.
10. Kenski, Hardy, & Jamieson, 2010; Kreiss, 2012; Plouffe, 2009.
11. CIRCLE, 2009; McKinney, 2011.
12. This classification of civic information builds on the learning typology developed by Bennett, Wells, & Rank, 2009, which revealed four civic skill set categories including knowledge and taking action. Foot & Schneider, 2006, similarly identify distinct categories of function for campaign websites, including "informing" and "mobilizing."
13. Websites are large, complex, and idiosyncratically organized, necessitating some degree of simplification in analysis. In the present case, the coders' task was simplified by only considering pages one link from the homepage. The assumption was that an organization would place its primary attempts to communicate with a visitor reasonably near to the page on which they arrived. Second, each coder was allowed to select not more than three pages per website for knowledge, and a further three for action. To ensure interrater reliability, coders' page selections were compared, and differences were resolved by collectively considering the websites and discussing them. For coding details, see Appendix C.
14. Kreiss, 2012; Ward & Gibson, 2009.

15. Earl & Kimport, 2011.
16. E.g., Earl & Kimport, 2009.
17. Cf. Papacharissi's (2010) notion of a "private sphere."
18. Bimber et al., 2012.
19. In fact, there were a further five pages identified in the mode of interaction coding process as dutiful action, but data errors caused these pages to be lost before activity coding could take place.
20. For coding details and reliabilities, see Appendix C.
21. Bimber et al., 2012; Earl & Kimport, 2011.
22. Kreiss, 2012.
23. Kreiss, 2012.
24. In fact, though a relatively youthful thirty-two, Barely Political creator Ben Relles was already a business school graduate and described himself as a "digital strategist" when the video was produced; Sklar, 2008.
25. Kreiss, 2012, p. 11.
26. Karpf, 2012.
27. Foot & Schneider, 2006.

Chapter 5

1. E.g., Foot & Schneider, 2006.
2. Boyd & Ellison, 2007.
3. E.g., Stromer-Galley, 2000.
4. West, 2011; Wortham, 2012.
5. Hempel, 2010.
6. Ibid.; Kazeniac, 2009.
7. Waters, Burnett, Lamm, & Lucas, 2009.
8. Delo, 2013; Inside Facebok, 2010; Madden & Zickuhr, 2011.
9. Zickuhr, 2010.
10. Notwithstanding, as Foot & Schneider, 2006, point out, that websites of political groups do tend to conform to community norms about what websites are for and how they should look.
11. Waters et al., 2009.
12. These were Servenet, from the online only category, and Youth Service America, from the community category. The Facebook Page was titled Youth Service America, and retained for this study in the community category.
13. It is thus a limitation of the present study that it considers only Facebook Pages, but the limitation is necessary to stay clearly within the bounds of Facebook's terms of service (see Appendix G). Analyzing only Pages also simplified the problem of identifying which are officially identified with the organizations under analysis.
14. In the process of selecting Facebook Pages, several minor amendments to the organizational list also had to be made. First, from the community category, because the local Girl Scouts chapter analyzed in the website study had no Facebook presence, it was replaced by the national Girl Scouts Page. Similarly, the local Boy Scouts chapter had created a Facebook Page, but clearly did not use it; it was also replaced by the organization's national page. Within the interest category, we similarly used the national NRA Page, the Greenpeace USA Page, the main UNICEF Page, and the national Sierra Club Page. In each of these cases, the decision to use a main Page rather than a specific youth-oriented Page was made either because no youth-specific Page had been created, one existed but displayed minimal activity, or the youth Page was dedicated to a very specific program (e.g., in the case of the NRA, a specific youth hunter education and competition program). In all, in line with our expectations about the Facebook context, it was clear that organizations expected young supporters to like and participate within the context of their main Page.

15. Thompson, 2008.
16. O'Connor, 2009.
17. To make the data-gathering and coding tasks manageable, from more prolific organizations (those posting 15 or more times per month, or, roughly, every other day) every third status update was gathered. From organizations that posted fewer than 15 times per month every status update was gathered and analyzed. The different rates of gathering were corrected for in analyses.
18. Drew, 2013.
19. In keeping with the spirit of Facebook's Statement of Rights and Responsibilities, images in this chapter are presented with names of individuals commenting on or liking an organization's post blacked out.
20. Bennett & Manheim, 2006.
21. It is worth noting that the EPA has a history of working with citizens and communities in a collaborative way. See Sirianni, 2009, chapter 5. See also Chapter 3.
22. Almond & Verba, 1963. See also Chapter 3.
23. The link analysis was applied to links contained in status updates—both those in which a status update specifically used Facebook's link function and those in which links were placed as hypertext directly in the status update text. Though now relatively rare owing to the improvement of Facebook's ability to recognize links, this was not uncommon in 2010. To determine intercoder reliability for these variables, the author and an assistant coded a subset of 184 (10%) of the 1,844 total status updates in the sample. In determining whether a link was internal or external, the reliability was 98.7%. The remaining sample was then coded by the author. In five cases (0.3% of the sample) the link had expired and it was no longer possible to analyze it. (See Appendix G.)
24. The coding process was as follows: the coder first viewed the text of the link. For most internal links, the name of the organization was visible in the link text—for example, it read something like www.facebook.com/dosomething/exampletext. In these cases, the coder could code the link without following it to its destination. If it was not clearly visible whether the link was internal or external, or what the link's destination was, the coder clicked the link and looked at the one page that was the link's destination. The coder read the entire page, and coded the link as internal if the organization's name appeared anywhere on the page, included as a sponsor of a project, an affiliate of another organization, or the subject of a news article. The reasoning behind this is that in such cases the organization is primarily linking to the page to tell its fans something about itself, or to advertise to fans what it is doing or has done. If the destination page did not contain the name of the linking organization, the link was coded as external. The one exception to the latter rule occurred in the government/party category, where cases in which politicians, the College Democrats, or the College Republicans offered links to websites sponsored by their own party were considered internal, even if the destination page did not specifically name the politician or college group. See also Appendix G.
25. Coleman, 2008.
26. Marwick, 2013.
27. Anderson, 2006.
28. O'Connor, 2009.

Chapter 6

1. Inglehart, 1997.
2. Tapscott, 2009; Zogby, 2008.
3. Gallagher, 2013.
4. Dalton, 2009.
5. Putnam, 2013.

6. Foroohar, 2011.
7. Judt, 2010; Packer, 2013; Sachs, 2011.
8. Wagner, Wells, Friedland, Cramer, & Shah, 2014.
9. Haidt, 2012; Reedy, Wells, & Gastil, 2014.
10. BBC, 2014.
11. Zukin et al., 2006.
12. Kreiss & Tufekci, 2012.
13. I am grateful to an anonymous reviewer for this observation; Savage, 1999; Sirianni, 2009, p. 114.
14. Karpf, 2012.
15. Livingstone, 2013.
16. E.g., Bennett, Wells, & Rank, 2009; Dalton, 2009; Mindich, 2004; Palfrey & Gasser, 2008; Patterson, 2007; Zukin et al., 2006.
17. Bimber et al., 2012; Earl & Kimport, 2011; Karpf, 2012; Kreiss, 2012.
18. See Bimber et al., 2012, for three case studies offering glimpses to answers of some of these.
19. Patterson, 2000.
20. Corburn, 2005; Sirianni, 2009.
21. Foot & Schneider, 2002; Stromer-Galley, 2000.
22. Foot & Schneider, 2006.
23. Cf. Kreiss, 2012.
24. Graham, Broersma, Hazelhoff, & van 't Haar, 2013; West, 2011.
25. Skocpol, 2003.
26. Cappella & Jamieson, 1997.
27. Zittrain, 2008.
28. Bimber, 2003, p. 106; Putnam, 2000.
29. E.g., Coleman & Blumler, 2009; Sirianni, 2009; West, 2011.
30. Bimber et al., 2009; Karpf, 2012.
31. Karpf, 2012, p. 169.
32. Kreiss & Tufekci, 2012, p. 5.
33. Kreiss, 2012; Polletta, 2013.
34. Kreiss & Tufekci, 2012, p. 4.
35. Kazin, 2011.
36. Putnam, 2000.
37. Gladwell, 2010; Hirschman, 1970.
38. E.g., Rainie & Wellman, 2012; Shah, Kwak, & Holbert, 2001.
39. Verba, Schlozman, & Brady, 1995.
40. Barakso, 2004.
41. Benkler, 2006; Shirky, 2008.
42. Chadwick, 2007; Flanagin et al., 2006, p. 43.
43. Chen, 2009; Polletta, 2013.
44. Wilson, 1973.
45. Chen, 2009.
46. Polletta, 2002.
47. Macedo, 2005, p. 119
48. Sirianni, 2009.
49. E.g., West, 2011.
50. Polletta, 2013, p. 41.
51. Castells, 2009; Papacharissi, 2010.
52. Bucy & Gregson, 2001.
53. Pingree, 2007.
54. Papacharissi, 2009.
55. Hirschman, 1970; though interestingly, one study exploring this question failed to find evidence for such a relationship: Rojas & Puig-i-abril, 2009.
56. Bucy & Gregson, 2001.

57. Shah, Thorson, Wells, Lee, & McLeod, forthcoming.
58. Mazzoleni & Schulz, 1999.
59. Gitlin, 2012.
60. Blumler & Kavanagh, 1999; Castells, 2009.
61. Williams & Delli Carpini, 2011.
62. Bond et al., 2012.
63. Drusch, 2013.
64. Dalton, 2009; Downs, 1957.
65. Papacharissi, 2009.
66. Gladwell, 2010.
67. Quoted by Bennett & Wells, 2009, p. 7.
68. Credit is due Lew Friedman for pointing me to the connections with Hirschman's work.
69. Hirschman, 1970; Lipset et al., 1956.
70. Kreiss & Tufekci, 2012.
71. E.g., by political consumption or volunteering—highly individualized activities; Zukin et al., 2006.
72. Tapscott, 2009, p. 75.
73. E.g., Corburn, 2005.
74. Paulson, 2014.
75. Jenkins & Carpentier, 2013; Livingstone, 2013.
76. Benkler, 2006; Shirky, 2008; Surowiecki, 2005.
77. Polletta, 2013, p. 48.
78. Tedesco, 2007; see Nisbet & Scheufele, 2004 for a similar result regarding online discussion.
79. Freelon, Wells, & Bennett, 2013.
80. Kazin, 2011; Schwartz, 2011.
81. Polletta, 2013.

Appendix

1. Montgomery, Gottlieb-Robles, and Larson's study (2004) provided 348 sites that passed an initial, automated test of having current activity. From the studies of Bennett and Xenos (2004; 2005; Xenos & Bennett, 2007) and Wells (2010) were drawn an additional 70 sites. After the compilation of those sites, all were checked manually, eliminating 161 that were duplicates, had not been active for more than a year, or were no longer online.
2. The list can be found in Clolery & Hrywna, 2006.
3. Key terms included: political positions (e.g., libertarian, socialist), political issues (gay rights, 2nd amendment), current issues of concern (sustainability, Darfur, media literacy), ethnicities (African American, Latino), and religions (Christian, Muslim).
4. Our process involved looking first on the homepage, then on an "About" page, for evidence that the site was for youth (e.g., references to youth, students, kids, age ranges under 30) and that it involved some form of public engagement (e.g., getting involved, improving one's community, speaking out, activism).
5. Following agreement that a learning goal was present on a site, agreement on the first page selected was as follows: knowledge, 91.6%; action, 95.6%. Looking at the second most-selected page, though slightly lower, the agreement is acceptable: knowledge, 79.6%; action, 73.9%. Coders only selected three pages for knowledge or action if all coders agreed, following deliberation, on all three pages.
6. Such agreement is in line with exploratory research of this sort: Bachen, Raphael, Lynn, McKee, & Philippi, 2008; Neuendorf, 2002.
7. Again, this level of reliability is in the accepted range for exploratory research with little precedent. As Bachen et al., 2008, note, though pairwise percent agreement has its limitations, in analyses of variables with limited variation more sophisticated metrics such

as Krippendorff's Alpha and Cohen's Kappa "produce extremely low (or incalculable) reliabilities" (n. 6); See also Riffe, Lacy, & Fico, 2005.

8. This reliability may also be calculated by collapsing the coders' decisions into measures of presence/absence of each of the three general activity categories. This measure also shows very high reliability: the coders' agreement on presence of one or more offline activity on a given page was 93.8%, of dutiful activity 100%, and of actualizing activity 87.5%.

9. As noted in Chapter 4, reliabilities in this range are very much within the accepted range for exploratory analytic methods such as this; see Appendix C.

10. There was one addition that needed to be made: following from the discussion of organization-driven action and fan-driven knowledge above, one type of activity that occurred in status updates but was not observed in the website context was an invitation to participate in a contest or organization-led process that involved contributing some kind of idea or content. This type of content was specifically coded for in activities coding in the following way: in the initial coding process an identical codesheet to that used in the website study was employed, and cases of entering contests or otherwise participating in institutional activities were grouped with the "join an online group" activity from the website study. That category was then separately analyzed to separate cases of merely joining from those in which the joining in some way involved a supporter creating some kind of novel content, or otherwise contributing some kind of idea (for instance, contributing a name to a nomination process).

11. Reliabilities when collapsing the individual actions into the three groups, as in Chapter 4, were similarly high: 89.7% for offline activities, 95.3% for dutiful activities, and 87.5% for networked/expressive activities. The process of bifurcating the one category that included some instances of supporter-produced content received 91.7% agreement.

12. Statement, Section 12, downloaded April 11, 2010.

References

Almond, G., & Verba, S. (1963). *The civic culture: Political attitudes and democracy in five nations.* Princeton, NJ: Princeton University Press.

Anderson, B. (1983/1991). *Imagined communities: Reflections on the origin and spread of nationalism.* London, New York: Verso.

Anderson, N. (2006, September 1). Tim Berners-Lee on Web 2.0: "Nobody even knows what it means." *Ars Technica.* Retrieved from http://arstechnica.com/business/2006/09/7650/

Arendt, H. (1958). *The human condition.* Chicago: University of Chicago Press.

Bachen, C., Raphael, C., Lynn, K., McKee, K., & Philippi, J. (2008). Civic engagement, pedagogy, and information technology on web sites for youth. *Political Communication, 25*(3), 290–310.

Bailyn, B. (1967). *The ideological origins of the American Revolution.* Cambridge, MA: Harvard University Press.

Barakso, M. (2004). *Governing NOW: Grassroots activism in the National Organization For Women.* Ithaca, NY: Cornell University Press.

Barakso, M., & Schaffner, B. F. (2008). Exit, voice, and interest group governance. *American Politics Research, 36*(2), 186–209. doi:10.1177/1532673X07306545

Barlow, J. P. (1993). The economy of ideas: A framework for patents and copyrights in the Digital Age. (Everything you know about intellectual property is wrong). *Wired, 2*(3). Retrieved from http://www.wired.com/wired/archive/2.03/economy.ideas_pr.html

Baym, G. (2009). *From Cronkite to Colbert: The evolution of broadcast news.* Boulder, CO: Paradigm Publishers.

BBC. (2014). Briton tells of his "fighting in Iraq." Retrieved from http://www.bbc.com/news/uk-28684671

Beck, U. (1999). *World risk society.* Cambridge: Polity.

Beck, U., & Beck-Gernsheim, E. (2002). *Individualization: Institutionalized individualism and its social and political consequences.* Thousand Oaks, CA: Sage Publications.

Benkler, Y. (2006). *The wealth of networks: How social production transforms markets and freedom.* New Haven, CT: Yale University Press.

Bennett, W. L. (1998). The uncivic culture: Communication, identity, and the rise of lifestyle politics. *PS: Political Science & Politics, 31*(4), 741–761.

Bennett, W. L. (2008). Changing citizenship in the digital age. In W. L. Bennett (Ed.), *Civic life online : learning how digital media can engage youth* (pp. 1–24). Cambridge, Mass.: MIT Press.

Bennett, W. L., Breunig, C., & Givens, T. (2008). Communication and political mobilization: Digital media and the organization of Anti-Iraq War demonstrations in the U.S. *Political Communication, 25*(3), 269–289. doi:10.1080/10584600802197434

Bennett, W. L., Freelon, D., & Wells, C. (2010). Changing citizen identity and the rise of a participatory media culture. In L. R. Sherrod, J. Torney-Purta, & C. A. Flanagan (Eds.), *Handbook of Research on Civic Engagement in Youth* (pp. 393–424). Hoboken, NJ: John Wiley and Sons.

Bennett, W. L., Lawrence, R. G., & Livingston, S. (2007). *When the press fails: Political power and the news media from Iraq to Katrina.* Chicago: University Of Chicago Press.

Bennett, W. L., & Manheim, J. B. (2006). The one-step flow of communication. *The ANNALS of the American Academy of Political and Social Science, 608*(1), 213–232. doi:10.1177/0002716206292266

Bennett, W. L., & Segerberg, A. (2011). Digital media and the personalization of collective action. *Information Communication & Society, 14*(5), 1–30.

Bennett, W. L., & Wells, C. (2009). Civic engagement: Bridging differences to build a field of civic learning. *International Journal of Learning and Media, 1*(3), 1–10.

Bennett, W. L., Wells, C., & Rank, A. (2009). Young citizens and civic learning: two paradigms of citizenship in the digital age. *Citizenship Studies, 13*(2), 105–120. doi:10.1080/13621020902731116

Bennett, W. L., & Xenos, M. (2004). *Young voters and the web of politics: Pathways to participation in the youth engagement and electoral campaign web sphere.* College Park, MD: Center for Information & Research on Civic Learning and Engagement (CIRCLE).

Bennett, W. L., & Xenos, M. (2005). *Young voters and the web of politics 2004: The youth political web sphere comes of age.* College Park, MD: Center for Information & Research on Civic Learning and Engagement (CIRCLE).

Benson, R. (2000). Tearing down the "wall" in American journalism. *Actes de la recherche en sciences sociales, 131-132*, 107–115.

Berners-Lee, T. (2010). Tim Berners-Lee. Retrieved November 12, 2010, from http://www.w3.org/People/Berners-Lee/Overview.html

Berry, J. M. (1999). *New liberalism: The rising power of citizen groups.* Washington, DC: Brookings Institution Press.

Berry, J. M., & Wilcox, C. (2005). *The interest group society.* New York: Pearson/Longman.

Bimber, B. (2003). *Information and American democracy: Technology in the evolution of political power.* Cambridge: Cambridge University Press.

Bimber, B., Flanagin, A. J., & Stohl, C. (2005). Reconceptualizing collective action in the contemporary media environment. *Communication Theory, 15*(4), 365–388.

Bimber, B., Flanagin, A., & Stohl, C. (2012). *Collective action in organizations: Interaction and engagement in an era of technological change.* Cambridge: Cambridge University Press.

Bimber, B., Stohl, C., & Flanagin, A. J. (2009). Technological change and the shifting nature of political organization. In A. Chadwick & P. N. Howard (Eds.), *Routledge Handbook of Internet Politics* (pp. 72–85). London: Routledge.

Blitzer, J. (2011, November 4). The aging of Spanish democracy. *The New York Times.* Retrieved from http://www.nytimes.com/2011/11/05/opinion/the-aging-of-spanish-democracy.html

Blumler, J. G., & Gurevitch, M. (1995). *The crisis of public communication.* New York: Routledge.

Blumler, J. G., & Kavanagh, D. (1999). The third age of political communication: Influences and features. *Political Communication, 16*(3), 209–230. doi:10.1080/105846099198596

Bond, R. M., Fariss, C. J., Jones, J. J., Kramer, A. D. I., Marlow, C., Settle, J. E., & Fowler, J. H. (2012). A 61-million-person experiment in social influence and political mobilization. *Nature, 489*(7415), 295–298. doi:10.1038/nature11421

Boy Scouts of America. (n.d.). Mission & Vision. Retrieved December 24, 2012, from http://www.scouting.org/scoutsource/Media/mission.aspx

boyd, d. (2014). *It's complicated: The social lives of networked teens.* New Haven, CT: Yale University Press.

boyd, d., & Ellison, N. B. (2007). Social network sites: Definition, history, and scholarship. *Journal of Computer-Mediated Communication, 13*(1). Retrieved from http://onlinelibrary.wiley.com/doi/10.1111/j.1083-6101.2007.0393.x/full

Boyte, H. C., & Kari, N. N. (1996). *Building America: The democratic promise of public work.* Philadelphia: Temple University Press.

Brinkley, D. (2012). *Cronkite.* New York: Harper Collins.

Brokaw, T. (1998). *The greatest generation.* New York: Random House.

Buckley, C., & Moynihan, C. (2011, November 4). Occupy Wall Street protest reaches a cross-roads. *The New York Times*. Retrieved from http://www.nytimes.com/2011/11/06/nyregion/occupy-wall-street-protest-reaches-a-crossroads.html

Bucy, E. P., & Gregson, K. S. (2001). Media participation: A legitimizing mechanism of mass democracy. *New Media & Society, 3*(3), 359–382.

Cappella, J. N., & Jamieson, K. H. (1997). *Spiral of cynicism: The press and the public good.* New York: Oxford University Press.

Carey, J. W. (1993). The mass media and democracy: Between the modern and the postmodern. *Journal of International Affairs, 47*(3), 1–21.

Carr, D. J., Gotlieb, M. R., Lee, N.-J., & Shah, D. V. (2012). Examining overconsumption, cop-metitive consumption, and conscious consumption from 1994 to 2004: Disentangling cohort and period effect. *Annals of the American Academy of Political and Social Science, 644*, 220–235.

Castells, M. (1996). *The rise of the network society.* Malden, MA: Blackwell Publishers.

Castells, M. (2009). *Communication power.* New York: Oxford University Press.

Chadwick, A. (2007). Digital network repertoires and organizational hybridity. *Political Communication, 24*(3), 283–301. doi:10.1080/10584600701471666

Chen, K. K. (2009). Enabling creative chaos: The organization behind the Burning Man event. Chicago: University Of Chicago Press.

CIRCLE. (2009). *New census data confirm increase in youth voter turnout in 2008 election.* Medford, MA: Tisch College, Tufts University. Retrieved from http://www.civicyouth.org/new-census-data-confirm-increase-in-youth-voter-turnout-in-2008-election/

Clemens, E. S. (1997). *The people's lobby: Organizational innovation and the rise of interest group politics in the United States, 1890–1925.* Chicago: University of Chicago Press.

Clemens, E. S. (1999). Organizational repertoires and institutional change: Women's groups and the transformation of American politics, 1890–1920. In T. Skocpol & M. P. Fiorina (Eds.), *Civic engagement in American democracy* (pp. 81–110). Washington, DC: Brookings Institution Press.

Clemens, E. S. (2005). Two kinds of stuff: The current encounter of social movements and orga-nizations. In G. F. Davis, D. McAdam, W. R. Scott, & M. N. Zald (Eds.), *Social movements and organization theory* (pp. 351–365). New York: Cambridge University Press.

Clolery, P., & Hrywna, M. (2006, November 1). Revenues of NPOs soaring. *Nonprofit Times*. Retrieved from http://www.nptimes.com/pdf/NPTTop1002006.pdf

Coleman, S. (2008). Doing IT for themselves: Management versus autonomy in youth e-citizenship. In W. L. Bennett (Ed.), *Civic life online: Learning how digital media can engage youth* (pp. 189–206). Cambridge, MA: MIT Press.

Coleman, S., & Blumler, J. G. (2009). *The Internet and democratic citizenship: Theory, practice and policy.* New York: Cambridge University Press.

Cook, T. E. (1998). *Governing with the news: The news media as a political institution.* Chicago: University of Chicago Press.

Corburn, J. (2005). Street science: Community knowledge and environmental health justice. Cambridge, MA: MIT Press.

Crowley, J. E., & Skocpol, T. (2001). The rush to organize: Explaining associational forma-tion in the United States, 1860s–1920s. *American Journal of Political Science, 45*(4), 813. doi:10.2307/2669326

Dahl, R. A. (1989). *Democracy and its critics.* New Haven, CT: Yale University Press.

Dalton, R. (2009). *The good citizen: How a younger generation is reshaping American politics.* Washington, DC: CQ Press.

Dalton, R. J. (2008). Citizenship norms and the expansion of political participation. *Political Studies, 56*(1), 76–98. doi:10.1111/j.1467-9248.2007.0718.x

Darnton, R. (2010). *Poetry and the police: Communication networks in eighteenth-century Paris.* Cambridge, MA: Belknap Press.

Davis, G. F., McAdam, D., Scott, W. R., & Zald, M. N. (Eds.). (2005). *Social movements and orga-nization theory.* Cambridge: Cambridge University Press.

Davis, G. F., & Zald, M. N. (2005). Social change, social theory, and the convergence of movements and organizations. In G. F. Davis, D. McAdam, W. R. Scott, & M. N. Zald (Eds.), *Social movements and organization theory* (pp. 335–350). New York: Cambridge University Press.

Della Porta, D., & Tarrow, S. (Eds.). (2005). *Transnational protest and global activism*. Lanham, MD: Rowman & Littlefield.

Delli Carpini, M., & Keeter, S. (1996). *What Americans know about politics and why it matters*. New Haven, CT: Yale University Press.

Delo, C. (2013, November 1). Marketers: Facebook still has way more teens than anyone else. *Ad Age*. Retrieved from http://adage.com/article/digital/marketers-facebook-teens/245073/

Deuze, M. (2006). Participation, remediation, bricolage: Considering principal components of a digital culture. *The Information Society, 22*(2), 63–75.

Downs, A. (1957). *An economic theory of democracy*. New York: Harper.

Drew, E. (2013, September 26). The stranglehold on our politics. *New York Review of Books*.

Drusch, A. (2013, August 24). 20-somethings jump into super PACs. *Politico*. Retrieved from http://www.politico.com/story/2013/08/super-pacs-twenty-somethings-95860.html

Earl, J., & Kimport, K. (2011). *Digitally enabled social change: Activism in the Internet age*. Cambridge, MA: MIT Press.

Earl, J., & Kimport, K. (2009). Movement societies and digital protest: Fan activism and other nonpolitical protest online. *Sociological Theory, 27*(3), 220–243.

Earl, J., & Schussman, A. (2008). Contesting cultural control: Youth culture and online petitioning. In W. L. Bennett (Ed.), *Civic life online: Learning how digital media can engage youth* (pp. 71–95). Cambridge, MA: MIT Press.

Eckholm, E. (2012, July 17). Boy Scouts reaffirm ban on gay members. *The New York Times*. Retrieved from http://www.nytimes.com/2012/07/18/us/boy-scouts-reaffirm-ban-on-gay-members.html

Edelman, M. (1988). *Constructing the political spectacle*. Chicago: University of Chicago Press.

BBC. (2012, January 21). Egypt's Islamists win elections. Retrieved from http://www.bbc.co.uk/news/world-middle-east-16665748

Eisinger, P. K. (1973). The conditions of protest behavior in American cities. *The American Political Science Review, 67*(1), 11–28. doi:10.2307/1958525

Entman, R. (1989). *Democracy without citizens: Media and the decay of American politics*. New York: Oxford University Press.

Fisher, D. (2006). *Activism, inc.: how the outsourcing of grassroots campaigns is strangling progressive politics in America*. Redwood City, CA: Stanford University Press.

Flanagin, A. J., Stohl, C., & Bimber, B. (2006). Modeling the structure of collective action. *Communication Monographs, 73*(1), 29–54.

Foot, K. A., & Schneider, S. M. (2002). Online action in Campaign 2000: An exploratory analysis of the U.S. political web sphere. *Journal of Broadcasting & Electronic Media, 46*(2), 222–244. doi:10.1207/s15506878jobem4602_4

Foot, K. A., & Schneider, S. M. (2006). *Web campaigning*. Cambridge, MA: MIT Press.

Foroohar, R. (2011). What ever happened to upward mobility? *Time*. Retrieved from http://content.time.com/time/magazine/article/0,9171,2098584,00.html

Franklin, C. (2009, July 17). Walter Cronkite, most trusted man in America. *Pollster.com—Political Surveys and Election Polls, Trends, Charts and Analysis*. Retrieved from http://www.pollster.com/blogs/walter_cronkite_most_trusted_m.php?nr=1

Franzen, C. (2011, October 19). Occupy Wall Street demographic survey results will surprise you. *Talking Points Memo*. Retrieved from http://talkingpointsmemo.com/idealab/occupy-wall-street-demographic-survey-results-will-surprise-you

Freelon, D., Wells, C., & Bennett, W. L. (2013). Participation in the youth civic web: Assessing user activity levels in web sites presenting two civic styles. *Journal of Information Technology & Politics, 10*(3), 293–309. doi:10.1080/19331681.2013.792309

Gallagher, L. (2013). *The end of the suburbs: Where the American dream is moving*. New York: Portfolio.

Gibson, R. K., & Ward, S. (2012). Political organizations and campaigning online. In H. A. Semetko & M. Scammell (Eds.), *Sage handbook of political communication* (pp. 62–74). London: SAGE Publications.

Giddens, A. (1991). *Modernity and self-identity: Self and society in the late modern age*. Redwood City, CA: Stanford University Press.

Gitlin, T. (2012, July 23). Was that the way it was? *The New Republic*. Retrieved from http://www.newrepublic.com/book/review/after-broadcast-news-bruce-williams-michael-dell-carpini

Gitlin, T. (2011, October 8). Occupy Wall Street and the Tea Party. *The New York Times*. Retrieved from http://www.nytimes.com/2011/10/09/opinion/sunday/occupy-wall-street-and-the-tea-party.html

Gladwell, M. (2010, October 4). Small change: Why the revolution will not be tweeted. *The New Yorker*. Retrieved from http://www.newyorker.com/reporting/2010/10/04/101004fa_fact_gladwell

Graham, T., Broersma, M., Hazelhoff, K., & van 't Haar, G. (2013). Between broadcasting political messages and interacting with voters. *Information, Communication & Society, 16*(5), 692–716. doi:10.1080/1369118X.2013.785581

Grimsted, D. (1972). Rioting in its Jacksonian setting. *American Historical Review, 77*(2), 361–397. doi:10.2307/1868697

Gueorguieva, V. (2008). Voters, MySpace, and YouTube: The impact of alternative communication channels on the 2006 election cycle and beyond. *Social Science Computer Review, 26*(3), 288–300. doi:10.1177/0894439307305636

Habermas, J. (1962/1989). *The structural transformation of the public sphere: An inquiry into a category of bourgeois society*. Cambridge, MA: MIT Press.

Haidt, J. (2012). *The righteous mind: Why good people are divided by politics and religion*. New York: Pantheon.

Hallin, D. (1992). The passing of the "high modernism" of American journalism. *Journal of Communication, 42*(3), 14–25.

Hallin, D. C. (2000). Commercialism and professionalism in American news media. In J. Curran & M. Gurevitch (Eds.), *Mass media and society* (3rd ed., pp. 218–237). New York: Oxford University Press.

Hallin, D. C. (2006). The passing of the "high modernism" of American journalism revisited. *Political Communication Report, 16*(1). Retrieved from http://www.jour.unr.edu/pcr/1601_2005_winter/commentary_hallin.htm

Hamilton, J. T. (2004). *All the news that's fit to sell: How the market transforms information into news*. Princeton, NJ: Princeton University Press.

Hayes, M. T. (1983). Interest groups: Pluralism or mass society. In A. J. Cigler & B. A. Loomis (Eds.), *Interest group politics* (pp. 111–136). Washington, DC: Congressional Quarterly Press.

Hempel, J. (2010, April 21). Facebook vs. Google: Game on. Retrieved from http://tech.fortune.cnn.com/2010/04/21/facebook-vs-google-game-on/

Hindman, M. (2008). *The myth of digital democracy*. Princeton, NJ: Princeton University Press.

Hirschman, A. O. (1970). *Exit, voice, and loyalty: Responses to decline in firms, organizations, and states*. Cambridge, MA: Harvard University Press.

Inglehart, R. (1997). *Modernization and postmodernization: Cultural, economic, and political change in 43 societies*. Princeton NJ: Princeton University Press.

Inside Facebook. (2010, January 4). December data on Facebook's US growth by age and gender: Beyond 100 million. Retrieved from http://www.adweek.com/socialtimes/december-data-on-facebook%E2%80%99s-us-growth-by-age-and-gender-beyond-100-million/233478?red=if

Ito, M., Baumer, S., Bittanti, M., boyd, danah, Cody, R., Herr-Stephenson, B., . . . Tripp, L. (2009). *Hanging out, messing around, and geeking out: Kids living and learning with new media* (1st ed.). Cambridge, MA: The MIT Press.

Iyengar, S., & McGrady, J. (2006). *Media politics: A citizen's guide*. New York: W. W. Norton & Company.

Jenkins, H. (2006). *Convergence culture: Where old and new media collide.* New York: New York University Press.

Jenkins, H., & Carpentier, N. (2013). Theorizing participatory intensities: A conversation about participation and politics. *Convergence: The International Journal of Research into New Media Technologies, 19*(3), 265–286. doi:10.1177/1354856513482090

Jenkins, H., Clinton, K., Purushotma, R., Robison, A. J., & Weigel, M. (2008). *Confronting the challenges of digital culture: Media education for the 21st century* (White paper). Chicago: John D. and Catherine T. MacArthur Foundation.

John, R. R. (1998). *Spreading the news: The American postal system from Franklin to Morse.* Cambridge, MA: Harvard University Press.

Jones, A. S. (2009). *Losing the news: The future of the news that feeds democracy.* New York: Oxford University Press.

Judt, T. (2010). *Ill fares the land.* New York: Penguin Press.

Karpf, D. (2012). *The MoveOn effect: The unexpected transformation of American political advocacy.* New York: Oxford University Press.

Kazeniac, A. (2009, February 9). Social networks: Facebook takes over top spot, Twitter climbs. Retrieved from http://blog.compete.com/2009/02/09/facebook-myspace-twitter-social-network/

Kazin, M. (2011, November 7). Anarchy now: Occupy Wall Street revives an ideology. *The New Republic.* Retrieved from http://www.tnr.com/article/politics/97114/anarchy-occupy-wall-street-throwback

Kenski, K., Hardy, B. W., & Jamieson, K. H. (2010). *The Obama victory: How media, money, and message shaped the 2008 election.* New York: Oxford University Press.

Kielbowicz, R. B. (1983). Party press cohesiveness: Jacksonian newspapers, 1832. *Journalism & Mass Communication Quarterly, 60*(3), 518–520. doi:10.1177/107769908306000321

Kirkpatrick, D. D. (2013, July 3). Army ousts Egypt's president; Morsi is taken into military custody. *The New York Times.* Retrieved from http://www.nytimes.com/2013/07/04/world/middleeast/egypt.html

Knoke, D. (1981). Commitment and detachment in voluntary associations. *American Sociological Review, 46*(2), 141. doi:10.2307/2094975

Koschnik, A. (2001). The democratic societies of Philadelphia and the limits of the American public sphere, circa 1793–1795. *The William and Mary Quarterly, 58*(3), 615–636. doi:10.2307/2674297

Kreiss, D. (2012). *Taking our country back: The crafting of networked politics from Howard Dean to Barack Obama.* New York: Oxford University Press.

Kreiss, D., Finn, M., & Turner, F. (2010). The limits of peer production: Some reminders from Max Weber for the network society. *New Media & Society, 20*(10), 1–17.

Kreiss, D., & Tufekci, Z. (2013). Occupying the political: Occupy Wall Street, collective action and the rediscovery of pragmatic politics. *Cultural Studies <=> Critical Methodologies, 13*(3).

Lankes, R. D. (2008). Trusting the Internet: New approaches to credibility tools. In M. J. Metzger & A. J. Flanagin (Eds.), *Digital media, youth, and credibility* (pp. 101–122). Cambridge, MA: MIT Press.

Lee, W. O., & Fouts, J. T. (2005). *Education for social citizenship: Perceptions of teachers in USA, Australia, England, Russia and China.* Hong Kong: Hong Kong University Press.

Lenhart, A., Purcell, K., Smith, A., & Zickuhr, K. (2010). *Social media & mobile Internet use among teens and young adults* (p. 37). Washington, DC: Pew Internet and American Life Project. Retrieved from http://pewresearch.org/pubs/1484/social-media-mobile-internet-use-teens-millennials-fewer-blog

Lessig, L. (2005). *Free culture: The nature and future of creativity.* New York: Penguin.

Levine, P. (2000). *The new Progressive Era: Toward a fair and deliberative democracy.* Lanham, MD: Rowman & Littlefield.

Levine, P. (2007). *The future of democracy: Developing the next generation of American citizens.* Medford, MA: Tufts University Press.

Linkins, J. (2009, August 22). Online poll: Jon Stewart Is America's most trusted newsman. *Huffington Post*. Retrieved from http://www.huffingtonpost.com/2009/07/22/time-magazine-poll-jon-st_n_242933.html

Lippmann, W. (1922). *Public opinion*. New York: Free Press.

Lipset, S. M., Trow, M. A., & Coleman, J. S. (1956). *Union democracy: The internal politics of the International Typographical Union*. New York: Free Press.

Livingstone, S. (2013). The participation paradigm in audience research. *The Communication Review, 16*(1-2), 21–30. doi:10.1080/10714421.2013.757174

Livingstone, S. (2009). *Children and the Internet*. Cambridge: Polity.

Lupia, A., & Sin, G. (2003). Which public goods are endangered? How evolving communication technologies affect the logic of collective action. *Public Choice, 117*(3), 315–331. doi:10.1023/B:PUCH.0000003735.7840.c7

Macedo, S. (Ed.). (2005). *Democracy at risk: How political choices undermine citizen participation, and what we can do about it*. Washington, DC: Brookings Institution Press.

Madden, M., & Zickuhr, K. (2011). *65% of online adults use social networking sites*. Washington, DC: Pew Internet & American Life Project. Retrieved from http://www.pewinternet.org/~/media//Files/Reports/2011/PIP-SNS-Update-2011.pdf

Marwick, A. E. (2013). *Status update: Celebrity, publicity, and branding in the social media age*. New Haven, CT: Yale University Press.

Mazzoleni, G., & Schulz, W. (1999). "Mediatization" of politics: A challenge for democracy? *Political Communication, 16*(3), 247–261. doi:10.1080/105846099198613

McCartney, S. (2010a, October). Using Twitter to pressure airlines: It works. *The Middle Seat Terminal—WSJ*. Newspaper. Retrieved from http://blogs.wsj.com/middleseat/2010/10/28/using-twitter-to-pressure-airlines-it-works/

McCartney, S. (2010b, October 26). The airlines' squeaky wheels turn to Twitter. *Wall Street Journal*. New York. Retrieved from http://online.wsj.com/article/SB10001424052702304173704575578321161564104.html

McGirt, E. (2009, April 1). How Chris Hughes helped launch Facebook and the Barack Obama campaign. *Fast Company*. Retrieved from http://www.fastcompany.com/magazine/134/boy-wonder.html

McKinney, M. S. (2011). *Communication in the 2008 U.S. Election: Digital natives elect a president*. New York: Peter Lang.

Michels, R. (1915). *Political parties: A sociological study of the oligarchical tendencies of modern democracy*. New York: Hearst's International Library Company.

Minder, R., & Erlanger, S. (2012, July 11). Spain's leader plans new austerity steps as miners clash with police. *The New York Times*. Retrieved from http://www.nytimes.com/2012/07/12/world/europe/spains-leader-plans-new-austerity-steps-as-miners-clash-with-police.html

Mindich, D. T. Z. (2004). *Tuned out: Why Americans under 40 don't follow the news*. New York: Oxford University Press.

Montgomery, K., Gottlieb-Robles, B., & Larson, G. O. (2004). *Youth as E-Citizens: Engaging the digital generation*. Washington, DC: Center for Social Media, American University.

Morozov, E. (2011). *The net delusion: The dark side of Internet freedom*. New York: Public Affairs.

Moynihan, C. (2012, April 12). Evicted from park, Occupy protesters take to the sidewalks. *The New York Times*. Retrieved from http://www.nytimes.com/2012/04/13/nyregion/evicted-from-park-occupy-protesters-take-to-the-sidewalks.html

Nerone, J. (2011). Representing public opinion: US newspapers and the news system in the long nineteenth century. *History Compass, 9*(9), 743–759. doi:10.1111/j.1478-0542.2011.0796.x

Neuendorf, K. A. (2002). *The content analysis guidebook*. Thousand Oaks, CA: Sage.

Newman, A., & Moynihan, C. (2012, May 1). May Day demonstrations lead to clashes and arrests. *The New York Times*. Retrieved from http://www.nytimes.com/2012/05/02/nyregion/may-day-demonstrations-lead-to-clashes-and-arrests.html

Nisbet, M. C., & Scheufele, D. A. (2004). Political talk as a catalyst for online citizenship. *Journalism & Mass Communication Quarterly, 81*(4), 877–896. doi:10.1177/107769900408100410

O'Connor, R. (2009). *Word of mouse: Credibility, journalism and emerging social media.* Cambridge, MA: Joan Shorenstein Center on the Press, Politics and Public Policy.

Odegard, P. H. (1928). *Pressure politics: The story of the Anti-Saloon League.* New York: Columbia University Press.

Olson, M. (1965). *The logic of collective action: Public goods and the theory of groups.* Cambridge, MA: Harvard University Press.

Packer, G. (2013). *The unwinding: An inner history of the new America.* New York: Farrar, Straus and Giroux.

Palfrey, J., & Gasser, U. (2008). *Born digital: Understanding the first generation of digital natives.* New York: Basic Books.

Papacharissi, Z. A. (2010). *A private sphere: Democracy in a digital age.* Cambridge: Polity.

Papacharissi, Z. (2009). The virtual sphere 2.0: The internet, the public sphere, and beyond. In A. Chadwick & P. N. Howard (Eds.), *Routledge handbook of Internet politics.* London; New York: Routledge.

Pasley, J. L. (2000). Party politics, citizenship and collective action in nineteenth-century America: A response to Stuart Blumin and Michael Schudson. *Communication Review, 4*(1), 39.

Pasley, J. L. (2002). *The tyranny of printers: Newspaper politics in the early American republic.* Charlottesville: University of Virginia Press.

Patterson, T. E. (2007). *Young people and news.* Cambridge, MA: Shorenstein Center for Press and Politics.

Patterson, T. E. (2000). *Doing well and doing good: How soft news and critical journalism are shrinking the news audience and weakening democracy—and what news outlets can do about it* (p. 28). Cambridge, MA: Shorenstein Center for Press and Politics.

Paulson, M. (2014, October 11). At forlorn urban churches, Mass gets crowded in a flash. *The New York Times.* Retrieved from http://www.nytimes.com/2014/10/12/us/at-forlorn-urban-churches-mass-gets-crowded-in-a-flash.html

Pingree, R. J. (2007). How messages affect their senders: A more general model of message effects and implications for deliberation. *Communication Theory, 17*(4), 439–461. doi:10.1111/j.1468-2885.2007.0306.x

Plouffe, D. (2009). *The audacity to win: The inside story and lessons of Barack Obama's historic victory.* New York: Viking.

Polletta, F. (2013). Participatory Democracy in the New Millennium. *Contemporary Sociology: A Journal of Reviews, 42*(1), 40–50. doi:10.1177/0094306112468718b

Polletta, F. (2002). *Freedom is an endless meeting: Democracy in the age of social movements.* Chicago: University of Chicago Press.

Prior, M. (2007). *Post-broadcast democracy: How media choice increases inequality in political involvement and polarizes elections.* Cambridge: Cambridge University Press.

Purcell, K., Rainie, L., Mitchell, A., Rosenstiel, T., & Olmstead, K. (2010). *Understanding the participatory news consumer.* Washington, DC: Pew Internet and American Life Project. Retrieved from http://www.pewinternet.org/Reports/2010/Online-News.aspx

Putnam, R. (1995). Tuning in, tuning out: The strange disappearance of social capital in America. *PS: Political Science and Politics, 28*(4), 664–683.

Putnam, R. D. (2000). *Bowling alone: The collapse and revival of American community.* New York: Simon & Schuster.

Putnam, R. D. (2013, August 3). Crumbling American dreams. *Opinionator.* Retrieved from http://opinionator.blogs.nytimes.com/2013/08/03/crumbling-american-dreams/

Rainie, L., & Wellman, B. (2012). *Networked: The new social operating system.* Cambridge, MA: MIT Press.

Raynes-Goldie, W. L., & Walker, L. (2008). Our space: Online civic engagement tools for youth. In W. L. Bennett (Ed.), *Civic life online: Learning how digital media can engage youth* (pp. 161–188). Cambridge, MA: MIT Press.

Reedy, J., Wells, C., & Gastil, J. (2014). How voters become misinformed: An investigation of the emergence and consequences of false factual beliefs. *Social Science Quarterly, 95*(5), 1399–1418. doi:10.1111/ssqu.12102

Reid, T. (2008, April 14). Barack Obama's "guns and religion" blunder gives Hillary Clinton a chance. *The Times of London*. London. Retrieved from http://www.timesonline.co.uk/tol/news/world/us_and_americas/us_elections/article3740080.ece

Reynolds, C. (2009, July 7). Smashed guitar, YouTube song—United is listening now. *Travel—LA Times.com*. Newspaper. Retrieved from http://travel.latimes.com/daily-deal-blog/index.php/smashed-guitar-youtu-4850/

Rheingold, H. (2003). *Smart mobs: The next social revolution*. Cambridge, MA: Perseus.

Rheingold, H. (1993). *The virtual community: Finding connection in a computerized world*. Boston: Addison-Wesley Longman.

Rojas, H., & Puig-i-Abril, E. (2009). Mobilizers mobilized: Information, expression, mobilization and participation in the digital age. *Journal of Computer-Mediated Communication*, 14(4), 902–927. doi:10.1111/j.1083-6101.2009.1475.x

Riffe, D., Lacy, S., & Fico, F. (2005). *Analyzing media messages: Using quantitative content analysis in research*. Hillsdale, NJ: Lawrence Erlbaum.

Sachs, J. (2011). *The price of civilization: Reawakening American virtue and prosperity*. New York: Random House.

Savage, D. (1999, December 9). Paul is dead. *The Stranger*. Seattle, WA. Retrieved from http://www.thestranger.com/seattle/paul-is-dead/Content?oid=2736

Scammell, M. (2003). Citizen consumers: Towards a new marketing of politics? In J. Corner & D. Pels (Eds.), *Media and the restyling of politics : consumerism, celebrity and cynicism*. Thousand Oaks, CA: Sage.

Schlozman, K. L., & Tierney, J. T. (1986). *Organized interests and American democracy*. New York: HarperCollins.

Schudson, M. (1978). *Discovering the news: A social history of American newspapers*. New York: Basic Books.

Schudson, M. (1998). *The good citizen: A history of American civic life*. New York: Martin Kessler Books.

Schwartz, M. (2011, November 28). Pre-Occupied. *The New Yorker*. Retrieved from http://www.newyorker.com/reporting/2011/11/28/111128fa_fact_schwartz

Scolari, C. A. (2012). Media ecology: Exploring the metaphor to expand the theory. *Communication Theory*, 22(2), 204–225. doi:10.1111/j.1468-2885.2012.1404.x

Shah, D., Kwak, N., & Holbert, R. L. (2001). "Connecting" and "disconnecting" with civic life: Patterns of Internet use and the production of social capital. *Political Communication*, 18(2), 141–162.

Shah, D.V., Thorson, K., Wells, C., Lee, N.J., & McLeod, J. (forthcoming). Civic norms and communication competence: Pathways to socialization and citizenship. In Kenski, K., & Jamieson, K.H. (Eds.), *The Oxford Handbook of Political Communication*. Oxford: Oxford University Press.

Shirky, C. (2008). *Here comes everybody: The power of organizing without organizations*. New York: Penguin Press.

Sirianni, C. (2009). *Investing in democracy: Engaging citizens in collaborative governance*. Washington, DC: Brookings Institution Press.

Sirianni, C., & Friedland, L. (2001). *Civic innovation in America: community empowerment, public policy, and the movement for civic renewal*. Berkeley: University of California Press.

Sheehan, C. A. (2009). *James Madison and the spirit of republican self-government*. New York: Cambridge University Press.

Sklar, R. (2008, March 28). A crush on Obama, and an eye on the prize. *Huffington Post*. Retrieved from http://www.huffingtonpost.com/2007/07/16/a-crush-on-obama-and-an-e_n_53057.html

Skocpol, T. (1999). How Americans became civic. In T. Skocpol & M. P. Fiorina (Eds.), *Civic engagement in American democracy* (pp. 27–80). Washington, DC: Brookings Institution Press.

Skocpol, T. (2003). *Diminished democracy: From membership to management in American civic life*. Norman: University of Oklahoma Press.

Skocpol, T. (2004). Voice and inequality: The transformation of American civic democracy. *Perspectives on Politics*, 2(01), 3–20.

Skocpol, T., & Fiorina, M. P. (Eds.). (1999). *Civic engagement in American democracy*. Washington, DC: Brookings Institution Press.

Skocpol, T., Ganz, M., & Munson, Z. (2000). A nation of organizers: The institutional origins of civic voluntarism in the United States. *The American Political Science Review*, 94(3), 527–546. doi:10.2307/2585829

Skocpol, T., & Williamson, V. (2012). *The Tea Party and the remaking of Republican conservatism.* New York: Oxford University Press.

Smith, A. (2013, February 20). Digital Politics: Pew Research findings on technology and campaign 2012. Retrieved from http://www.pewinternet.org/2013/02/20/digital-politics-pew-research-findings-on-technology-and-campaign-2012/

Smith, A. (2009). *The Internet's role in Campaign 2008.* Washington, DC: Pew Internet & American Life Project. Retrieved from http://www.pewinternet.org/Reports/2009/6--The-Internets-Role-in-Campaign-2008.aspx

Smith, A., Schlozman, K. L., Verba, S., & Brady, H. (2009). *The Internet and civic engagement.* Washington, DC: Pew Internet & American Life Project. Retrieved from http://www.pewinternet.org/Reports/2009/15--The-Internet-and-Civic-Engagement.aspx

Spiegel. (2011, May 19). Spain's lost generation finds its voice. Retrieved from http://www.spiegel.de/international/europe/0,1518,763581,00.html

Starr, P. (2004). *The creation of the media: Political origins of modern communications.* New York: Basic Books.

Stolle, D., Hooghe, M., & Micheletti, M. (2005). Politics in the supermarket: Political consumerism as a form of political participation. *International Political Science Review*, 26(3), 245–69.

Stromer-Galley, J. (2000). On-line interaction and why candidates avoid it. *Journal of Communication*, 50(4), 111–132. doi:10.1111/j.1460-2466.2000.tb02865.x

Surowiecki, J. (2005). *The wisdom of crowds.* New York: Random House.

Tapia, J. E. (1997). *Circuit Chautauqua: From rural education to popular entertainment in early twentieth century America.* Jefferson, NC: McFarland.

Tapscott, D. (2009). *Grown up digital: How the net generation is changing your world.* New York: McGraw-Hill Education.

Tarrow, S. G. (2005). *The new transnational activism.* Cambridge: Cambridge University Press.

Tedesco, J. C. (2007). Examining Internet interactivity effects on young adult political information efficacy. *American Behavioral Scientist*, 50(9), 1183–1194. doi:10.1177/0002764207300041

The Onion. (2013, January 16). Internet users demand less interactivity. Retrieved from http://www.theonion.com/articles/internet-users-demand-less-interactivity,30920/

Thompson, C. (2008, September 7). Brave new world of digital intimacy. *The New York Times.* Retrieved from http://www.nytimes.com/2008/09/07/magazine/07awareness-t.html

Thorson, K. (2010). *Finding gaps and building bridges: Mapping youth citizenship.* PhD dissertation, University of Wisconsin-Madison.

Tocqueville, A. de. (1835/1964). *Democracy in America.* New York: Washington Square Press.

Toma, C. L., & Hancock, J. T. (2010). Looks and lies: The role of physical attractiveness in online dating self-presentation and deception. *Communication Research*, 37(3), 335–351. doi:10.1177/0093650209356437

Tremlett, G. (2011, November 20). Spain election: People's party sweeps to crushing victory over Socialists. *The Guardian.* Retrieved from http://www.guardian.co.uk/world/2011/nov/20/spain-election-peoples-party-victory

Trippi, J. (2004). *The revolution will not be televised: Democracy, the Internet, and the overthrow of everything.* New York: Regan Books.

Truman, D. B. (1951). *The governmental process: Political interests and public opinion.* New York: Knopf.

Tufekci, Z., & Wilson, C. (2012). Social media and the decision to participate in political protest: Observations from Tahrir Square. *Journal of Communication*, 62(2), 363–379. doi:10.1111/j.1460-2466.2012.1629.x

Turner, F. (2006). *From counterculture to cyberculture: Stewart Brand, the Whole Earth Network, and the rise of digital utopianism.* Chicago: University of Chicago Press.

Van Laer, J., & van Aelst, P. (2010). Internet and social movement action repertoires: Opportunities and limitations. *Information Communication & Society*, 13(8), 1146–1171.

Verba, S., Schlozman, K. L., & Brady, H. E. (1995). *Voice and equality: Civic voluntarism in American politics.* Cambridge, MA: Harvard University Press.

Vromen, A. (2007). Australian young people's participatory practices and Internet use. *Information, Communication and Society, 10*(1), 48–68.

Wagner, M. W., Wells, C., Friedland, L. A., Cramer, K. J., & Shah, D. V. (2014). Cultural worldviews and contentious politics: Evaluative asymmetry in high-information environments. *The Good Society, 23*(2), 126–144. doi:10.5325/goodsociety.23.2.0126

Walker, J. L., Jr. (1991). *Mobilizing interest groups in America: Patrons, professions, and social movements*. Ann Arbor: University of Michigan Press.

Walker, J. L., Jr. (1983). The origins and maintenance of interest groups in America. *The American Political Science Review, 77*(2), 390. doi:10.2307/1958924

Ward, S., & Gibson, R. (2009). European political organizations and the internet: Mobilization, participation, and change. In A. Chadwick & P. N. Howard (Eds.), *Routledge handbook of Internet politics*. New York: Routledge.

Waters, R., Burnett, E., Lamm, A., & Lucas, J. (2009). Engaging stakeholders through social networking: How nonprofit organizations are using Facebook. *Public Relations Review, 35*(2), 102–6.

Wattenberg, M. P. (2008). *Is voting for young people?* New York: Pearson Longman.

Wellman, B. (2001). Physical place and cyberplace: The rise of personalized networking. *International Journal of Urban and Regional Research, 25*(2), 227–252.

Wells, C. (2010). Citizenship and communication in online youth civic engagement projects. *Information Communication & Society, 13*(3), 419–441.

West, D. M. (2011). *The next wave: Using digital technology to further social and political innovation*. Washington, DC: Brookings Institution Press.

Willard, F. E. C. (1883). *Woman and temperance*. Hartford, CT: Park Publishing Company.

Williams, B. A., & Delli Carpini, M. X. (2011). *After broadcast news: Media regimes, democracy, and the new information environment*. New York: Cambridge University Press.

Wilson, J. Q. (1973). *Political organizations*. Princeton, NJ: Princeton University Press.

Wojcieszak, M. (2010). Cyber racism: White supremacy online and the new attack on civil rights. *Sociological Inquiry, 80*(1), 150–152. doi:10.1111/j.1475-682X.2009.0320.x

Wortham, J. (2012, October 8). Presidential campaign on social media. *The New York Times*. New York. Retrieved from http://www.nytimes.com/interactive/2012/10/08/technology/campaign-social-media.html

Xenos, M., & Bennett, W. L. (2007). The Disconnection In Online Politics: the youth political web sphere and US election sites, 2002–2004. *Information, Communication Society, 10*(4), 443–464.

Zaller, J. (2003). A new standard of news quality: Burglar alarms for the monitorial citizen. *Political Communication, 20*(2), 109–130.

Zaller, J. (1999). *A theory of media politics: How the interests of politicians, journalists and citizens shape the news*. Retrieved from http://www.sscnet.ucla.edu/polisci/faculty/zaller/media%20politics%20book%20.pdf

Zickuhr, K. (2010). *Generations 2010*. Washington, DC: Pew Internet & American Life Project. Retrieved from http://pewinternet.org/Reports/2010/Generations-2010.aspx

Zittrain, J. L. (2008). *The future of the Internet and how to stop it*. New Haven, CT: Yale University Press.

Zogby, J. (2008). *The way we'll be: The Zogby report on the transformation of the American dream*. New York: Random House.

Zukin, C., Keeter, S., Andolina, M., Jenkins, K., & Delli Carpini, M. X. (2006). *A new engagement: Political participation, civic life, and the changing American citizen*. New York: Oxford University Press.

Index

Page numbers in italics refer to illustrations.

affiliation with, 24; online communication strategies of, 89; online engagement and, 126; political parties vs., 16; as producers of information, 8, 16; as prominent civic communicators, 59; social networking sites and, 126; as sources of information, 52, 59, 62–65, 95, 167; structural elements of, 59; transformation of, 62; variety of, 85; young citizens desert, 35, 164
civic participation. *See* participation
civic skills, 174, 222n12
civic web, 27–28, 91, 92, 102, 103, 116, 122
civil society, 4, 23, 25, 34, 35
classic era of civic association, 67–72
class lines, hardening of, 163
Clemens, Elisabeth, 72
clicktivism, 183
climate change, 23, 163
Clinton, Hillary, 95, 190
coffeehouses, 11
cognitive engagement, of youth, 39
Coleman, Stephen, 85–86, 153
collective action, 22, 33, 61, 77; communication and, 6, 78; digital media and, 4, 76
College Democrats, 113, 224n24
College Republicans, 94, 224n24; external status updates links of, 154–55, *155*
comment features: on Facebook, 126, 132; as sharing tool, 52
commitment question of, 182–85
communication: actualizing citizens' preferences for, 55–56; actualizing features of, 81; choices of, 42; dynamics of, 25; engagement and, 7; environment, 24, 27, 45; expectations of, 26, 44; innovations in, 10; of interest groups, 19; intraorganizational, 65; logics of, 28, 77; mass, 76; media of, 11; modes of, 6, 62; post-Revolutionary system of intranational, 13; power of, 44, 46, 47; processes of, 4, 50; reduced costs of, 4, 21, 22; relationships of, 23, 26; styles, 5, 85. *See also* digital communication; digital media
communication patterns: actualizing, 27; of civic organizations, 27; dutiful, 27; engagement modes and, 79; of media politics, 19; types of, 98, 99
communicative autonomy, 26, 27, 29; bureaucratic civic participation and, 172; increase in, 80–81
communicative behavior on web, 86
communicative practice, 42
communicative relationships, 65–67; between civic organizations and young citizens, 3, 23, 59, 63, 167; civic organization websites and, 116–22; definition of, 66; fluidity of, in networked movements, 21; removal of interpersonal connections from, 74; unidirectional, 75
communicative risk aversion, 74, 170

communicative style, 49
community organizations, 62; activity offerings of, 111; actualizing communications of, 159, 165; examples of, 94; participatory opportunities and, 169; websites of, 96–97, 116
US Congress: Capitol Hill, 108; contacting, 112
connectedness: global, 34; hyper-, 35; of network society, 33
conservativism, conservatives, 131, 133, 155
constituents, politicians' relationships with, 20
consumer politics, as lifestyle politics, 39
contentious action, 106
content sharing, 125
convergence culture, 44
Cook, Timothy, 19
coordination costs, of formal organizations, 78
Cornish, Samuel E., 70
corporations: in civic organizations' networks, 156–57; external status update links to content of, 156; targeted by young citizens, 218n52; transnational, 34
corruption, 19, 35
cosmopolitanism, 34
credibility, 45, 63
Cronkite, Walter, 30, 31, 51
crowd sourcing, 119
cultural changes, 92, 104, 122
cultural globalization, 33
current affairs, 11

DailyKos, 21, 172, 175
Dalai Lama, 135
Dalton, Russell, 24, 38, 40, 218n44
Dean, Howard, 2004 campaign of, 20, 79, 83, 86, 177
Declare Yourself, 112
deference, 12, 17
democracy, 11, 65–66; direct, 17; as discourse, 11; duties in, 15; in Egypt, 2; future of, 32; history of, 10; institutional players in, 4; mechanics of, 2; participation in, 2–3, 44; process of, 177, 188; reform of, 164; without citizens, 19, 73; young citizens and, 5, 37–38
Democracy for America, 172
Democratic Party, 133, 134; Occupy movement and, 2; status updates on Facebook Page of, 148, *148*, 149; website of, 113
Deuze, Mark, 43–44, 45, 52
Digg, 125
digital activists, 107
digital citizens, young as, 6, 21, 42, 89
digital communication, 89; civic organizations and, 66; cost reductions of, 21, 77; culture of, 42; infrastructure of, 7, 19; technology of, 32
digital culture: definition of, 43–44; elements of, 44–46; newness of, 42; norms of, 82, 83, 89, 121, 127, 128, 157; participatory ethos of, 186; practices of, 121